EDOUARD MANET

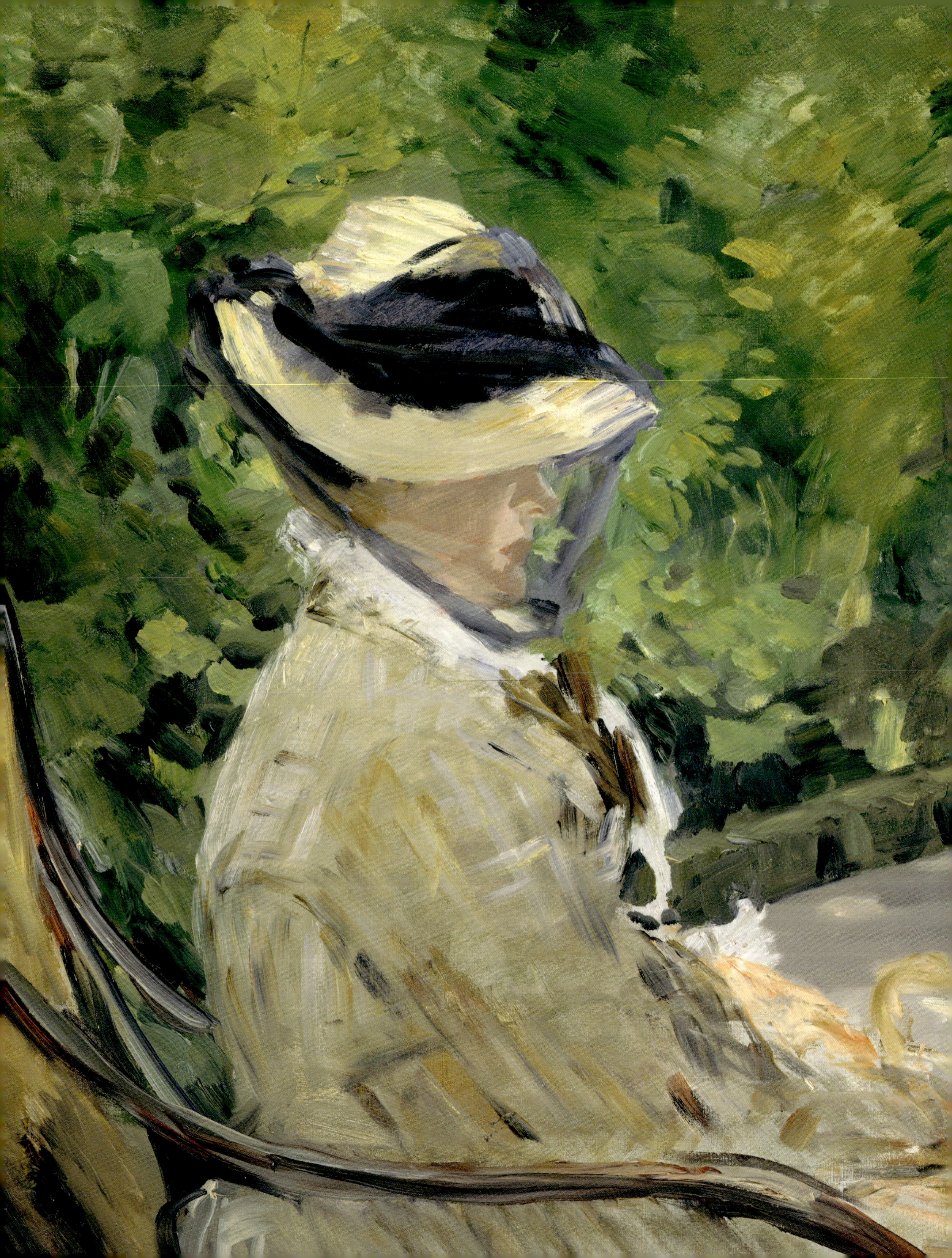

ART MASTER

EDOUARD MANET

ANN SUMNER

SIRIUS

SIRIUS

This edition published in 2024 by Sirius Publishing, a division of
Arcturus Publishing Limited,
26/27 Bickels Yard, 151–153 Bermondsey Street,
London SE1 3HA

ISBN: 978-1-3988-5095-8
AD007301UK

Printed in China

CONTENTS

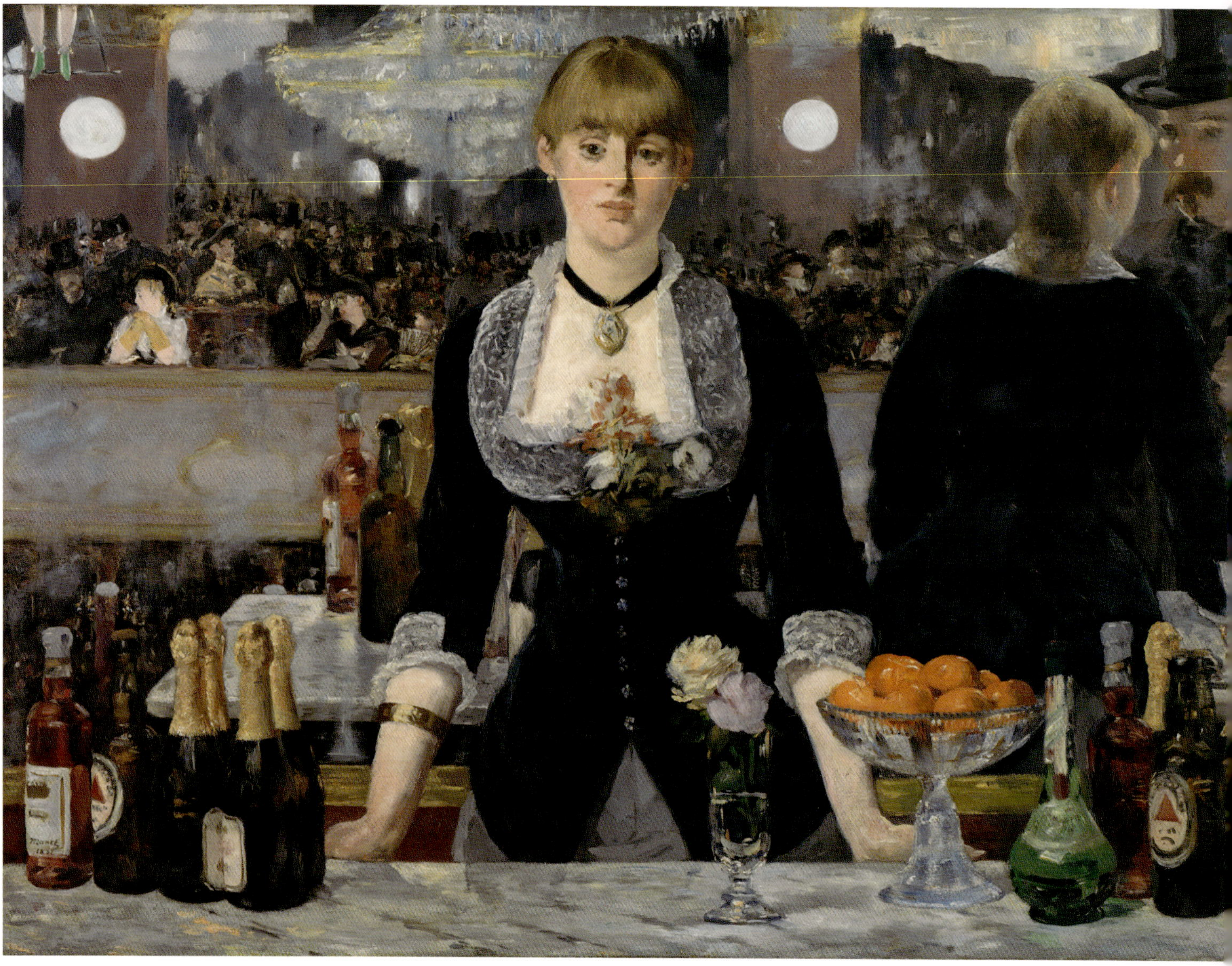

A Bar at the Folies-Bergère, *1881–2. Manet's late, great masterpiece, it shows a renowned bustling music hall in Paris, the* Folies-Bergère, *and yet the barmaid looks wistful and detached. The model, known only as Suzon, may have also worked as a prostitute. The mirror behind her reflects the packed music hall, the man she is serving and the green-clad legs of a trapeze artist performing above. It was shown at the 1882 Salon but not appreciated by the critics who preferred his other work,* Jeanne (Spring).

INTRODUCTION

Manet is often seen as the father of Impressionism – an older revolutionary artist admired by this younger group. They met and discussed art with him in Parisian cafés. With the notoriety surrounding the reception of his works, he quickly became a natural leader of the avant-garde artists. However, despite the friendship he shared with Monet, Renoir, Sisley and Bazille, and the fact that he quickly mastered painting figures in gardens *en plein air*, Manet was never to become a member of the Impressionist group and did not exhibit with them. In fact, he was only a few years older than most of them and actually younger than one of the group, Camille Pissarro. His period of painting what might be defined as Impressionist pictures was relatively short-lived. Manet's primary interest was the depiction of figures, carefully arranged compositions in his studio, where he could control the lighting. By the close of the 1870s, he had moved away from the Impressionists artistically and he returned to *plein-air* paintings only in the last years of his life, but his impact upon, and influence over, the Impressionist group, and subsequent artists, was transformational.

Manet's influence was great, but his life was not long, since he died in 1883, at the age of just 51, the year after painting one of his most famous works, *A Bar at the Folies-Bergère*, which was exhibited posthumously at the Salon. The pall-bearers at his funeral included Antonin Proust, Émile Zola, Alfred Stevens, Théodore Duret and Claude Monet. Degas is said to have muttered as he left the cemetery that Manet was 'greater than we thought'. While Manet did not receive the official recognition he had so strived for during his lifetime, the French government posthumously awarded him the Legion of Honour. His legacy continued, with artists such as the Swiss painter Félix Vallotton paying homage to him by reinterpreting *Olympia* in 1913 (*see* page 90) and Matisse acknowledging his admiration of Manet's impact on him in an interview in the 1930s: 'Manet is the first painter to have made an immediate translation of his sensations and thus given free rein to instinct, and he was the first to act through his reflexes and thus to simplify the painter's technique.'

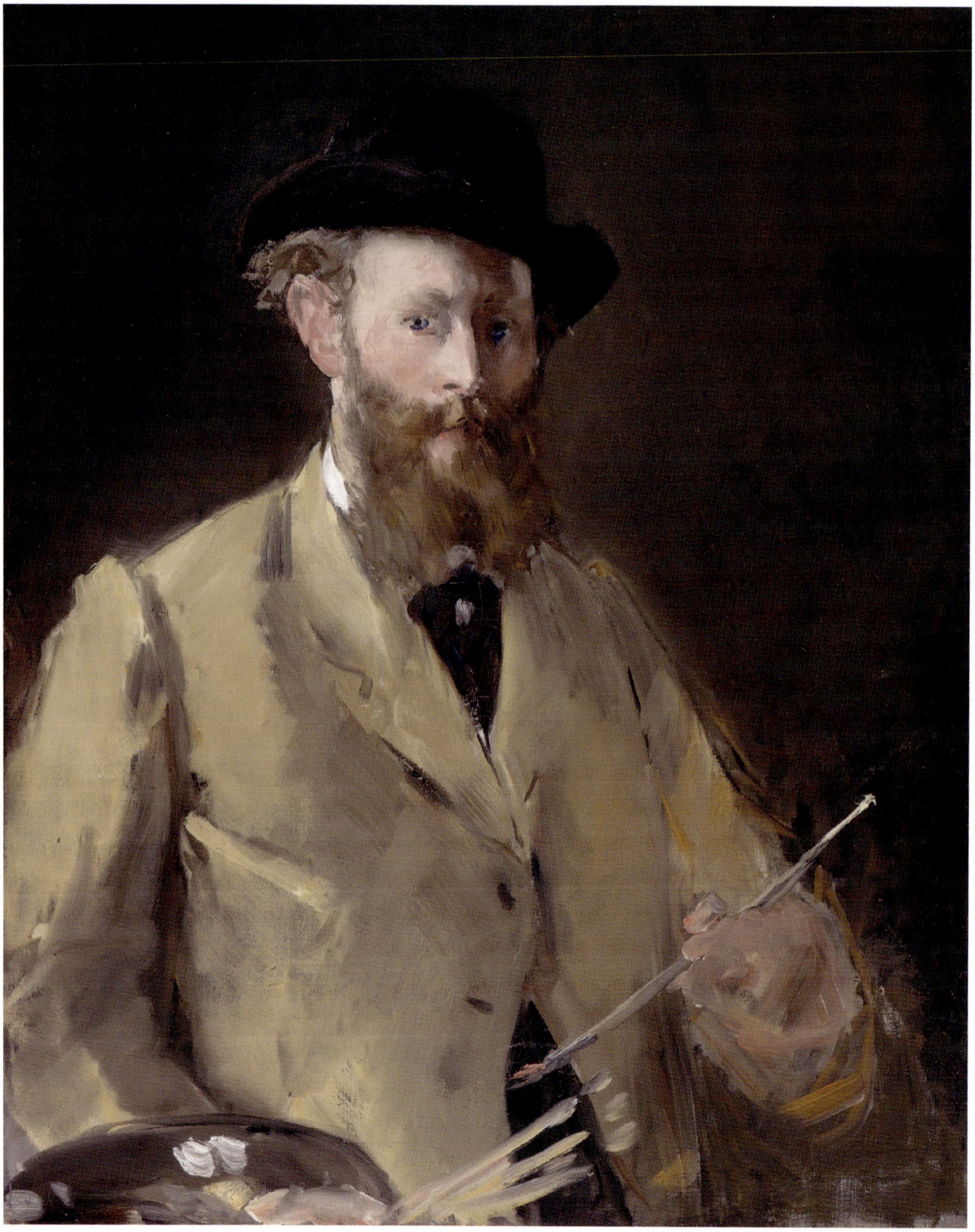

Self-Portrait with a Palette, *1878–9. This is the only self-portrait by Manet in which he shows himself as an artist, although he is dressed in a jacket and hat, which he would not have worn to paint. His only other individual self-portrait shows him full-length wearing a cap and dates from the same period.*

CHAPTER 1
Context and Reputation

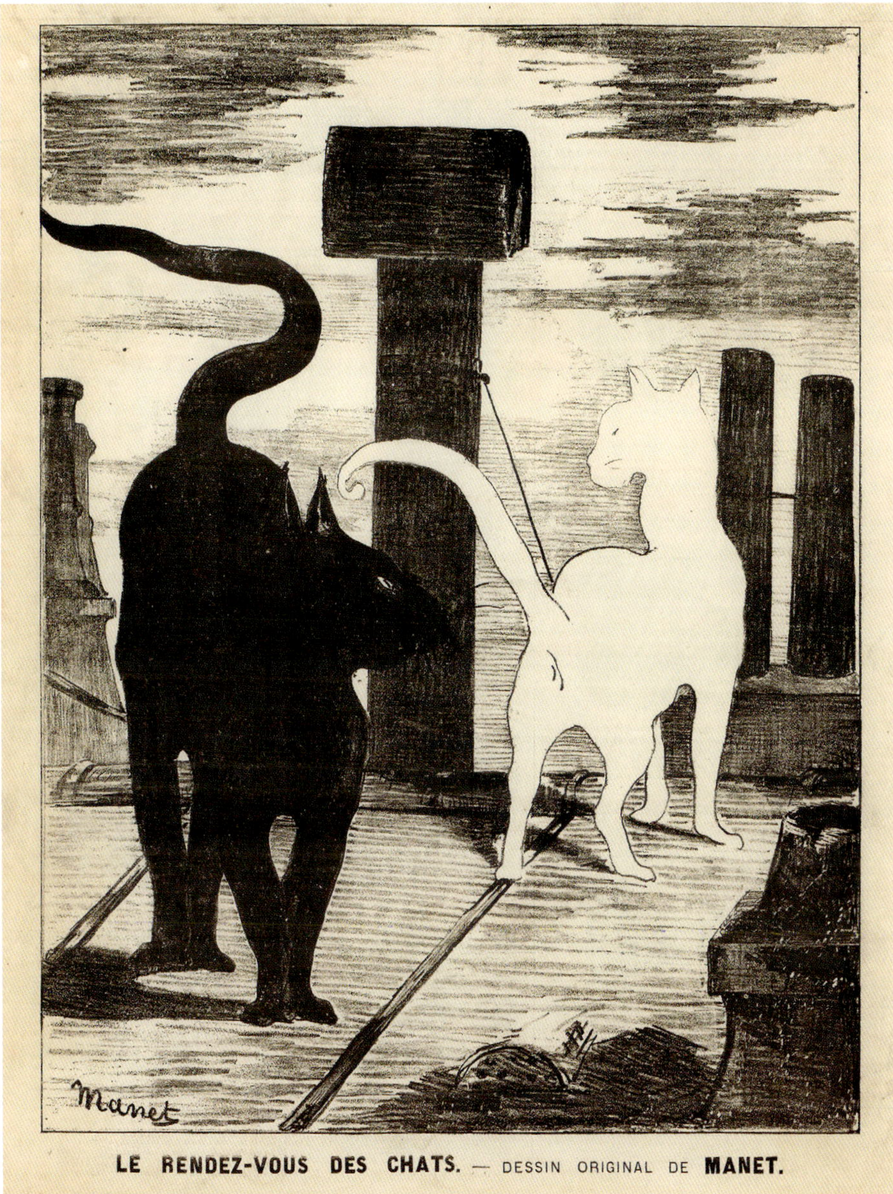

The Cat's Rendezvous, *1869. Manet's sketchbooks contain many studies of cats. In 1868, he collaborated with the writer Jules Champfleury on his amusing book* Les Chats *(1869), and produced this publicity poster.*

Throughout his career, Édouard Manet both shocked and confounded official artistic circles, critics and the public alike with his unorthodox subjects and virtuoso technical ability. Today, he is best known for his scenes of everyday life in Paris, from his early masterpiece *Music in the Tuileries Gardens* (1860–1), to the late *A Bar at the Folies-Bergère* (1881–2). His paintings shed light on the sophisticated Parisian life he knew and loved. Manet was prolific and in a relatively short career painted around 430 oil paintings as well as watercolours and, in his later years, pastels. He was also a talented printmaker, producing around 100 etchings and lithographs between 1860 and 1882. His unique approach to his art influenced many contemporary painters, as well as the evolution of modern art in Paris. Today, he is recognized as one of the great masters of modern art.

Manet's life and art are full of contradictions. Apparently happily married, he was renowned as a ladies' man, having numerous mistresses. He was born into a well-connected Parisian bourgeois family, but his politics were firmly Republican. His paintings suggested that he was an outsider, a Bohemian rebel artist, when in fact he was a good-looking, witty, fashionable man about town, at home in Parisian café society. His reputation as a radical artist, and painter of modern life, overlooks his early work, which is steeped in admiration for the Old Masters: he admired Spanish art in particular, but he also owed a great debt to the Italian Renaissance and Dutch schools.

Finally, he sought approval from the official French Salon, being ambitious for medals and accolades, but loathed the constraints of academicism.

The Salon grew steadily in importance for contemporary artists, attracting increasing numbers of submissions, critical reviews and visitors, particularly during the French Second Empire from 1852 to 1870, which was exactly when Manet was establishing his career. Independent and less conventional artists were routinely excluded from the Salon, hampering their success; there were few other possible exhibiting spaces. Manet knew this, but failed to conform in the way that French artistic officialdom required. Rather, he continued to produce works that were strongly lit, flat in their modelling and bright in colour. Still, he was shocked and hurt by their rejection and the outrageous reception some of his paintings received. Paul Mantz, writing in the *Gazette des Beaux-Arts* in 1863, noted that some works by Manet, such as *Music in the Tuileries Gardens* (*see* pages 25–6) 'reveal in him an abounding vigour, but which, with their medley of red, blue, yellow and black, are but caricatures of the colours and not the colours themselves. To sum up, such art may well be extremely honest, but it is not sound, and we can feel under no obligation to plead Manet's cause before the Exhibition jury.' Manet did, however, enjoy the support of some of the greatest writers and critics of the day, such as Baudelaire, Zola and Mallarmé.

In 1867, Manet set up his own exhibition rather than submit his works to the Salon jury, anticipating further rejection. Using the third person, he wrote, 'Mr Manet has never wanted to make a protest... He claims neither to have overthrown the art of the past nor to have created a new order.' Yet, in reality, this is just what he did. Influenced by his friend Charles Baudelaire, he began from the 1860s to embrace scenes of modern life.

In 1950, the Italian art historian Lionello Venturi published his book *From Manet to Lautrec*, and identified clearly what was unique about Manet's technique and which set him apart: 'He felt the necessity to consider line as a means of separation, rather than as a contour, to reduce chiaroscuro to its smallest terms and to disregard three-dimensional space. In this way, he obtained a strong sharpness of figures, a rich colouration, even in black, and an emergence of the figure (in reflief, as it were) which was both compelling and more externally presented, reduced to flattened relief and detached from atmosphere.' Five years later, the intellectual French thinker and art historian Georges Bataille concluded in his biography: 'Manet is not

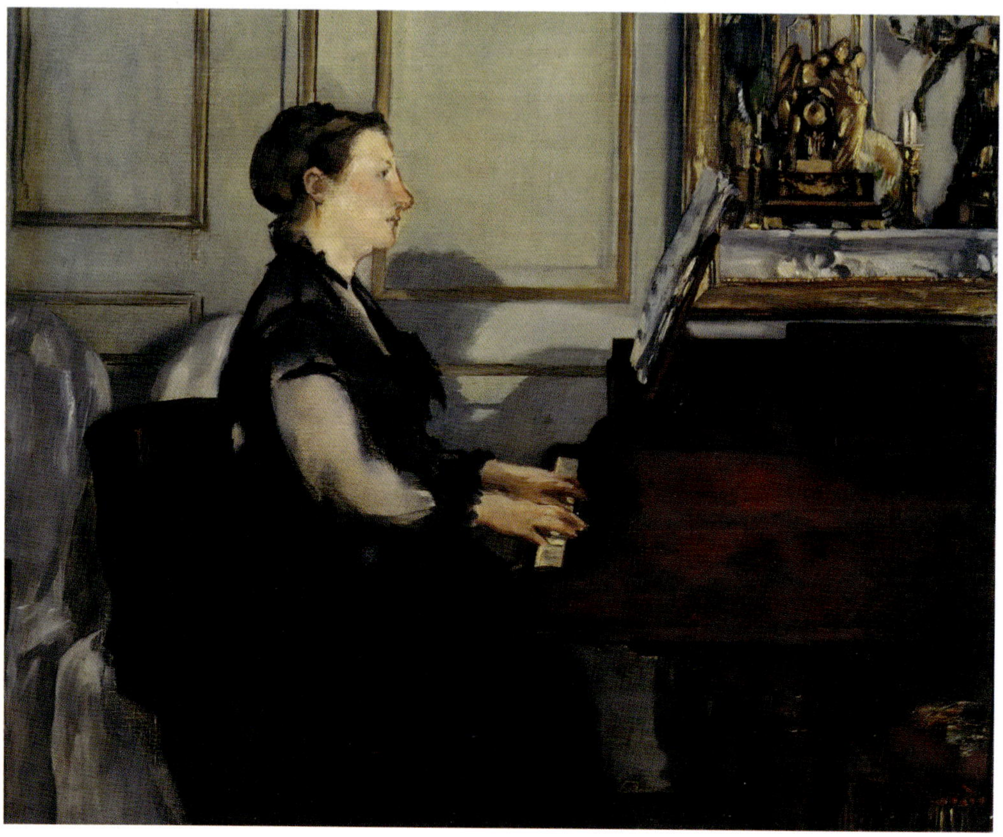

Madame Manet at the Piano, *1867. Manet met his future wife, Suzanne Leenhoff, in 1850, when she arrived in his parents' household as a piano teacher. She was Dutch, the daughter of an organist and herself a talented pianist. She gave birth to a son, Léon-Édouard Koëlla, in 1852 and eventually married Manet at Zalt-Bommel on 28 October 1863. She often sat as a model for her husband and was immensely tolerant of his womanizing.*

only a very great painter; he broke with those who went before him… Manet's paintings brought about a sudden change – a sharp upset for which the word revolution would be fitting, did it not give rise to ambiguity.' And by the 1960s, Phoebe Pool was concluding that 'Manet refreshed art by confronting his own times with neither stale dogma nor too stifling a hatred of tradition.'

In more recent years there has been a tendency not only to reassess his relationship with Impressionism and his legacy, exploring some works in detail, but also to focus on less well-known aspects of his art, including specific genres in which he excelled, such as his portraiture and still-life painting. A number of excellent exhibitions have celebrated the breadth of his abilities. 'Manet and Still-Life Paintings' (Musee D'Orsay, Paris and Walters Art Gallery, Baltimore 2000–01) celebrated not only the many individual still lifes he created, but also the numerous still-life elements included in his most famous paintings. 'Manet: Portraying Life (Toledo Museum of Art and Royal Academy, London 2012–13) focused on his brilliance as a portrait painter and the array of sitters, from his own family to his wide circle of fellow artist friends, as well as critics, writers and intellectuals and his favourite models. Manet's own *Self Portrait* (1878) as well as tender portraits of his wife, such as *Madame Manet in the Conservatory* (1879) or *…at the Piano*, and remarkable depictions of *Eva Gonzalès* (1870) and *Berthe Morisot with a Bouquet of Violets* (1872) demonstrate his outstanding talents in this genre. Equally, some exhibitions explored thoughtfully just one work, such as 'Manet and the Execution of Maximilian' (MOMA, New York 2006), which brought together eight paintings on a single theme: the death by firing squad of the Austrian archduke Ferdinand Maximilian in Mexico. The Mannheim painting (*see* page 49) had first been exhibited in New York in 1879 and in Boston but found no American buyer. Most recently, the stunning, wide-ranging exhibition 'Manet and Modern Beauty: The Artist's Last Years' (J. Paul Getty Museum, Los Angeles and The Art Institute of Chicago, 2019–20) focused on his work of the 1870s and early '80s, drawing on many paintings in private collections and acknowledging contemporary fashion as central to Manet's late depictions of Parisian women. It emphasized his continued commitment to the Salon as well as the great influence of the eighteenth-century French masters Chardin, Boucher and Watteau on Manet's later work, suggesting that the artist was exploring his own position in the French School even as his health deteriorated.

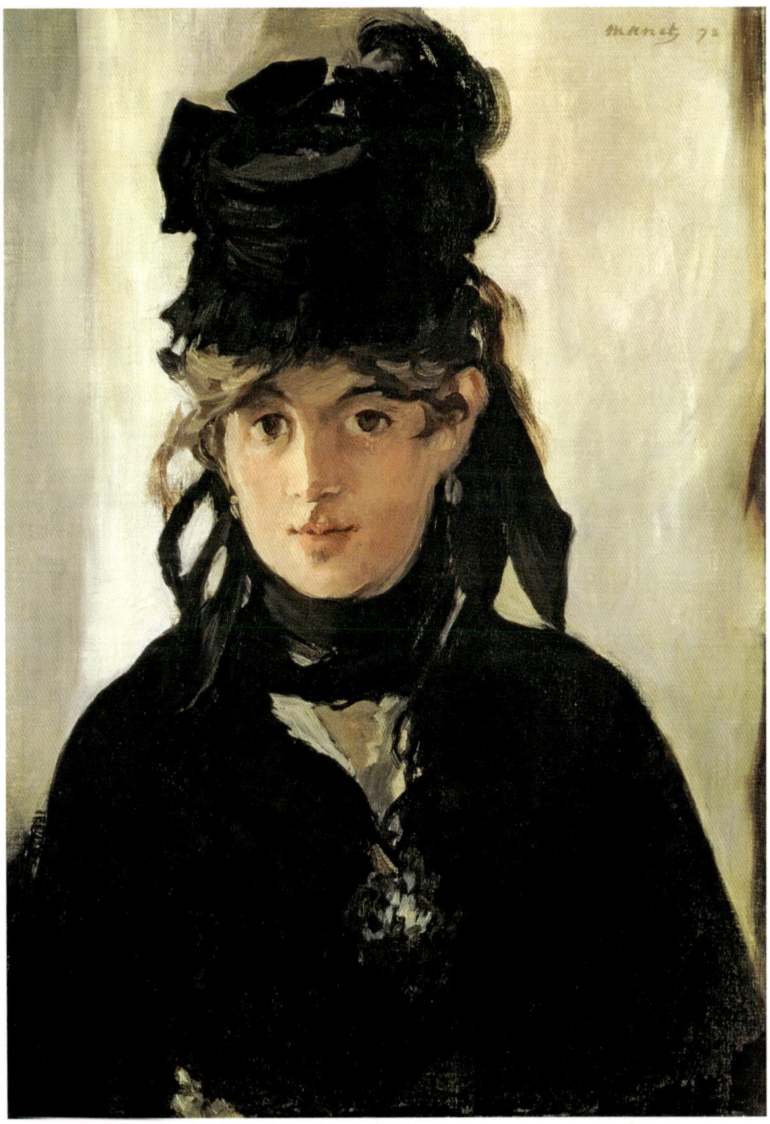

Berthe Morisot with a Bunch of Violets, *1872. Morisot was the great niece of the painter Jean-Honoré Fragonard (1732–1806). Dressed in mourning clothes, the violets are barely discernible as the light comes from the left, illuminating Morisot's face, but leaving much of the torso in shadow.*

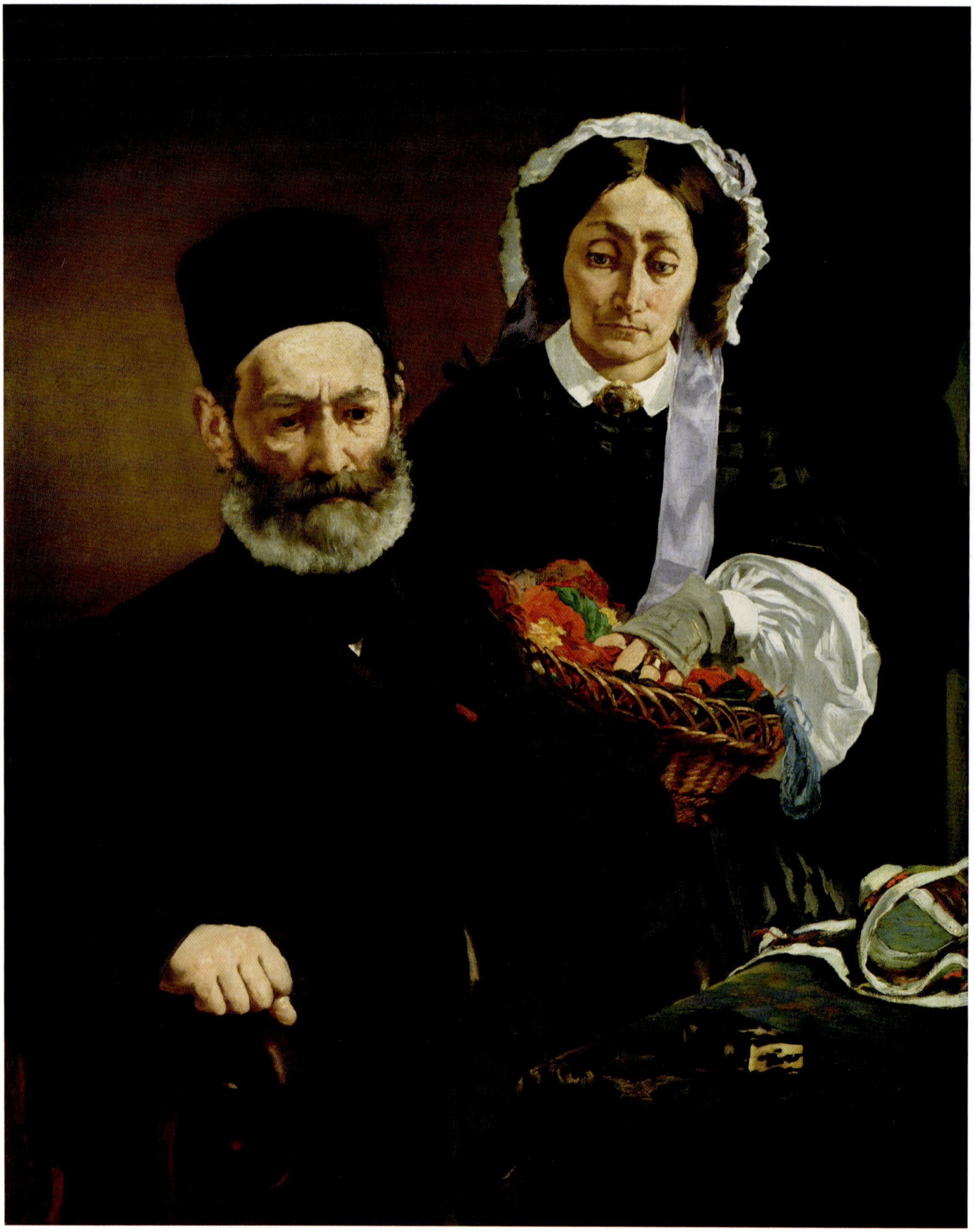

Portrait of Monsieur and Madame Auguste Manet, *1860. Manet's parents were affluent and well-connected. His father became paralyzed and lost his capacity to speak in 1857. Clearly unwell, his son shows him wearing the ribbon of the Legion of Honour of which he was so proud. The painting was accepted for the 1861 Salon.*

CHAPTER 2
The Young Artist

EARLY LIFE AND FAMILY BACKGROUND

Manet tends to be an artist who is appreciated for being a bold pioneer, a painter of modern life who broke new ground and influenced a younger generation of artists following him. Thus there has been a concentration upon his mature years, rather than his family background and significant early career, which was steeped in the traditional study of the Old Masters and particularly the artists of Spain. It is important to understand Manet's upbringing and how he matured into a fashionable, sociable artist who had such impact. Doing so allows us to appreciate his motivations, particularly his desire to triumph at the official annual Salon in Paris. Behind the façade of respectability, the Manet household was a tightly closed unit that held many secrets, some of which have never been resolved. As Sue Roe wrote in her book *The Private Lives of the Impressionists*, 'Manet was a complex character… he was a true Parisian.'

Édouard Manet was born on 23 January 1832 at 5, rue des Petits Augustins (now 5, rue Bonaparte) in Paris, into a well-connected bourgeois family. His father Auguste Manet (1797–1862), was a senior judge at the court of Seine, employed by the Ministry of Justice, and his mother Eugénie-Desirée Fournier (1811–95) was the daughter of a diplomat and boasted as her godfather the Swedish crown prince, who became Charles XIV of Sweden. He had two younger brothers: Eugène (1833–92), who went into the army and studied law but who is best known as the husband of the Impressionist painter Berthe Morisot, and Gustave (1835–84), who became a lawyer and politician. Manet painted his parents in a famous double portrait of 1860, and both his brothers acted as models for Édouard in his later artistic career.

The family were very much establishment – affluent, property owning and well-connected – and his education reflects their status. He attended the Institut Poiloup in Vaugirard from 1839 to 1844, where he first demonstrated a skill at drawing and was encouraged initially by his maternal uncle Captain Edmond-Édouard Fournier, who took him to the Louvre regularly and paid for him to attend a drawing class.

In 1844, he entered the Collège Rollin, where he met Antonin Proust, who would become a renowned journalist and politician and remained a lifelong friend of the artist. Finishing school in 1848 at the age of 16, Manet went to sea to train as a sailor, at his father's suggestion. He spent three months on the *Le Havre et Guadeloupe* bound for Brazil. On board, he drew caricatures of fellow sailors. In April 1849, however, in Rio de Janeiro he failed his first naval examinations and began to realize that life at sea was not for him. Having experienced the sea so intimately, it did provide later inspiration for his many accomplished marine pictures.

In June 1849, after failing his training school's entrance exam a second time, the teenager returned to Le Havre and eventually managed to persuade his parents to allow him to train as an artist in Paris. It was in the same year that Suzanne Leenhoff (1829–1906) was employed by his wealthy parents to give his two young brothers piano lessons. A young woman, just two years his senior, she would play a key part in his life as his future wife.

FORMAL TRAINING AND EARLY INFLUENCES

From 1850 to 1856, Manet studied under the academic history and genre painter Thomas Couture on rue Laval in Paris. Arriving with Couture at the age of 18, Manet embarked on a rigorous, six-year-long, traditional training with an artist who admired Venetian Renaissance art. These were turbulent political years in Paris: Louis Napoleon Bonaparte staged a military coup at the end of 1851 and declared himself Napoleon III in 1852, establishing the Second Empire.

THOMAS COUTURE

Couture was a painter of large historical paintings such as *The Romans During the Decadence*, which took him three years to complete and is a commentary on what he saw as the moral decadence of France under the July Monarchy. For his work, he won several medals at the Paris Salon, but he was also a fine portraitist. These include his *Portrait of Antoine Étex* and the historian *Jules Michelet*, and this emphasis on portraiture may have influenced his pupil. Despite Couture's eagerness to challenge traditional academic practice, which appealed to Manet, the pupil often found the training frustrating and the two did not always see eye to eye. However, Couture's sharp use of tonal contrasts undoubtedly influenced Manet's artistic development: although there are fundamental differences between teacher and student, it is clear that the younger artist learned from Couture a good grasp of drawing and pictorial technique. Other famous pupils of Couture included Puvis de Chavannes (1824–1898) and Henri Fantin-Latour (1836–1904).

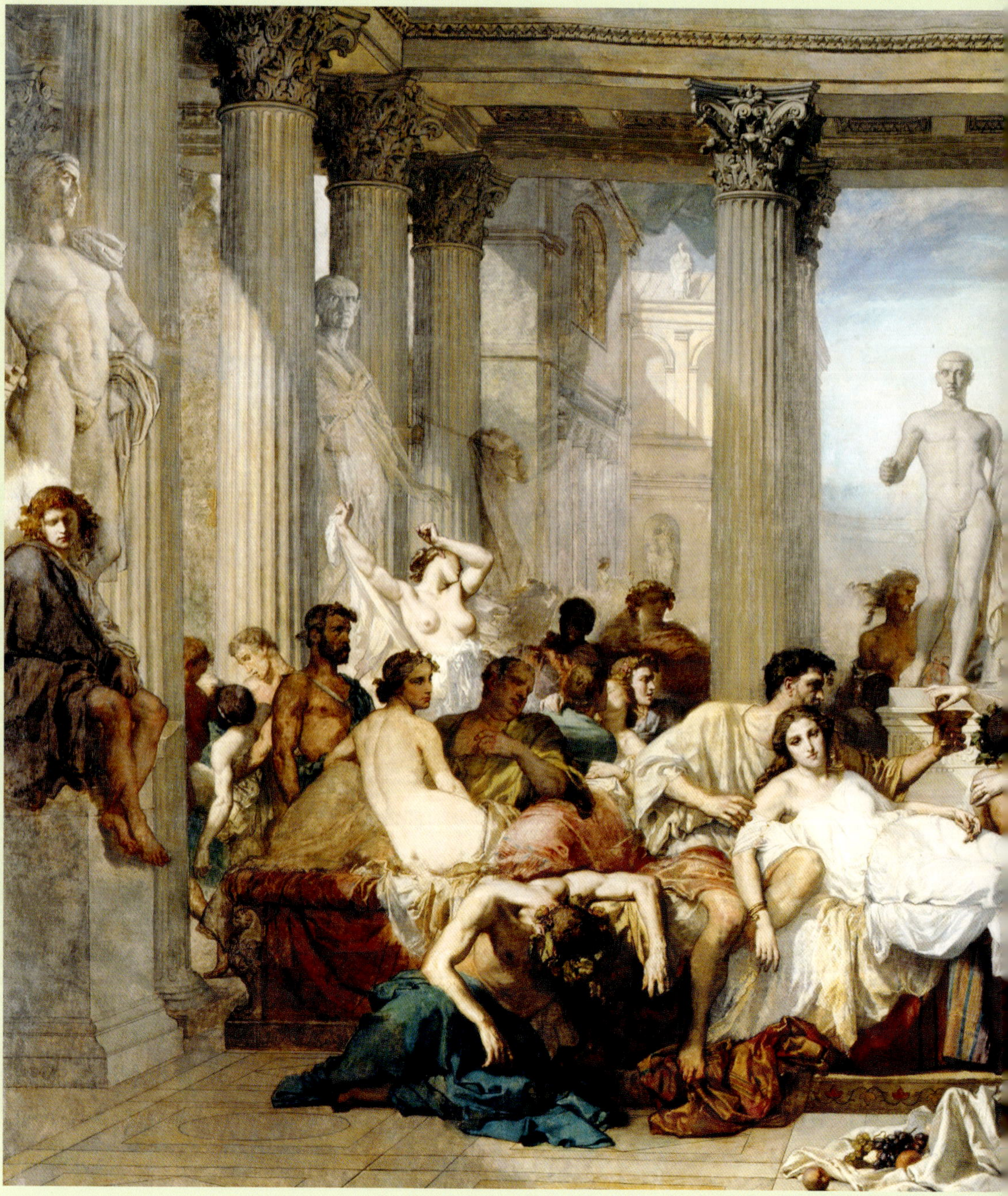

Below: The Romans During the Decadence, *Thomas Couture, 1847. Couture took three years to complete this work and quoted two lines from the Roman poet Juvenal, in the catalogue for the 1847 Salon when it was exhibited: 'Crueller than war, vice fell upon Rome and avenged the conquered world', referencing his thoughts on the state of French society at the time. A Republican, he criticized the moral decadence of France under the July monarchy and Manet's family would have been well aware of Courture's politics when they decided to send their son to train with him..*

Right (above): Portrait of Antoine Étex, *Thomas Couture, 1845–55. Étex was a French academic sculptor, whom Courture captured in this confident pose suggesting his ambitious aspirations. Such assured portraiture would have impressed the young Manet.*

Right (below): *Thomas Couture, photographed by Étienne Carjat* c. 1860.

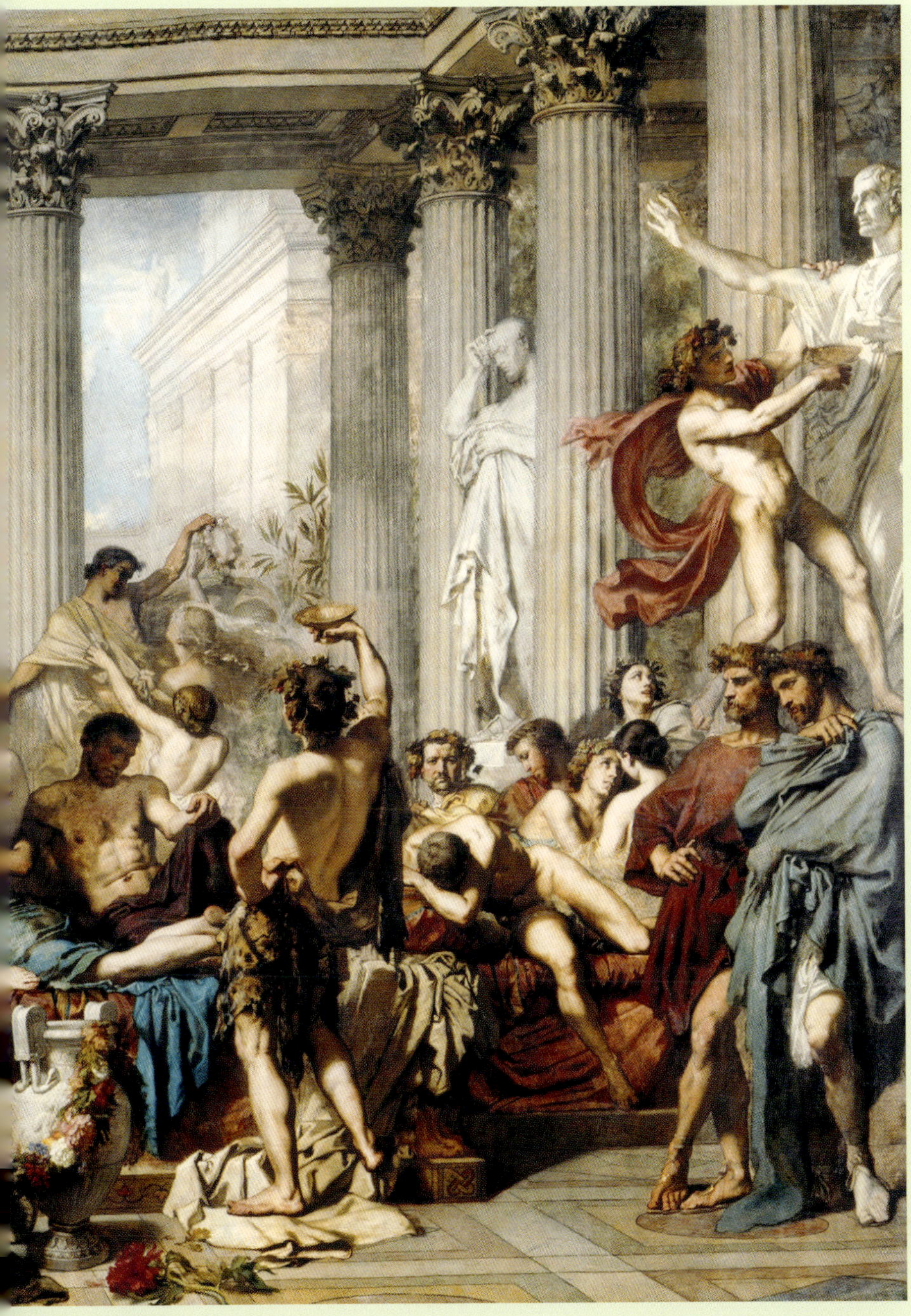

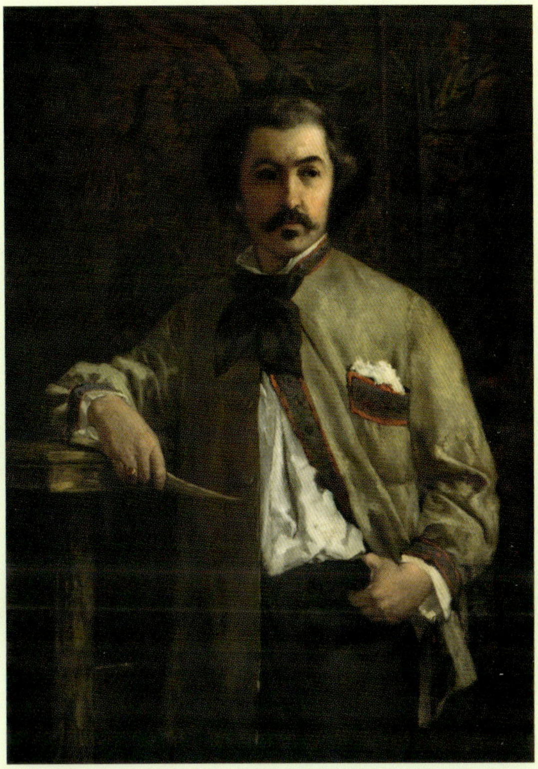

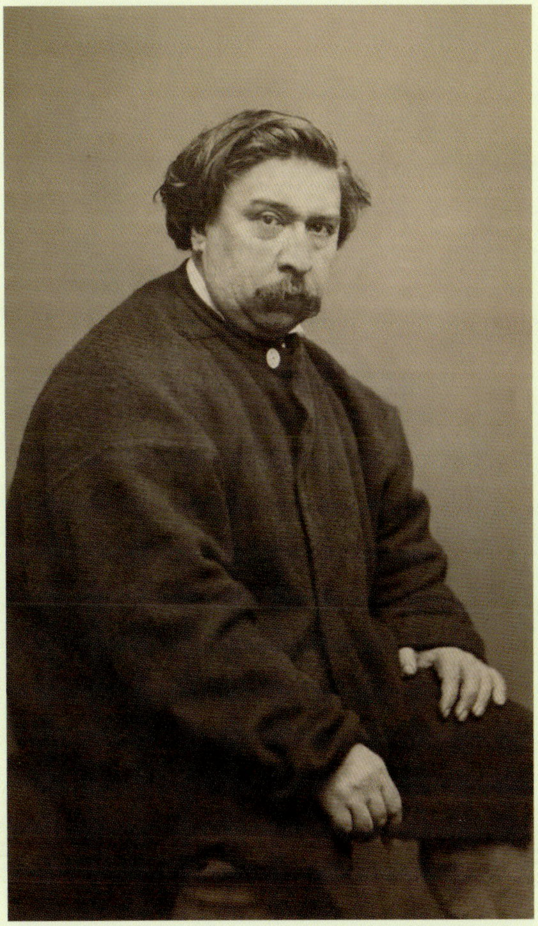

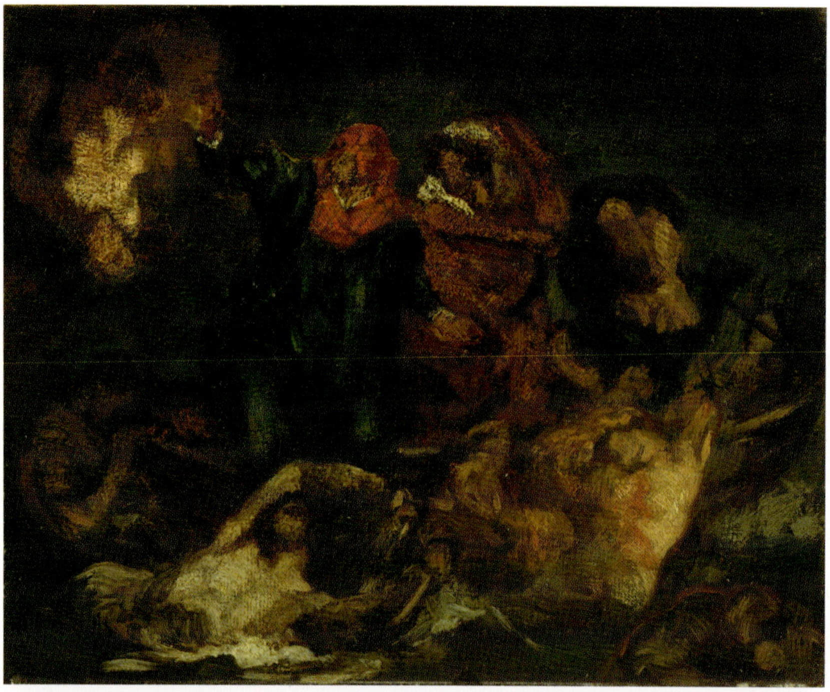

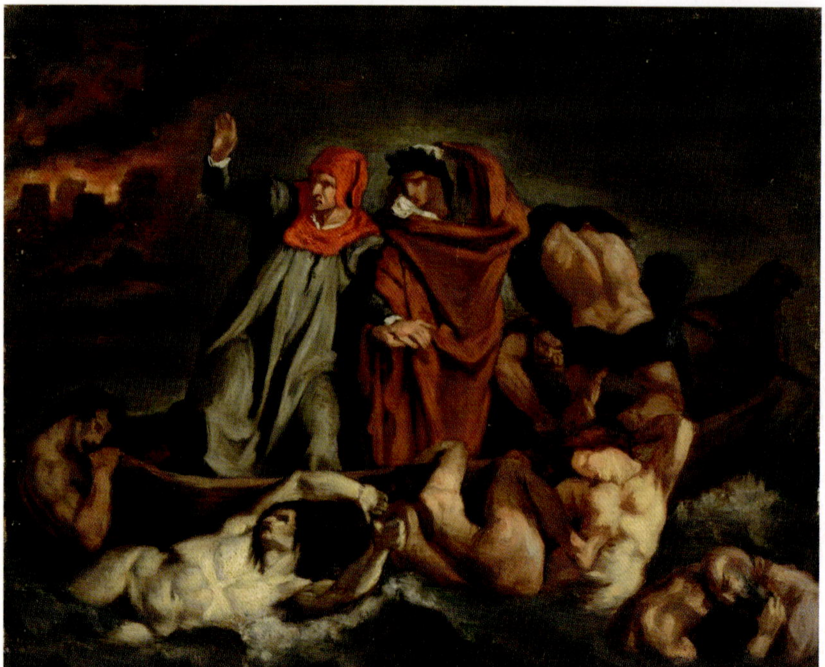

Above (top) The Barque of Dante (after Delacroix), *1859*.
Above (bottom): The Barque of Dante, *Eugène Delacroix, 1822. This was Delacroix's first major work and illustrates canto eight of Dante's* Inferno. *Manet made two copies of Delacroix's celebrated painting which is now in the Musée du Louvre, Paris.*

The few surviving works from Manet's student period are mostly copies after the Old Masters. He diligently copied works at the Musée du Louvre, his first registration to copy there dating from January 1850. There, he encountered great Italian art, and encouraged by Couture, he went on a study trip to Italy in 1853, visiting Florence and Venice. Gradually he was coming under the influence of Gustave Courbet, whose work could be seen in 1855 at the independent Pavillon du Réalisme at the Exposition Universelle. That same year, Manet visited Eugène Delacroix's studio and requested permission to copy his masterpiece *The Barque of Dante*. In 1857, Delacroix recommended that Manet copy Rubens' work, specifically the *Portrait of Hélène Fourment and her Children* in the Louvre in Paris, and the young man also much admired the Dutch painter Frans Hals, who clearly influenced his style.

In 1856, as he came to the end of his training with Couture, Manet embarked on more travel to study art in Holland, Germany and Austria before returning to Florence in 1857. His new admiration for Spanish art occurred at about the same that he left Couture's studio in 1856, and he turned particularly to Velázquez and Goya. In Austria, he had particularly admired Velázquez's beautiful portraits, sent to Vienna by Philip IV. Back in Paris, he copied works attributed to Velázquez in the Louvre, including the *Portrait of the Infanta Margarita* and *The Little Cavaliers,* which was then attributed to Velázquez. Some commentators feel that the composition influenced *The Spanish Cavaliers* (1859) and the later *Music in the Tuileries*.

In this Lyon work, Manet clearly references elements from his copy of *Little Cavaliers*. The background figure wearing a pink cloak clearly relates to the fifth from the right in his copy after the *Little Cavaliers*. The open door is further an obvious tribute to Velázquez's *Las Meninas*. The child in the right foreground is probably the seven- or eight-year-old Léon Koëlla, who appears again in other works.

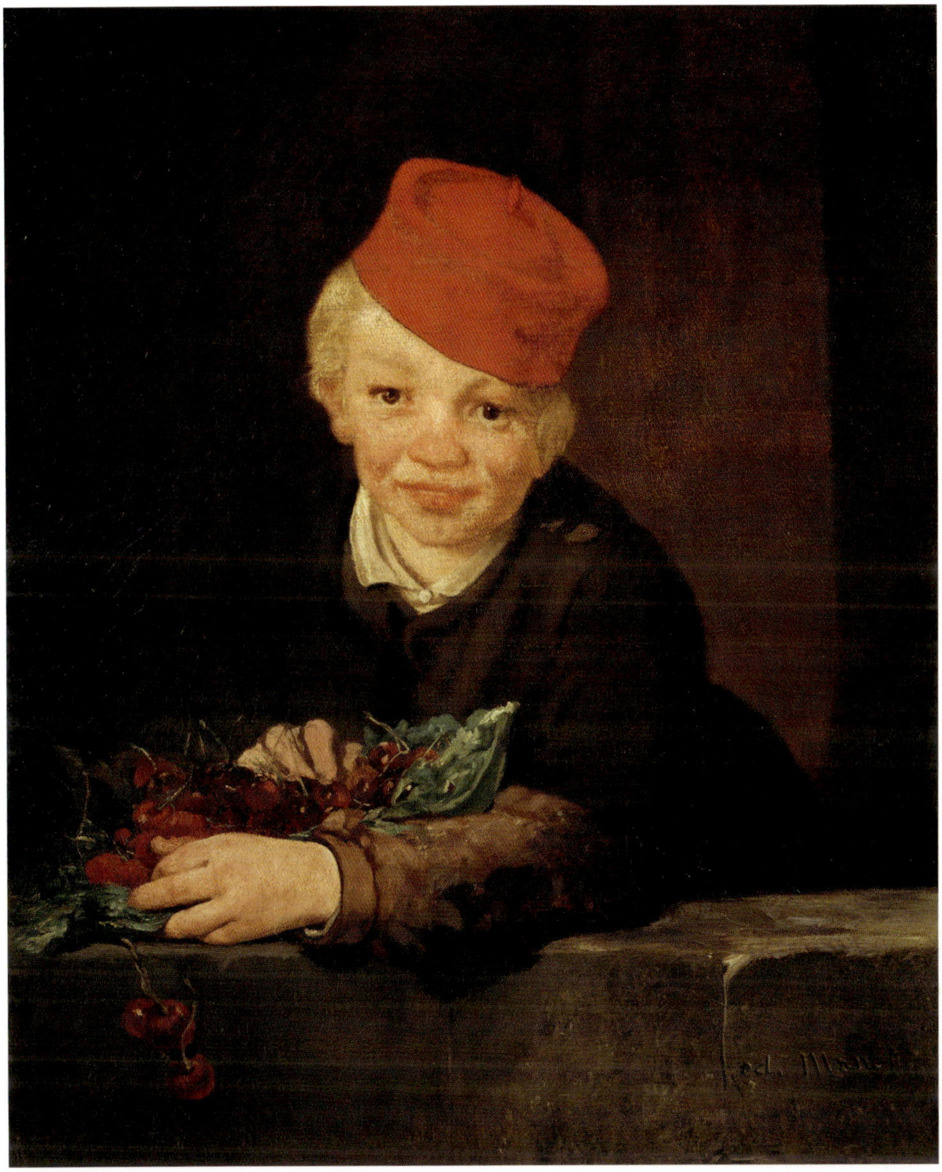

Boy with Cherries, c. *1858. This charming work is clearly influenced by the Italian master Caravaggio as well as Dutch seventeenth-century artists. The model was a tragic young studio assistant. It was first exhibited at the Galerie Martinet in Paris in September 1859. Manet continued to contribute to exhibitions organized by the Galerie Martinet during the early 1860s. This picture remained in his own collection and was sold by the art dealer Paul Durand-Ruel after the artist's death.*

WORKING INDEPENDENTLY

In 1856, Manet set up a studio on rue Lavoisier, which he shared with Albert de Balleroy (1828–72), a painter of animals and military subjects. There he painted *The Boy with Cherries* (*c.* 1858). His style in this period was characterized by loose brush strokes, simplification of details, and the suppression of tone, as he came under the influence of realist artists such as Gustave Courbet and turned to subjects such as beggars, singers, Gypsies and models in cafés and bars.

Boy with Cherries is clearly influenced by the Italian master Caravaggio and his depictions of young boys, as well as Dutch genre painting of the seventeenth century, perhaps even by Rembrandt's famous *Girl at a Window*. Such Dutch works use the stone parapet to establish the spatial definition of the composition. In Manet's painting, the cherries seem to represent an allegory for the senses. Behind the direct gaze and fresh-faced smile of the young boy lies tragedy. Alexandre, who washed Manet's paintbrushes and occasionally posed for him, ended up committing suicide at the age of 15 in the artist's studio at rue Lavoisier. The episode inspired Charles Baudelaire to write *La Corde*, a short story he dedicated to Manet and which was initially published in *Le Figaro* on 7 February 1864 and later published in the compilation *Le Spleen de Paris*.

While *Boy with Cherries* reflects Italian and Dutch

influences, other works such as *Woman with a Jug (Suzanne Leenhoff)*, 1858–60, clearly show the impact of Italian Renaissance painting, especially the Venetian School: note the poetic way Suzanne is depicted. The colouring, as well as the placing of the figure in front of a window with a view of a Classical landscape, clearly references Italian Renaissance pictures, including the work of Titian. This series of paintings shows Manet exploring the traditional Old Masters, which he had studied on his travels. This particular painting testifies to his increasing attachment to the young piano teacher who lived at his parent's home. In 1852, she had moved to live with her mother and given birth to a son for whom Manet would maintain a strong attachment throughout his life and who would feature as a model in these paintings too.

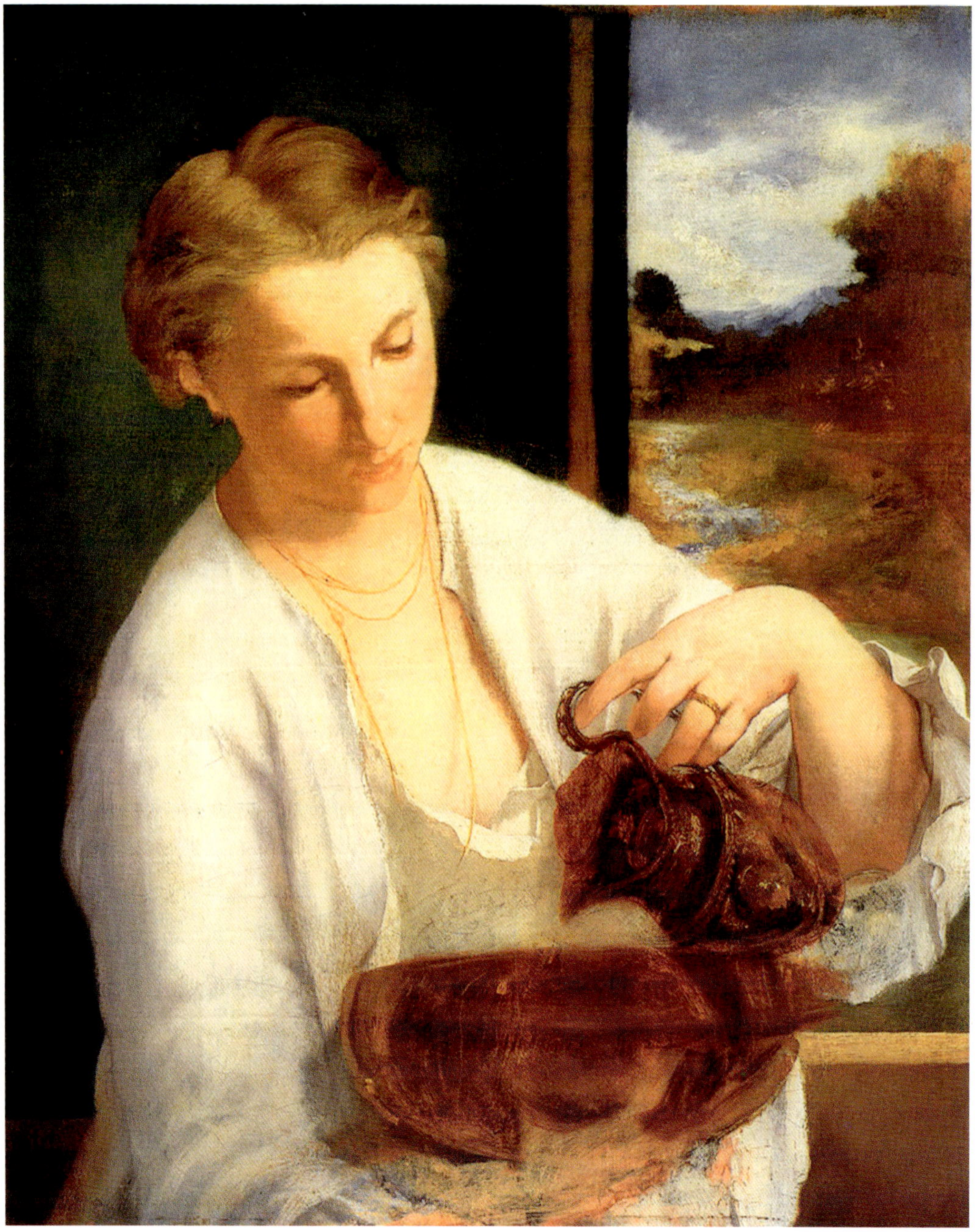

Woman with a Jug (Suzanne Leenhoff), *1858–60. This early work is obviously influenced by Italian Renaissance painters such as Titian in the colour palette, the positioning of the figure in front of a window and the distant landscape. The model is his lover and future wife Suzanne Leenhoff. X-ray and infra-red photos of the picture have revealed that the canvas has been reworked and is a fragment of a larger composition, possibly a monumental work Manet was preparing for the Salon in a grand architectural setting in line with his master Courture's example.*

Like every young ambitious artist in Paris, his main aim was to have his works accepted at the official Salon, and this would naturally have been encouraged, both by Couture and by his own his family. Dating back to 1667, the Salon had been firmly established by the early 1860s as a huge exhibition of contemporary painting held in lofty galleries of the Palais d'Industrie, intended to foster all that was good in French art. Paintings were selected by a jury and there was a prestigious programme of honours and awards made. The high walls were hung floor to ceiling with paintings arranged in alphabetical order. The public were admitted by payment of an entrance fee and the majority of works accepted were for sale. For Manet, acceptance into the Salon remained a career-long obsession: he later wrote that 'the Salon is the real field of battle. It is there that one must take one's measure'.

In 1859, Manet moved to a new studio at 58, rue de la Victoire and continued work on his controversial *The Absinthe Drinker,* 1859. Velázquez's influence and even Honoré Daumier's are plain, with its brown, grey and black tonality. The man is shown full length, wearing a black top hat, wrapped in a brown cloak and sitting on a stone ledge, one foot extended forward with an empty bottle discarded on the floor. Manet later added a half-full glass of absinthe on the ledge. Influenced by the realism of Gustave Courbet, the work shows a mundane subject on a large scale – a lost soul painted to the size of an aristocratic portrait. The sitter was a well-known alcoholic, Collardet, known by many in the area around the Louvre. The full glass and empty discarded bottle on the floor make it clear that this is a man with addictive issues, a familiar sight in Paris at the time. Manet lamented to his friend Antonin Proust that 'I have done a Parisian type, studied in Paris, putting into it the simplicity of craft which I discovered in Velázquez. No one understands it. If I painted a Spanish type, it would be better understood.' Indeed, Couture did not approve of Manet's experiments in realism. In 1859, the painting came before the Salon Committee, Manet's first submission to the Salon. Despite the support of the great Delacroix himself, it failed to find approval amongst the jury and was rejected. This was the first of his paintings to shock and confound

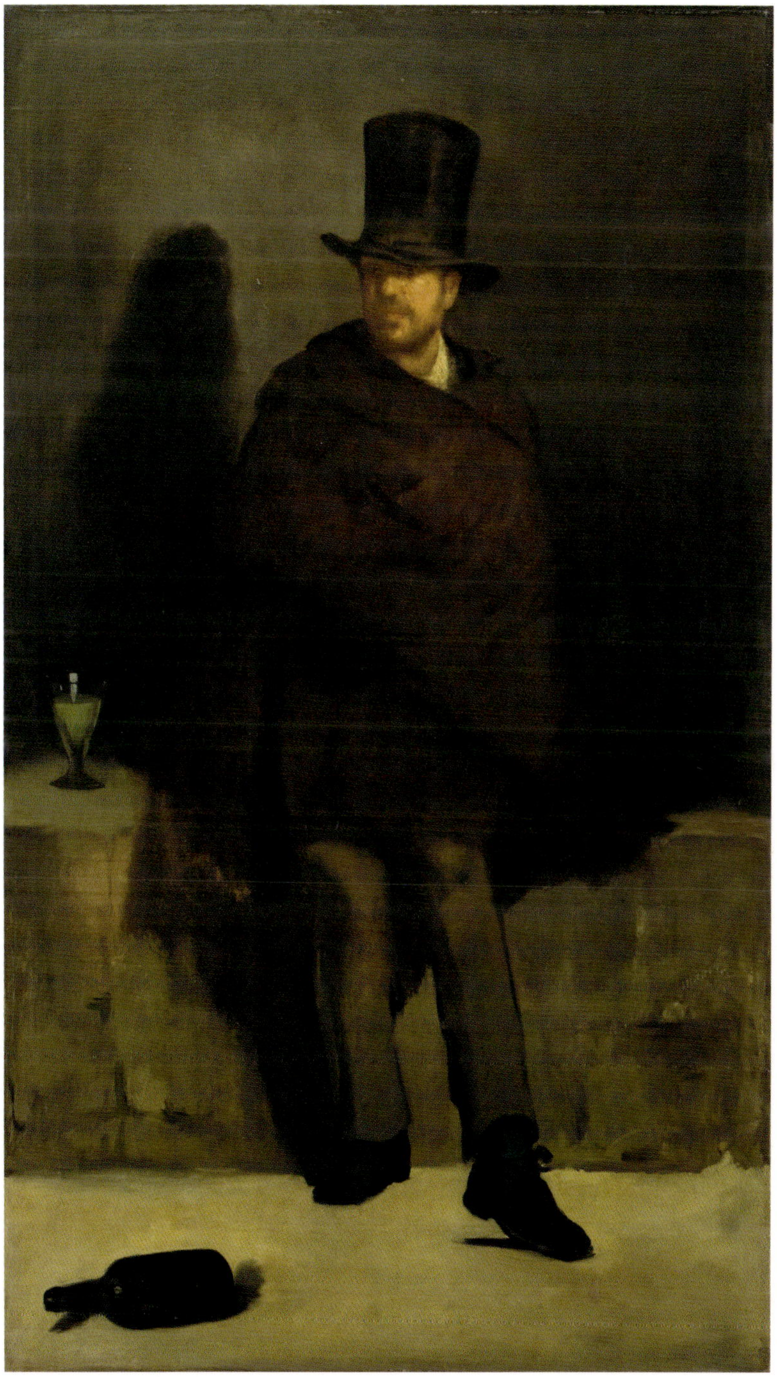

The Absinthe Drinker, *1858. The alcoholic rag picker depicted was well known in the Louvre area and called Collardet. The work is influenced by the realism of Velázquez and Gustave Courbet, but did not find the approval of Couture. It was the first work Manet submitted to the Paris Salon in 1859, being rejected with only Eugène Delacroix voting in its favour.*

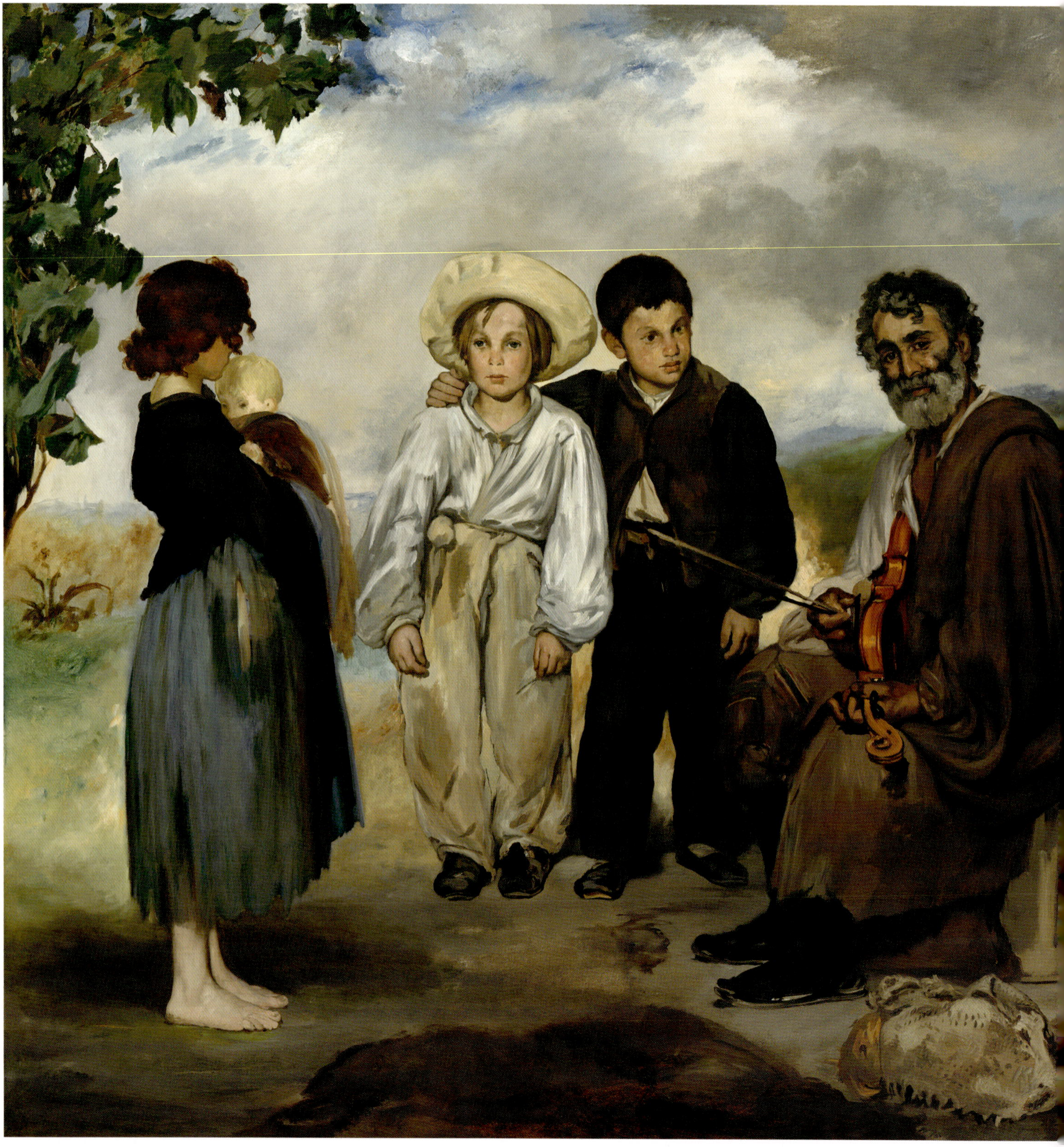

The Old Musician, *1862. Manet observed the street life of Paris in a series of studies. Here, he shows a strolling musician with his grey, bearded and weathered face. In his 60s, Jean Lagrène was well known as the leader of a local gypsy gang in the Batignolles area. The work reflects the influence of the seventeenth-century Le Nain brothers.*

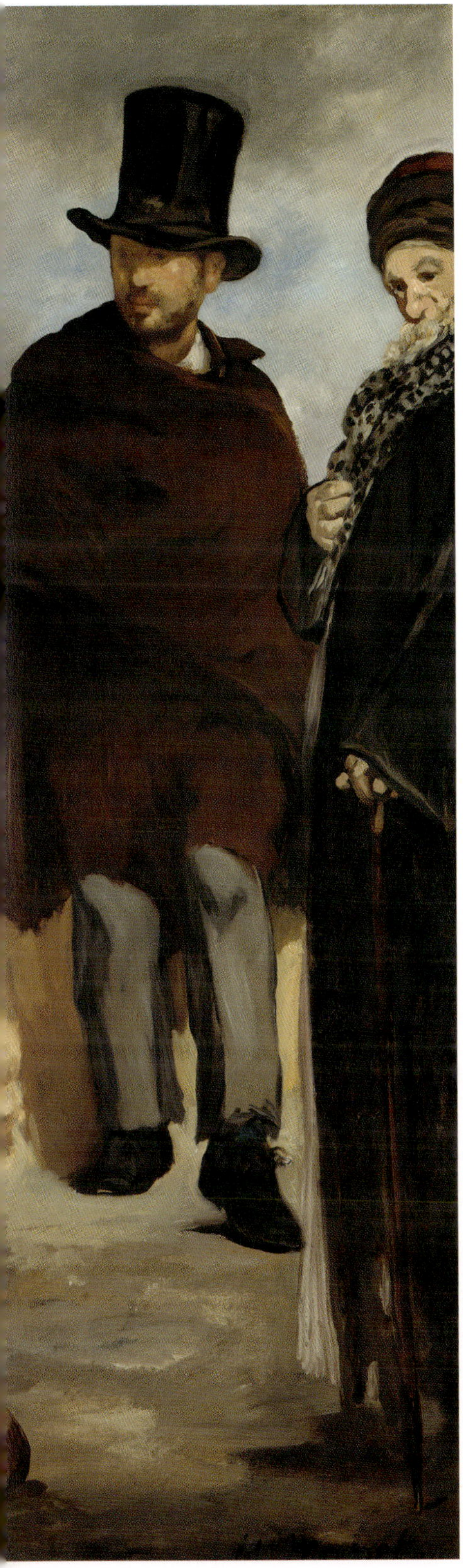

critics, with his bold technique and unorthodox approach to subject matter. Undaunted, he began a few years later a larger ambitious work which has some debt to Le Nain and more still to Velázquez's *The Triumph of Bacchus*, also known as *The Drinkers*. This was *The Old Musician* (1862), in which he reproduces the *Absinthe Drinker* again, but this time as part of a coherent group of figures set within a landscape.

Once again Manet used real models. The old musician himself, with his bearded and weathered face, was a man in his mid 60s called Jean Lagrène, leader of a local gypsy band in the Batignolles. At the right, the elderly figure has traditionally been identified as Guéroult, an elderly Jew who lived in the ghetto area of Paris known as Little Poland in the Batignolles. It was here in 1862 that Manet moved his studio, to 81, rue Guyot. The absinthe drinker with his top hat was, of course, Collardet, who is shown this time without his glass and bottle. Manet's representation of the urban poor involved not only the central strolling musician but a gypsy girl with a baby and gypsy boys. These were the type of urban poor who were literally displaced by the major urban public works programme ordered by Emperor Napoleon III in the early 1860s to rid Paris of large, unhealthy, overcrowded slum areas. These slums were replaced by wide tree-lined boulevards, new parks and squares, with a new sewer system, under the eye of Baron Haussmann. In fact, Lagrène himself, the central figure here, had initially found work on a building site but was injured in an accident and became an organ grinder. He would have been recognizable to many who saw this painting.

Manet observes this group with a detached gaze and distinctly modern ambiguity. Technically, the painting demonstrates his approach to oil painting, placing pigments side by side rather than blending tones, creating a sense of immediacy which would usually be associated with a sketch rather than a finished work. His observations are in sharper and crisper focus than the traditional academic approach of his fellow artists. It was this very approach, characteristic of Manet's style in the early 1860s, that Monet and Renoir admired when they first saw his paintings. It was exhibited at the Galerie Martinet in 1863, along with 14 other works in his first solo exhibition in Paris, but it did not sell and remained in his studio until his death.

EARLY SUCCESS AT THE SALON AND FAMILY MYSTERY

From the summer of 1860 Manet set up a studio in rue de Douai for some 18 months and began work on two key paintings, *The Spanish Singer* and a double portrait of his parents. As he turned 30, he began to frequent the fashionable Café Tortoni and Café de Bade, on the boulevard des Italiens. There he often held court, enjoying being the centre of attention, and surrounding himself with a wide circle of artistic, literary and musical friends.

When the double portrait of his parents and *The Spanish Singer* were finished, he submitted them to the Salon. Both were accepted. By the time Manet painted the famous portrait of his parents, his ailing father was then 63 years old and his mother 48, although she looks much older in this portrait. His father's arm grips the chair of his seat, and the technique used on his beard may reference Manet's study of Rembrandt and Frans Hals. The couple sat for their son in their apartment at 69, rue de Clinchy.

Both sitters look down and appear tense and although they are wearing everyday dress, his father's jacket displays the ribbon of the Legion of Honour, which contrasts with the domestic detail of his mother's basket of colourful yarn. Perhaps she is asking her husband to help select a wool colour to continue her work which is on the table. Her face is particularly anxious and strained. Her dark dress is enlivened by a vivid blue ribbon falling from her headdress. Preparatory drawings show the artist initially portrayed his father looking straight out at the viewer, which would have changed the atmosphere of the finished portrait.

By 1857, Manet's father Auguste, suffering from tertiary syphilis, had become paralyzed. Manet captures his ailing father, with his concerned mother at his shoulder. Behind the scene Manet's relationship with his parents was an interesting one. In 1851 Suzanne Leenhoff, the attractive Dutch piano teacher who taught his brothers, became pregnant. Her mother quickly arrived from Holland on the news and was supporting Suzanne when her son was born on 29 January 1852. He was registered as Koëlla, Léon Édouard, the son of Koëlla and Suzanne Leenhoff. It is unclear to whom the name Koëlla refers, but the boy was raised as the youngest son of Suzanne's parents, and he was presented in society as her brother. Suzanne, her mother and the baby set up home on the boulevard des Batignolles and Manet spent as much time with them as possible. It was clear to his mother that he had fallen in love with the Dutch girl and she accepted and assisted this arrangement. The parentage of Léon, who appears in so many of Manet's paintings, has always been questioned. Was he the child of the young artist, or was his father the formidable Judge Manet shown in the double portrait? The situation was a delicate one. An illegitimate child would have presented challenges for an established family such as the Manets. It seems a solution was found: Manet lived a double life, dividing his time between Suzanne and her son and his own parents, a situation that lasted for ten years until 1862, when the Judge died. In October of that year, Manet and Suzanne departed for a visit to Holland and returned man and wife. Having now inherited from his father, he and Suzanne set up home at 34, boulevard des Batignolles, with Léon. Once they were man and wife, Suzanne became the most frequently painted of his sitters and Léon too featured regularly in Manet's paintings. It was also in 1862 that Manet met Victorine Meurent, who would become one of his favourite models and his mistress.

The portrait of his parents had been accepted at the 1861 Paris Salon alongside *The Spanish Singer*, which was hung prominently and actually won an honourable mention. This was his first major success, and the sitter, who posed in Manet's studio, may have been the Spanish singer Jerome Bosch, who was playing with a troupe in Paris at the time. Despite the embrace of the Salon, both works were overlooked by some of the most important critics of the time, including Théodore de Banville. But his work was noticed by the poet Charles Baudelaire, and *The Spanish Singer* drew the attention of the critic Théophile Gautier, who had recently returned from Spain himself. Writing in *Le Moniteur Universel* and noting the debt to Velázquez and Goya, he dubbed the sitter a 'Guitarero, who has not stepped out of a comic opera… How heartily he sings as he plucks away at his guitar!' and continued that 'there is a great deal of talent in this life-size figure, painted with a full brush in courageous strokes and really true colour.' In fact, the pose of the singer is unnatural and he appears to be trying to tap his foot while also playing the guitar and singing. It feels as if at any moment he might tip over the bench on which he is sitting. The depiction of his mouth is also unnerving. Furthermore, Manet appears to have painted a left-handed guitarist playing an instrument strung for a right-handed player and yet the work was deemed a success. *The Spanish Singer* was etched by Manet in 1861 and printed in five states between 1861 and 1863. The influence of Velázquez is clear in the foreground pitcher and fruit.

Spanish art continued to be a major influence in the next decade for Manet's art, and in 1865 he finally visited the country himself. Having begun to establish a name for himself with success at the Salon, Manet was now poised to make a real impact.

The Spanish Singer, *1860. This life-sized painting was hung prominently at the 1861 Salon, and actually won an honourable mention, becoming Manet's first painting to receive wider critical attention. The sitter was the Spanish singer Jerome Bosch, who was playing with a troupe in Paris at the time. It was painted in Manet's studio and his outfit was drawn from costumes and props the artist had acquired and which appear in other works.*

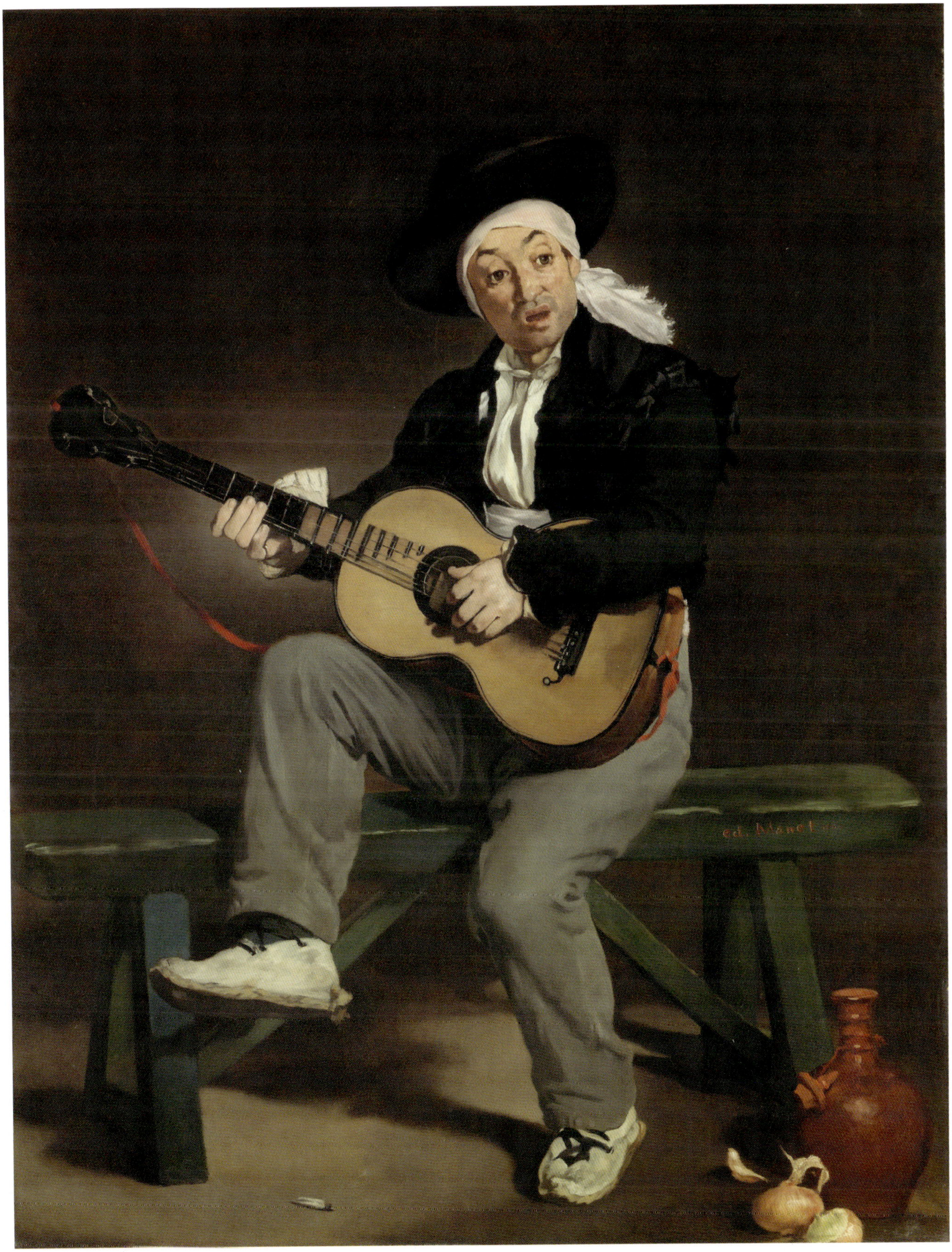

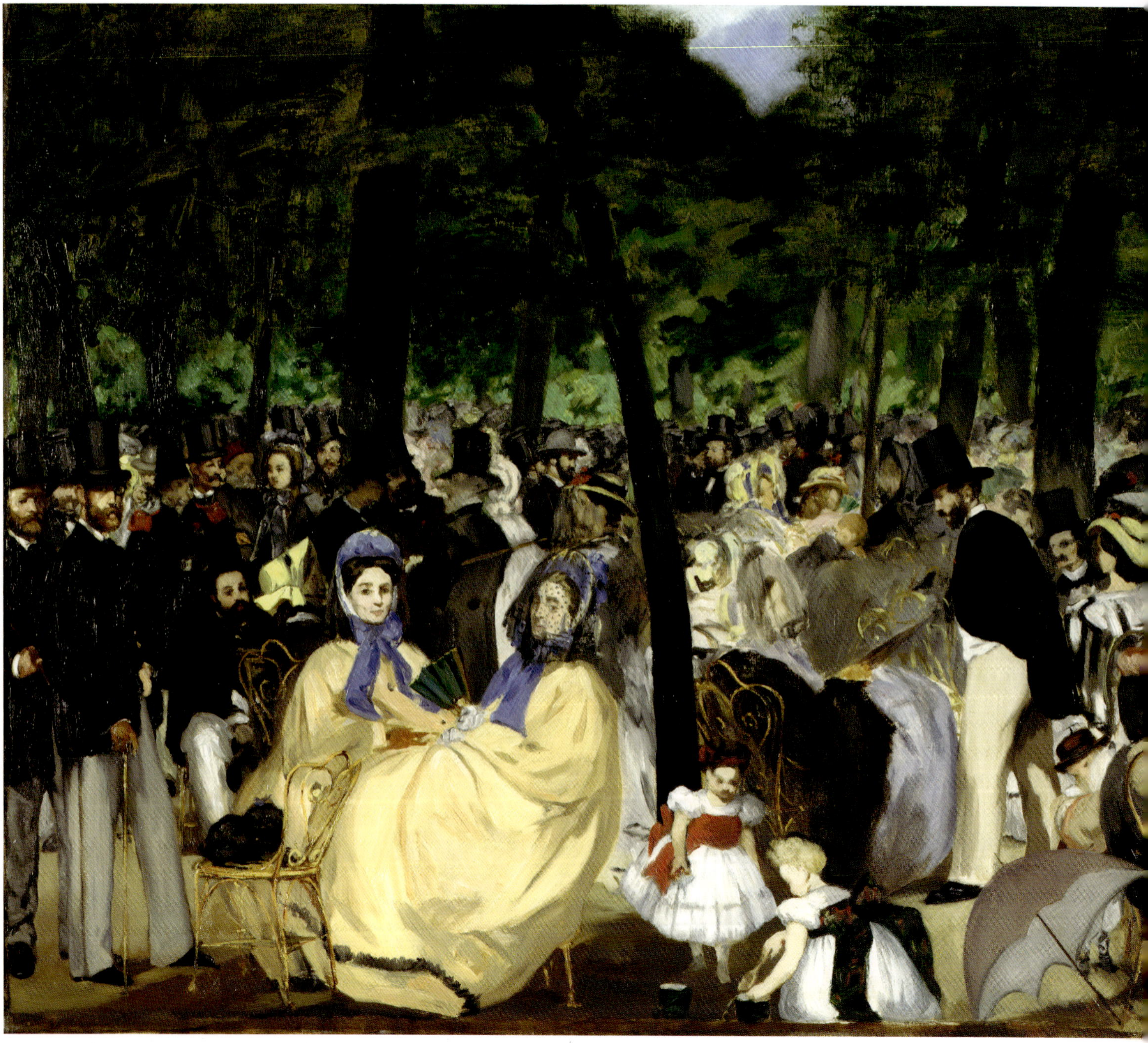

Above: Music in the Tuileries Gardens, *1862.*
Opposite: *A detail from* Music in the Tuileries Gardens. *A bearded Édouard Manet is shown on the extreme left, holding his cane.*

CHAPTER 3
Making an Impact

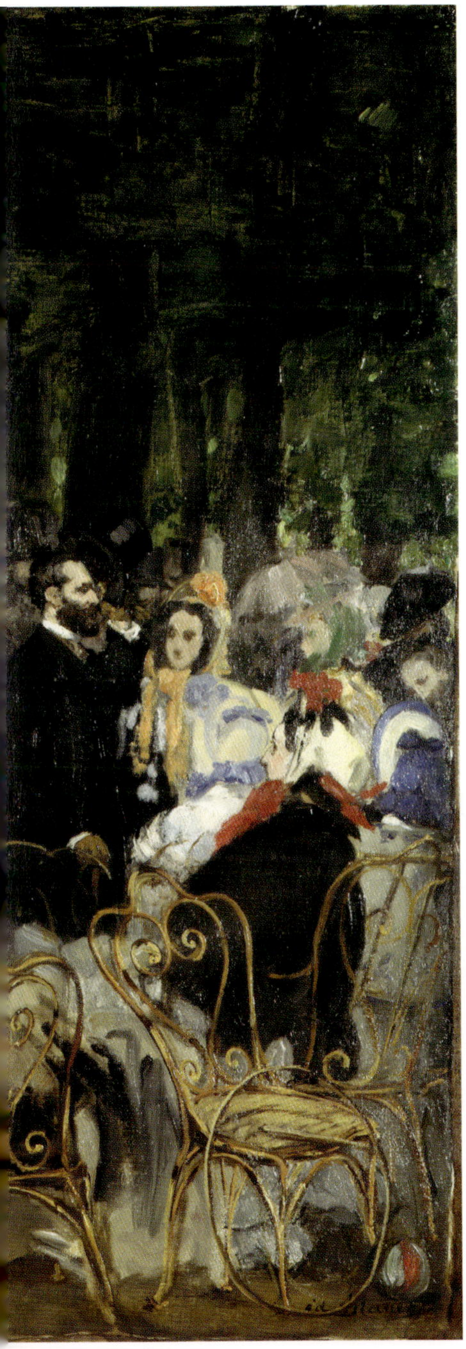

OBSERVING FASHIONABLE PARIS

For Manet, the 1860s were a crucial period when he established his career with a series of paintings, some of them controversial with the critics and public alike, but which are today renowned. Paris continued to be transformed by Haussmann's building project for Napoleon III. The cramped medieval city was for a while a building site, gradually emerging as a new, planned, modern capital city with open spaces. Following much demolition, a new network of interconnecting wide boulevards lined with cafés, restaurants and theatres emerged, while railways connected the city itself with the rest of France. Manet was already a regular member of the emerging café society and central to the evening gatherings at the Café Guerbois, where animated discussions on modern art took place. New railway stations opened – the Gare de Lyon in 1855 and the Gare du Nord in 1864. Four new parks were created and the original parks such as the Jardin du Luxembourg were refurbished and replanted.

Manet was a sophisticated man about town, who observed the changing modern city around him and who would find inspiration in the contemporary society of the city for his work. He had already observed certain aspects of city life and in the same year that he had painted the *Old Musician*, he also turned his attention to modern and fashionable society. In his elegant painting *Music in the Tuileries Gardens*, he captured the stylish and sophisticated bourgeois crowd who gathered at the Tuileries Gardens, an extension of Napoleon III's palace, where music was played in the open air twice a week. Many of those who attended such events were part of Manet's extensive cultured circle and he would have experienced such scenes first hand.

He worked on *Music in the Tuileries Gardens* over the summer and early autumn of 1862 in his studio at 81, rue Guyot, visiting the gardens regularly to make observations. The composition can almost be read as a self-portrait, among friends enjoying listening to music. The sophisticated Manet had many artistic and cultured contacts, from painters to musicians, intellectuals and art critics. In *Music in the Tuileries*

Gardens, he included some of his closest friends and he subtly included himself – standing at the far left with a cane, although partly obscured by another figure, his friend the animal painter Albert de Balleroy, with whom he had recently shared a studio. Other painters we recognize include Gustave Courbet, Charles Monginot and Fantin-Latour, as well as the sculptor and critic Zacharie Astruc, one of the first to recognize Manet's talents. Other critics and writers can be identified, such as Champfleury, Théophile Gautier, Charles Baudelaire, Aurélien Scholl (known as the 'journalist of the boulevards') and Baron Taylor (a great admirer of Spanish art, as was Manet), as well as the composer Jacques Offenbach. Seated in the foreground are two society figures: Madame Loubens and, wearing a veil, Madame Lejosne, the wife of Commander Lejosne. It was at her salon that Manet was introduced to the critic Charles Baudelaire, a key supporter for him. Manet's younger brother Eugène, is also present, wearing cream trousers and a top hat, situated just right of centre. It has been suggested that for some of these sitters, Manet used *cartes de visite* to capture likenesses, although family members and friends would no doubt have been happy to sit for him.

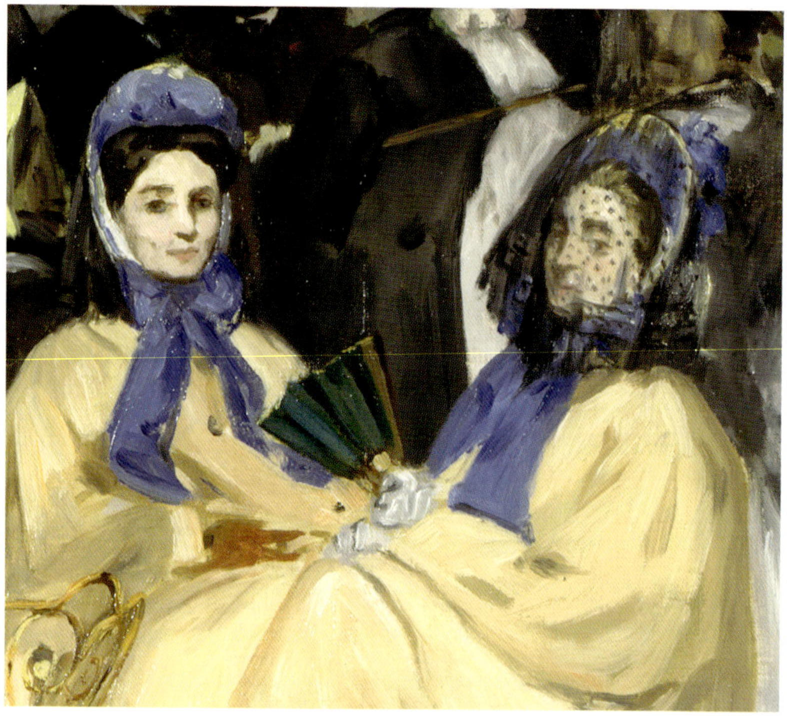

Above and below: *Details from* Music in the Tuileries Gardens. *Above are two society figures – Madame Loubens (left) and Madame Lejosne (veiled, right). Below is Édouard Manet's brother, Eugène, with the composer Jacques Offenbach seen behind, by the tree.*

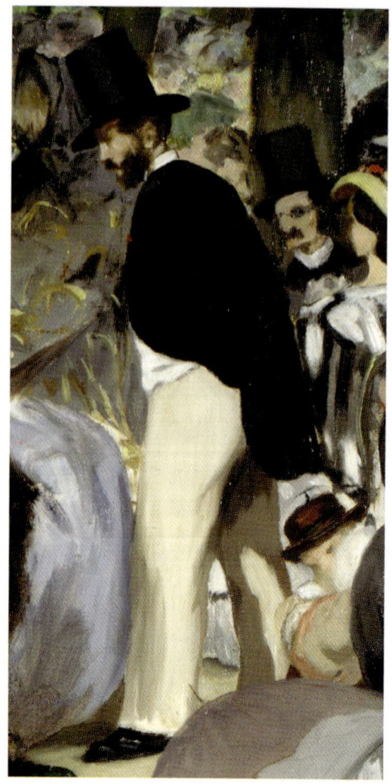

This fashionable set are posed by Manet in the famous garden with its chestnut trees, listening to music from the band and dressed in the height of Parisian fashion. Some are sitting on the recently introduced wrought-iron furniture. It is Manet's first attempt to depict contemporary life in Second Empire Paris and demonstrates his early interest in how city dwellers spent their leisure time. Later, such subjects representing modern life would also, of course, attract the Impressionists. The informality of Manet's composition would have stuck contemporary onlookers, and it has been suggested that this could have come about as a result of his study of etchings by artists such as Paul Gavarni and Constantin Guys, two artists favoured by Baudelaire. Although this work would appear to be less influenced by Spanish art than many of his pictures of this period, the way in which Manet situates himself at the very edge of the picture may still reflect the influence of Velázquez. Manet had recently made a copy in the Louvre of *The Little Cavaliers*. It shows an imaginary gathering of seventeenth-century Spanish artists, including the great Velázquez with Murillo, standing in relatively similar positions to those in which Manet depicted himself and de Balleroy. Like Velázquez, Manet is continually interested in the relationship between the observer and the observed. Baudelaire argued that modern life was as heroic and worthy of painting as any literary subject, insisting: 'Modernity is the transient, the fleeting, the contingent.' Some critics maintain that this painting by Manet was a direct response to Baudelaire's call for images of transient beauty within contemporary urban life. At the time in contemporary Paris, showing a fashionable

Right: *A detail from* Music in the Tuileries Gardens. *This group of figures behind Madame Loubens and Madame Lejosne, consist of the artist Fantin-Latour, famous for his still life and flower paintings, who can be identified staring straight ahead, and Charles Baudelaire (in profile), captured in much less detail, in this group of fashionably dressed Parisian men enjoying an open air concert in the Tuileries Gardens.*

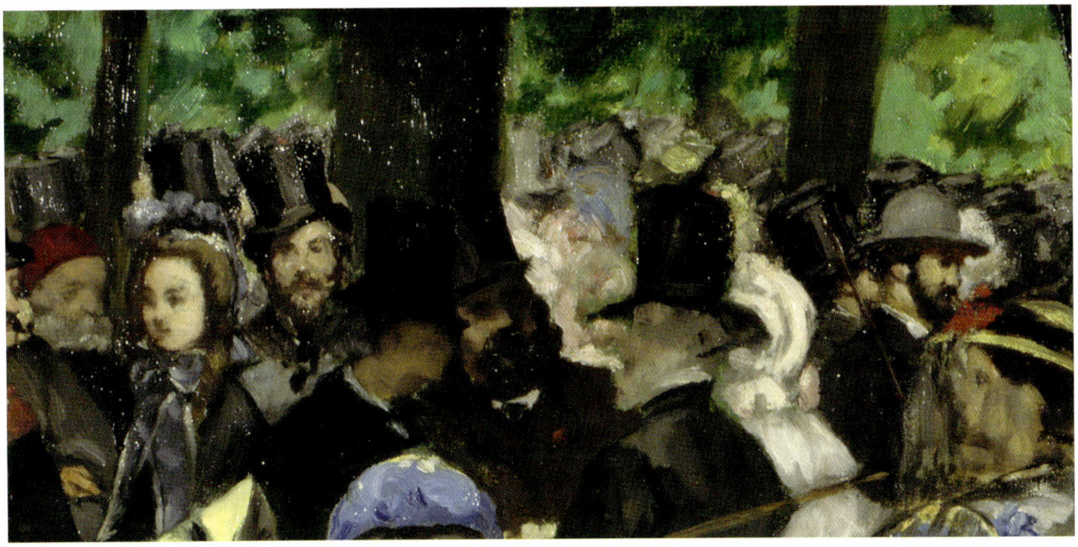

The Little Cavaliers, *1861–2. Manet copied many works in the Louvre, and was particularly attracted to the paintings by the seventeenth-century Spanish master Velázquez.* The Little Cavaliers *is Manet's interpretation of a work that was attributed to the great Spanish artist at the time but which has since been re-attributed. The original showed an imaginary gathering of seventeenth-century Spanish artists, including Velázquez with Murillo, standing in relatively similar positions to those in which Manet depicted himself and de Balleroy in* Music in the Tuileries Gardens.

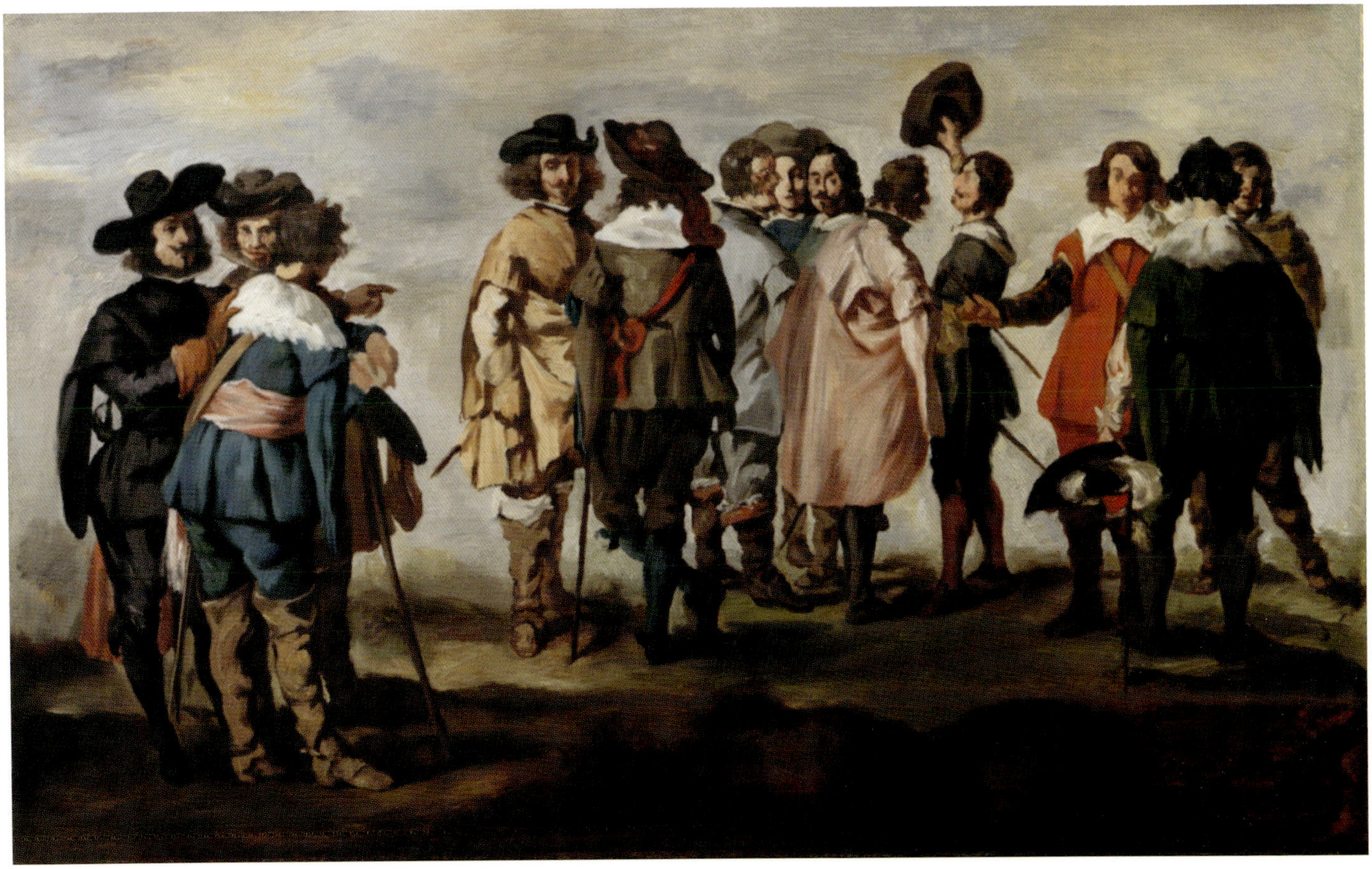

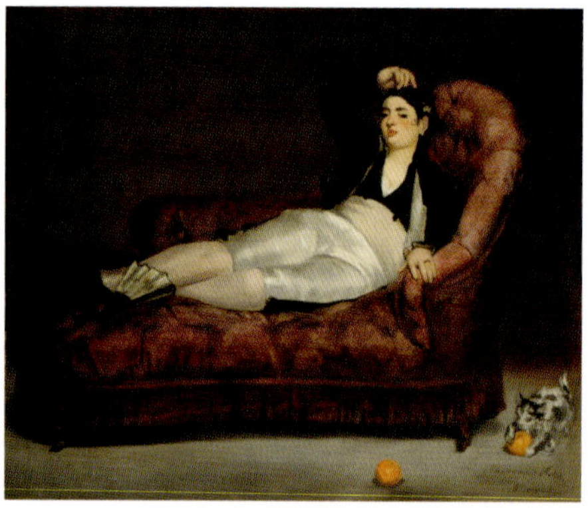

Young Woman Reclining in a Spanish Costume, *1862. Both the pose and costume of this female model reflect the work of Francisco de Goya.*

Spanish Ballet, *1862. The luscious colours reflect once more Manet's debt to Spanish seventeenth-century art.*

crowd attending a concert in oil paint was groundbreaking; this was a scene more commonly shown in prints and watercolours.

Compositionally the picture also broke new ground. Manet distributed the figures in a frieze-like manner without an obvious focal point. The central area is painted in an impressionistic manner, the crowd depicted with daubs of colour and only a few faces in focus, while the foreground figures to the left side of the painting are shown in more detail. A number of figures are arbitrarily cropped, including the depiction of the artist himself. The depiction of the foreground faces are shown flat without modelling, and he does not make use of halftones. This was modern life in Paris as seen and experienced by Manet, and it was a subject that would occupy him for the rest of his life.

Music in the Tuileries Gardens was exhibited at the Galerie Martinet in 1863, in his first solo exhibition in Paris. Also shown were 14 other works, including *The Old Musician* and *The Absinthe Drinker*. Émile Zola recalled that *Music in the Tuileries Gardens* outraged the gallery clients, one threatening violence if 'Musique

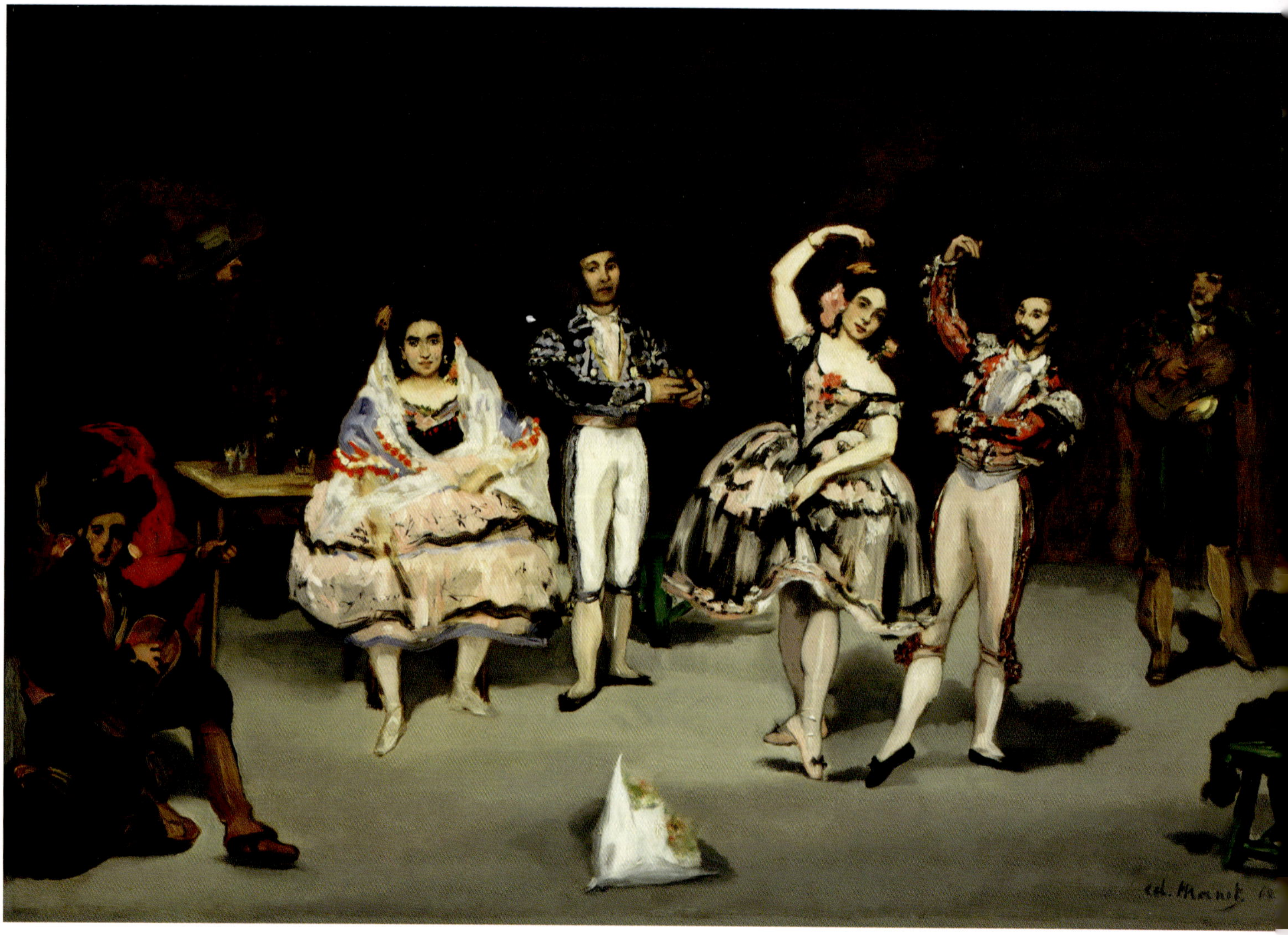

aux Tuileries were left in the room any longer'. The painting did not sell, though it would later be purchased by the dealer Paul Durand-Ruel in 1872. Manet's continued interest in Spanish art was evident among other paintings he exhibited at the Galerie Martinet exhibition. *Young Woman Reclining in a Spanish Costume* (1862) was another wonderful homage to Goya, and he had been working on *Spanish Ballet* (1862) at the same time as *Music in the Tuileries Gardens*.

Between August and November 1862, the Spanish National Ballet company was performing at the Hippodrome in Paris, where they were much admired by Manet's friend Charles Baudelaire. The artist managed to obtain permission to sketch the troupe when they were not performing. He persuaded the dancers to come to the studio of his friend the Belgian painter Alfred Stevens, and pose for him there. He produced numerous sketches detailing the exotic costumes, which informed this final work. The troupe are shown on stage, with two guitarists at the side, and on the left, seated, is the striking Lola de Valence (Lola from Valencia), the principal dancer with a pink and black skirt. Don Mariano Camprubi, the principal male lead, wears a sumptuous bolero jacket of red, black and white, and stands beside the young dancer Anita Montez, who had been so well received in Paris. The luscious silky colours somewhat contrast with the slightly awkward poses on the stark stage, on to which a bouquet of flowers has been thrown by an appreciative audience. By painting the Spanish ballet, Manet was again capturing a scene of modern Parisian life.

His individual painting of the exotic, intoxicating *Lola de Valence* (1862 – *see* page 30) is perhaps more successful and was also on display at the Galerie Martinet in the early spring of 1863. The dancer Lola Melea, known as 'Lola de Valence', is depicted wearing traditional Spanish dress with a ruffled skirt of bright orange and red, a fan in her hand and a gauze mantilla with red trimmings, with a veil over her head. It is a realistic portrayal of this striking dark beauty, showing her short in stature and with muscular legs. Originally, the background of this work was plain but Manet changed this, so that Lola appears to be in the theatre wings, about to go on stage; the audience can just be seen at the extreme right of the picture. Lola's confident pose may echo Goya, but Manet also appears to have observed her as she posed for him, a ballerina in her prime. Baudelaire wrote a poem, which he hoped would be included on the canvas itself, but in the end it accompanied the work attached to the frame in a cartouche:

My friends, I know desire to range among
The beauties that surround us;
But the charm
Of Lola de Valence does all
Disarm
The unexpected charm of a red and black jewel

The work was popularized through an etching Manet produced incorporating the poem. This demonstrates just how much admired such works were within Manet's own personal circle. The critics, though, were already starting to struggle with some aspects of Manet's production. Paul de Saint-Victor, writing in *La Presse* in 1863, concluded: 'Never has anyone distorted lines so appallingly and made tones howl. His *Bullfighters* would frighten the Spanish cows; his *Smugglers* would only have to appear to put the most fearless customs men to flight. His *Music in the Tuileries* hurts the eye as carnival music assaults the ear.' Paul Mantz, writing of the exhibition in the *Gazette des Beaux-Arts* in 1863, observed:

'The whole thing is nothing but a shrieking contrast of plaster with white and black tones. The effect is lurid, hard and sinister. Sometimes, when M. Manet is in a joyful mood, he paints Musique aux Tuileries, Ballet Espagnol or Lola de Valence, that is, pictures which reveal his generous fertile vigour, but which in their medley of red, blue and yellow, are the caricature of colour rather than colour itself. Really, such art may be strong and faithful but it is not healthy, and we are not disposed to plead M. Manet's cause before the jury of the Exhibition.'

COURTING CONTROVERSY

The display at Galerie Martinet launched in March, before the Paris Salon opened in May 1863, to which Manet had submitted a truly controversial modern work strongly referencing the Old Masters. According to Antonin Proust, the idea for *Le Déjeuner sur l'herbe* came to him on a sunny Sunday afternoon on the Ile Saint-Ouen on the River Seine in 1862, near the Manet family's summer home at Gennevilliers to the west of Paris. Watching women bathing, he vowed to reinterpret the lyrical *Le Concert champêtre* in the Louvre (then attributed to Giorgione but now thought to be by Titian), giving it a contemporary theme and initially calling it *Le Bain*. For the composition of the central group in his work, Manet was clearly also inspired by the three figures to the right in Marcantonio Raimondi's engraving after Raphael's *Judgement of Paris*. Created in his studio at rue Guyot, with Victorine Meurent posing for the nude woman. One of the clothed male figures is Karl Adolph Constantin Leenhoff, the sculptor brother of Suzanne Leenhoff, his soon-to-be wife. The other figure is modelled by his younger brother Gustave Manet. Despite the obvious homage to Italian Renaissance art, Manet's style and treatment, as well as the subject, were shocking – not only for the Salon jury but for the public at large. The direct gaze of the nude woman was provocative and placing her in a contemporary setting, with no literary or mythological context, was disturbing. The style also unsettled, considered stark since he made no attempt at transition between the light and dark tones, and the figures seem to be situated uncomfortably in a sketchy wooded landscape setting, with a detailed still life in the foreground. Perhaps not surprisingly, it was rejected by the Salon but it would gain considerable attention at the new Salon des Refusés.

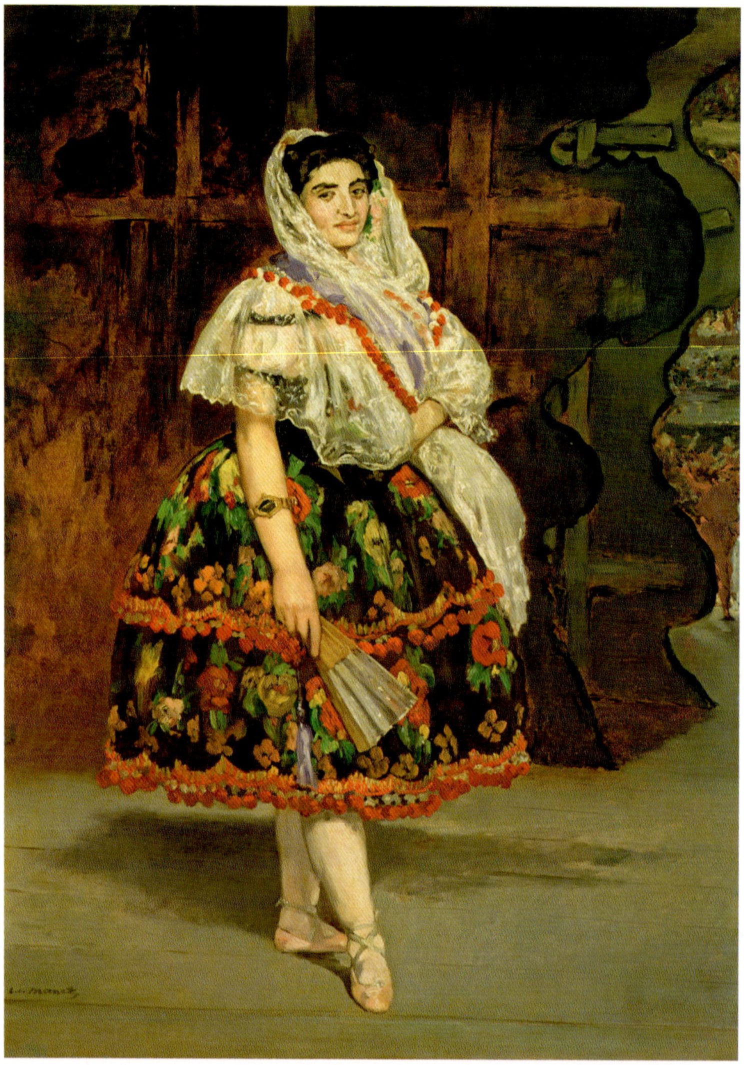

Lola de Valence, *1862. The sitter was Lola Melea, better known as Lola de Valence, the premier dancer with the Camprubi company that had performed at the Hippodrome in Paris in 1862. Manet later altered the work to situate Lola clearly in the wings and show a glimpse of the audience awaiting her.*

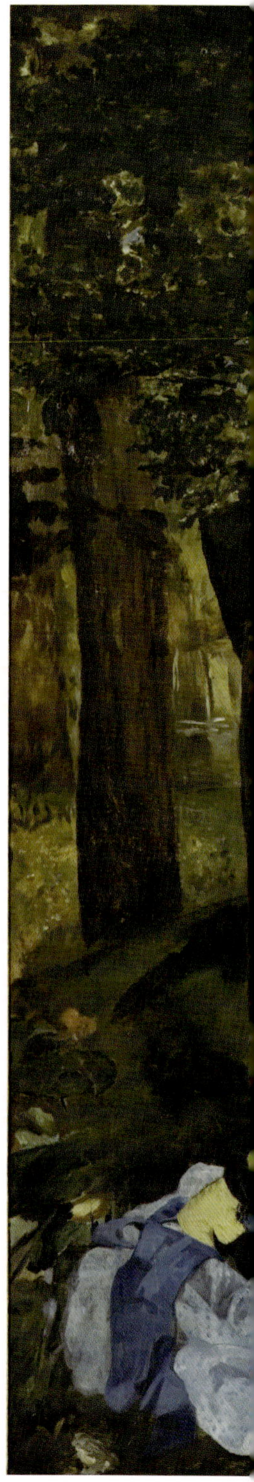

The Salon was, of course, the official exhibition of art sponsored by the French government whose jury favoured academic landscapes, portraits and history subjects. When the decisions were announced in April 1863, it was clear that the jury had been even more conservative than usual and Napoleon III, seeing the scale of discontent, feared a political backlash. Fewer than 2,218 pictures out of a total of more than 5,000 were accepted. Many artists protested and so the Emperor arrived at the Palais de l'Industrie, where the Salon paintings had been assessed, to view all the works submitted, including those which had been rejected. He decided that there should be a new exhibition, a Salon des Refusés (Exhibition of Rejected Art) to allow the public to judge the merits of these works for themselves. This Salon

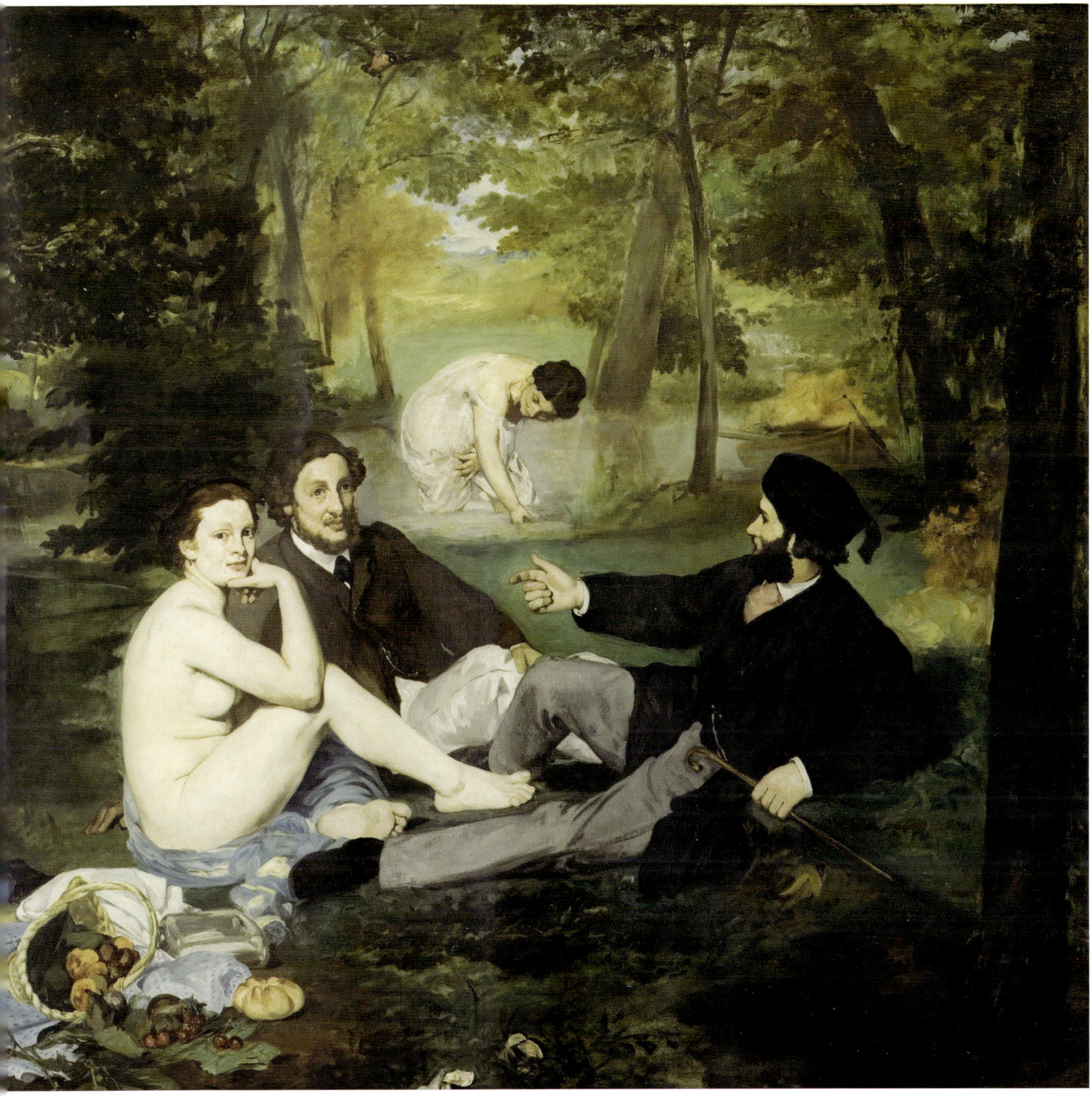

Le Déjeuner sur l'herbe, *1862–3. Compositionally this work was a re-interpretation of the lyrical* Le Concert champêtre *in the Louvre (then attributed to Giorgione but now thought to be by Titian), giving it a contemporary make-over and initially the title,* Le Bain. *The central group was clearly drawn from Marcantonio Raimondi's engraving after Raphael's* Judgement of Paris. *It was ridiculed by many critics in 1863 at the Salon des Refusés and the public crowds were bewildered.*

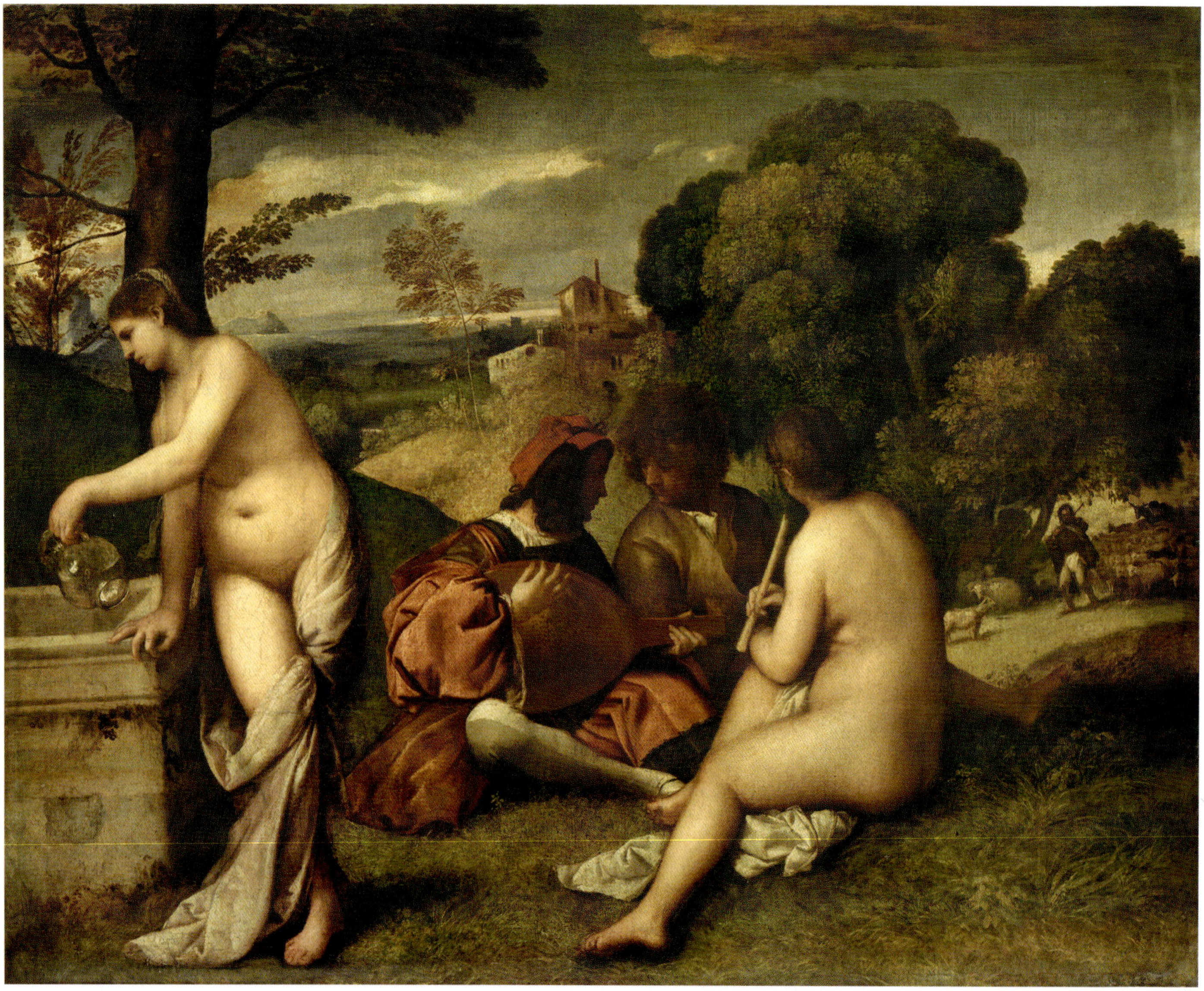

Above: Le Concert champêtre, *Titian (originally attributed to Giorgione)*, c. *1509.*

Below: The Judgement of Paris, *Marcantonio Raimondi (after Raphael), 1884.*

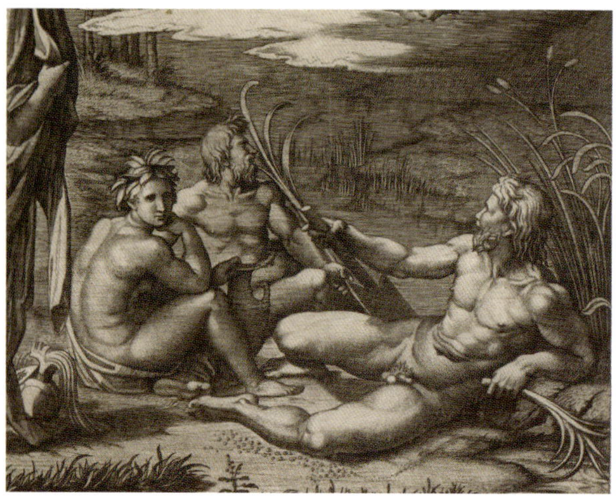

des Refusés which would open two weeks after the Salon, still at the Palais de l'Industrie but in adjoining galleries. Works by Courbet, Cézanne, Fantin-Latour, Pissarro, Jongkind and Whistler were all included in this new display, which proved to be extremely popular with the public, but the exhibition will forever be remembered because of the reaction to the controversial *Dejeuner sur l'herbe,* which hung in the furthest room.

Manet also exhibited *Mademoiselle Victorine in the Costume of an Espada* (1862) at the Salon des Refusés and one other work, but it was his *Dejeuner sur l'herbe* which was centre stage, shocking not only the critics but the public at large. Many critics simply savaged the work and the public found the naked woman's lack of modesty unnerving. Louis Étienne wrote in *Le Jury et les exposants*: 'A commonplace woman of the demi-monde, as naked as can be, shamelessly lolls between two dandies dressed to the teeth', continuing: 'This is a young man's practical joke, a shameful open sort not worth exhibiting this way.' The critic Ernest Chesneau felt that 'M. Manet will show talent on the day when he learns drawing and prespective; he will show taste on the day when he abandons these subjects which have been chosen with scandal in mind... M. Manet wishes to achieve fame by shocking the bourgeois.' It was he who revealed to the public that Manet had lifted the seated group directly from Raimondi's engraving after Raphael. His intention, it would seem, was to expose the artist as a plagiarist, apparently unaware that Manet may actually have wanted to make that artistic reference obvious. Fernand Desnoyers, writing in *La Peinture*, noted perhaps more positively: 'You can consider it evil but not mediocre', though he concluded: 'Mr Manet has the qualities needed to make him be refused unanimously by every hanging committee in the world. His shrill colours penetrate the eye like a steel saw; his characters are sharply punched out with crudity which no compromise can soften.'

The artist's friend, the sculptor Zacharie Astruc, came to the rescue in May 1863, writing,

'Manet's talent has a striking and decisive side to it – its biting, sober, energetic quality, revealing a temperament both restrained and fiery, and above all sensitive to heightened impressions. He handles its effects carefully: it is his nature to concentrate on the truth without too much subtle detail, with little regard for brilliance, yet [he] is inspired by everything that arouses his passion... Above all he is a beloved son of the natural world that he worships. Nature has so much more to teach than any school – Manet knows this very well. His powerful intelligence, as yet a green and sour fruit, demands the right to come to maturity in a new sphere which he will invigorate.'

Three more Salons des Refusés were held, in 1874, 1875 and 1886, but the novelty faded as other art exhibitions began to emerge, such as those organized by the Impressionists. Manet had certainly gained the attention of the crowds in 1863, as well as many of the young future Impressionists, but his ambition was not just for notoriety. He wanted to find success at the official Salon and public accolade.

After the furore following the reception of *Dejeuner sur l'herbe*, Manet was saddened to hear of the death of the great artist Delacroix on 13 August 1863. The ailing artist had been absent from the recent Salon Jury Committee and therefore not involved in the decision to reject Manet's works. Manet attended his funeral with Baudelaire and many of Delacroix's admirers. They were struck by the modesty of Delacroix's funeral arrangements, considering it as an insult to all those who recognized him as one of France's greatest artists. Fantin-Latour, especially, was outraged that no official tribute had been made, and a year after Delacroix's death, he painted a group portrait *Homage to Delacroix*, to acknowledge the influence he had had on a whole new generation of artists and thinkers. In it, both writers and artists are clustered around a portrait of Delacroix executed from a photograph taken ten years before. Fantin-Latour himself is in a white shirt and holding a palette, James Whistler (1834–1903) is standing in the foreground, and Manet with one hand in his pocket is easily recognizable standing right by the portrait. Baudelaire is seated on the right. By the time this portrait had been painted, Manet had himself completed a very significant new work for exhibition, another work that would prove even more controversial – his *Olympia*.

Homage to Delacroix, *Henri Fantin-Latour, 1864.*

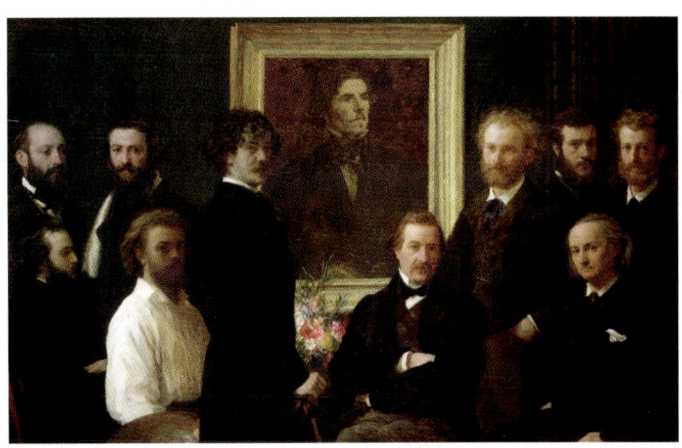

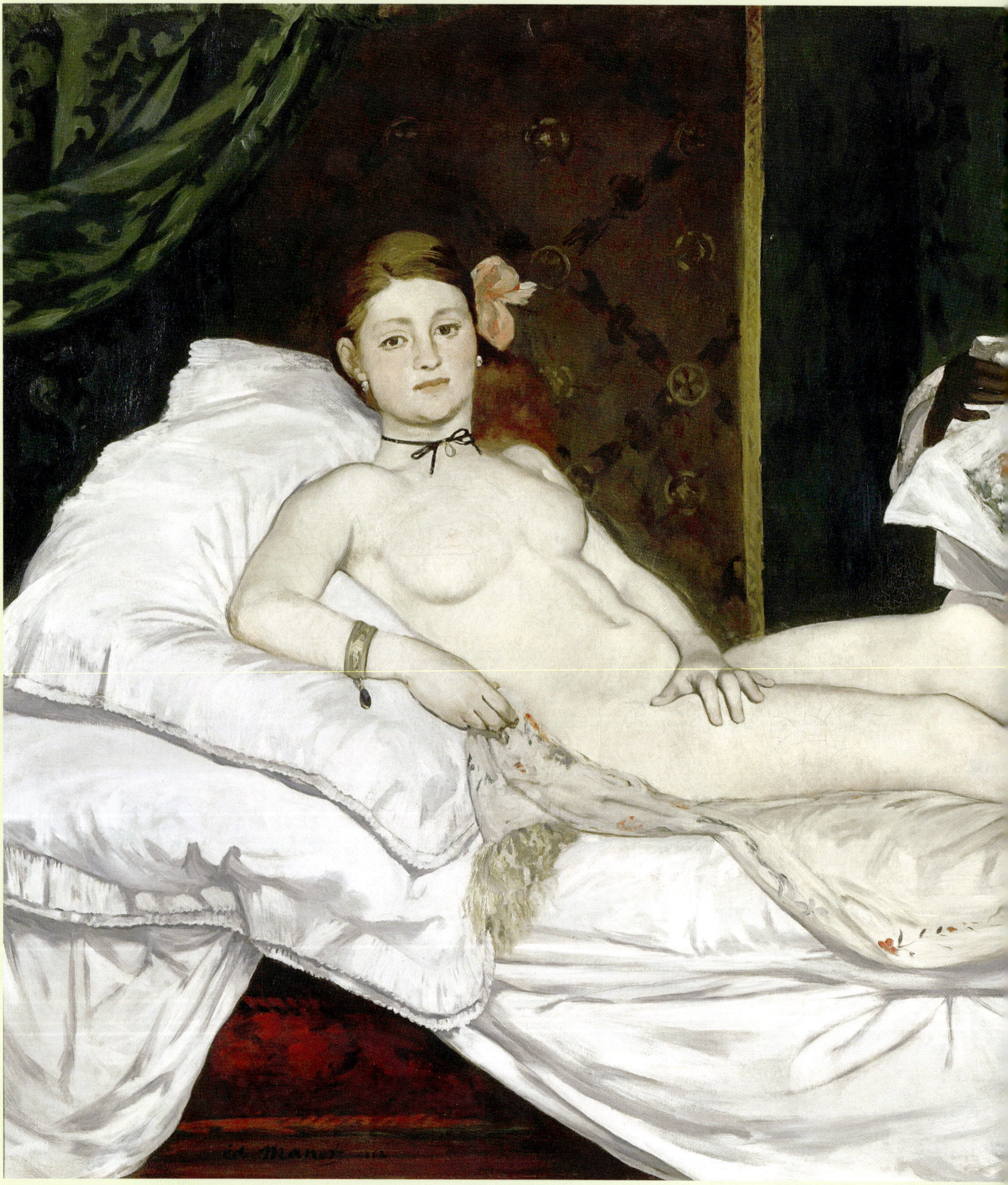

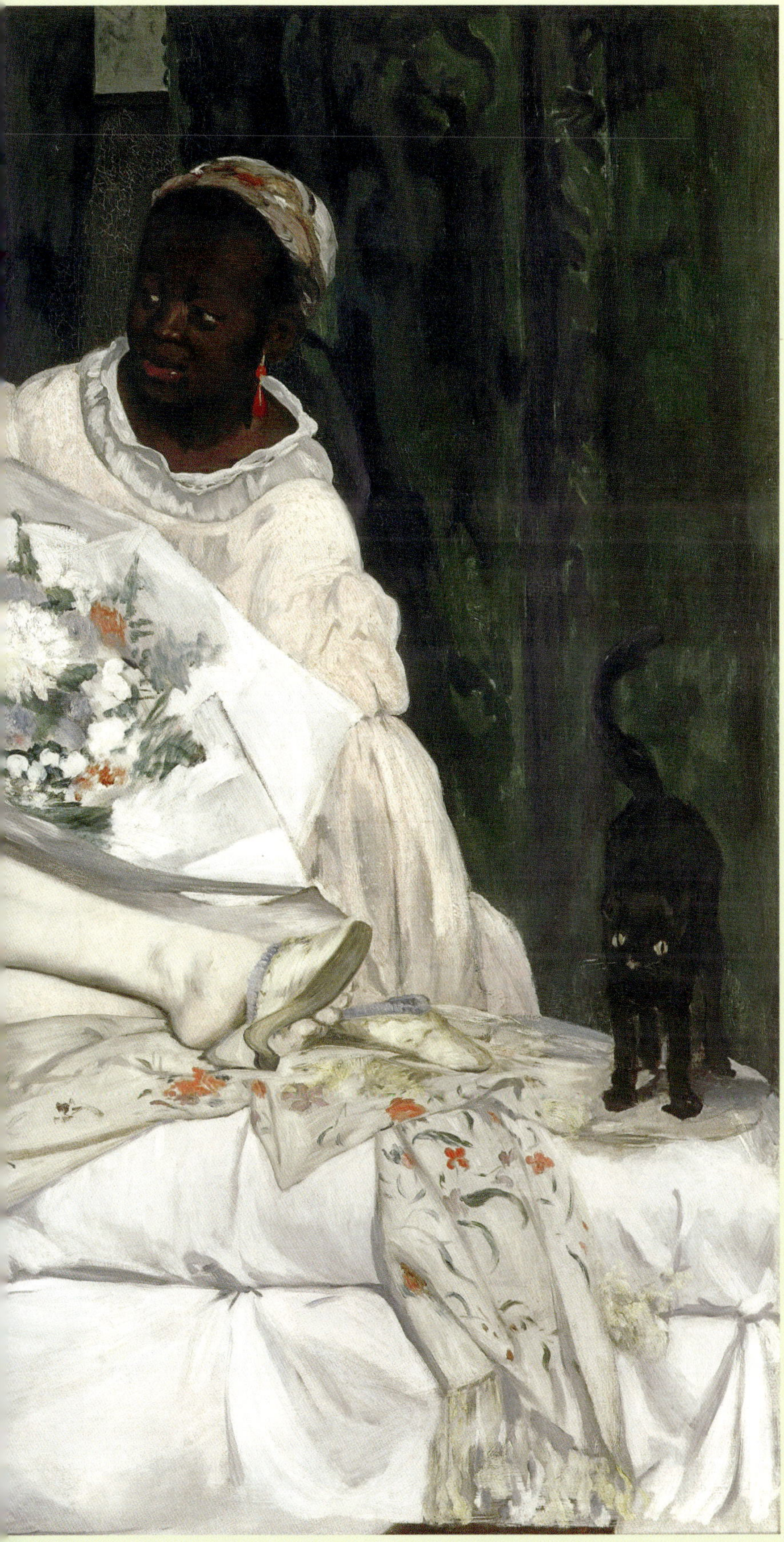

OLYMPIA

Manet had been working on his tribute to Titian's *The Venus of Urbino* throughout 1863 and was influenced too by Goya's *Maja desnuda* in his approach to painting a major nude. Again, Victorine Meurent was the model who posed for him, and she was recognized by some from the *Dejeuner sur l'herbe* when the painting was shown at the Salon two years later. This reclining pale female nude with her direct gaze has, since her debut, sparked controversy. A confident young redhead, she wears only a black ribbon around her neck, a gold bracelet on her wrist, a pink flower in her hair and expensive dainty slippers, one of which is discarded on the bed – all symbolizing wealth and sensuality. And by her feet, instead of Titian's little loyal dog, there is a small black cat, with piercing green eyes, almost invisible against the dark green background. In art, the cat is a traditional symbol of prostitution. By Olympia's side is a fully clothed black servant, posed by the art model Laure, who is attempting to draw her attention to a huge bouquet of flowers.

Olympia, *1863. Manet clearly used as his source for* Olympia, *one of the best-known Renaissance paintings in the Louvre – Titian's* Venus of Urbino. *Manet had copied this work as a student in or around 1853. Shown at the Paris Salon in 1865, it was quickly nick-named 'Venus with a Cat', referencing the famous black cat at Olympia's feet.*

Manet appears to have required only two or three sittings to complete this assured work, one of his most famous paintings, originally displayed at the 1865 Salon under the title 'Venus with a Cat'. The title *Olympia* was attached to it only 15 months later as the result of a quirky poem written by Astruc. Once again Manet's style and technique deviate from the academic approach, as can be seen by comparing the work with Alexandre Cabanel's *The Birth of Venus*, which enjoyed critical success at the Salon that year (so much so that a number of versions were painted afterwards by the artist). Cabanel offers a smooth finish and idealized approach, while Manet once again eliminates mid-tones and uses broad brushstrokes, and realistic full lighting creates an intentionally shallow depth. The contrast explains why both the critics and the public felt so shocked. It feels as if Manet is trying to be deliberately provocative, but in fact he was stung by the criticism and withdrew from his usual café society, taking long reflective walks alone. The acceptance of his work at the Salon must have felt like a triumph, but the violent reaction of the critics who felt Titian's *Venus* had been transformed into a confident courtesan brazenly displayed on a bed, challenging the very foundations of the academic tradition, must have been desperately disappointing for him. He wrote for support to his friend Baudelaire, who was at the time in Brussels, 'I wish you were here with me, my dear Baudelaire; I'm bombarded with insults… I should have liked your verdict on my pictures.'

Théophile Gautier, writing in *Le Moniteur universel* in 1865, summarized the general response: '*Olympia* cannot be understood from any point of view, even if

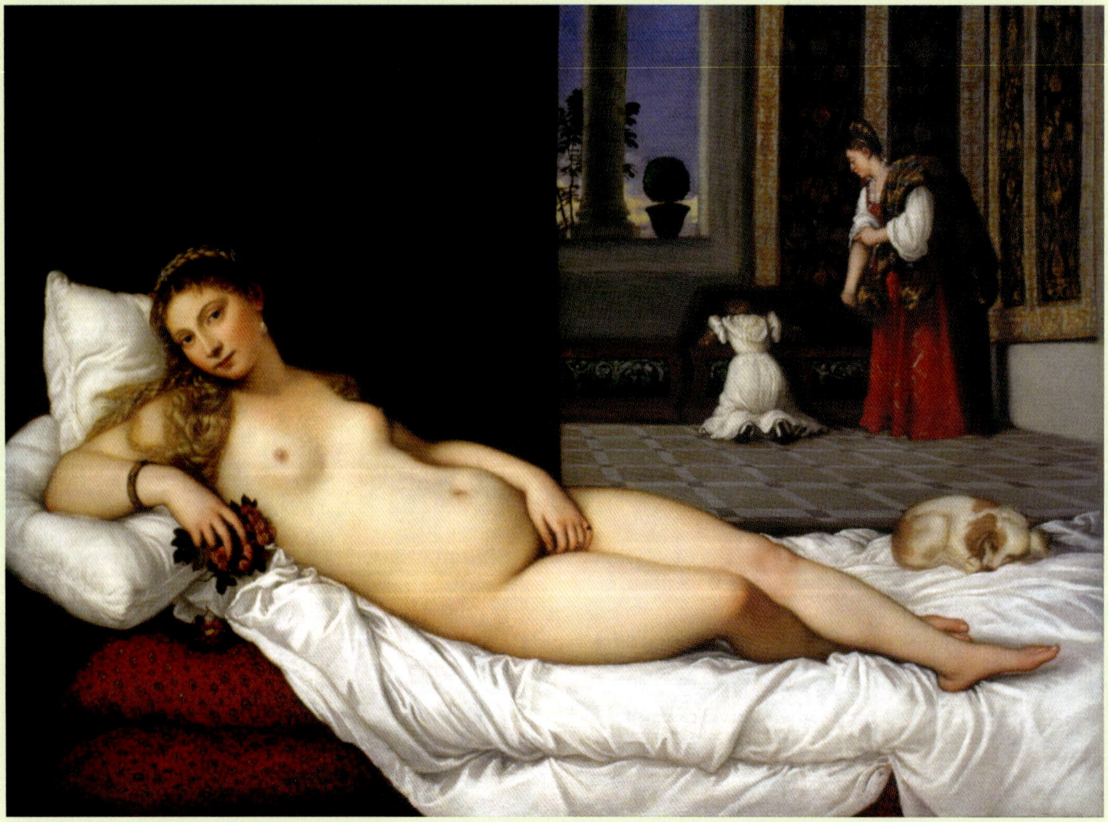

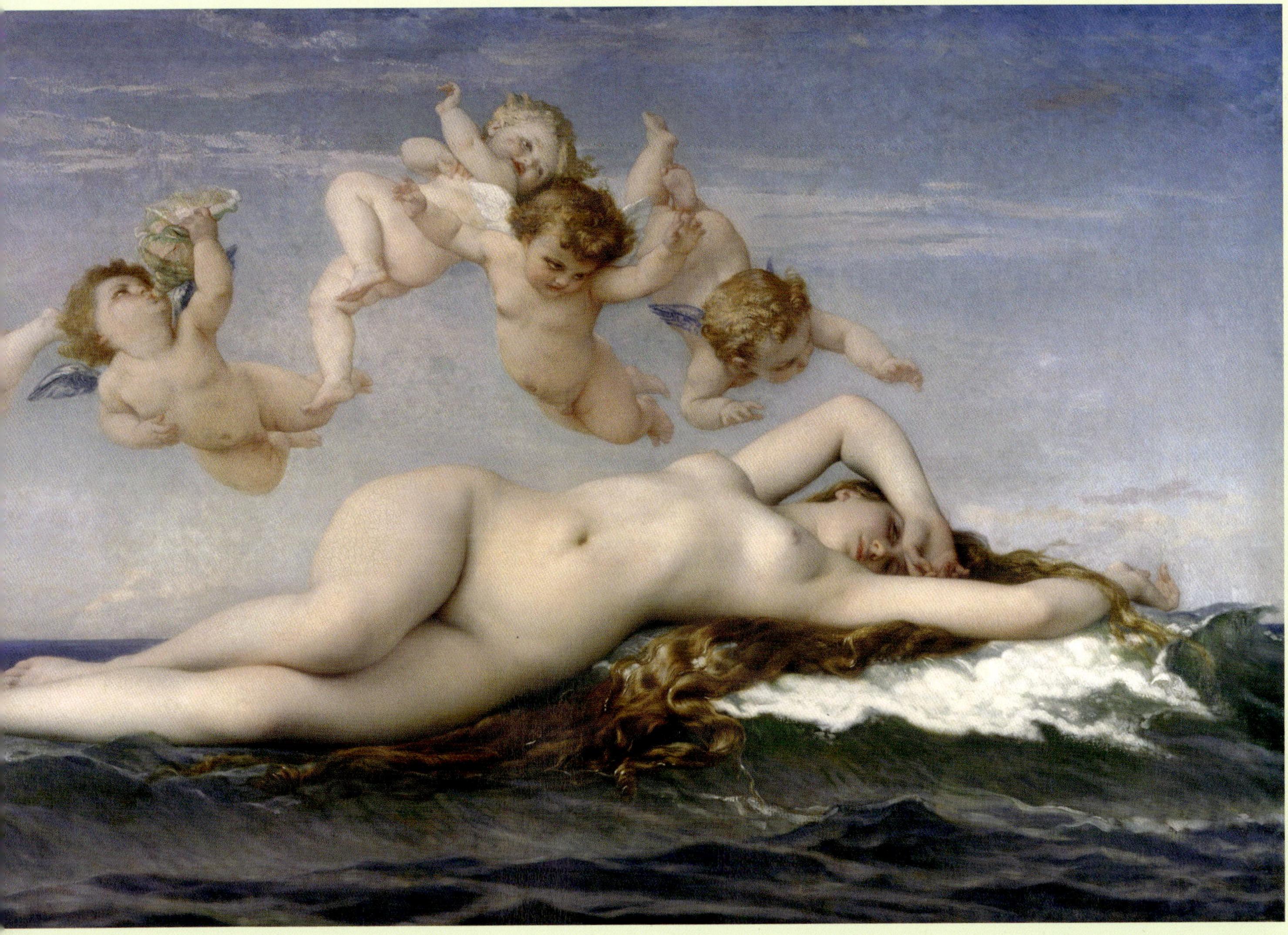

Above: The Birth of Venus, *Alexandre Cabanel, 1863. Cabanel's work was a real success at the Paris Salon of 1863 and was purchased by Napoleon III for his own collection. Cabanel shows the moment from classical mythology when Venus is born of sea foam and carried ashore. It was typical of the many nudes on display that year, with the artist employing a pale smooth palette, in great contrast to Manet's flatly painted* Olympia *shown just two years later.*

Opposite: Venus of Urbino, *Titian, 1534. The original voluptuous classical goddess, Venus is shown by Titian in a richly atmospheric, imaginary setting that was transformed by Manet into his Olympia, who is flatly painted, and seemingly inhabits the contemporary world of Parisian prostitution.*

you take it for what it is, a puny model stretched out on a sheet... We would still forgive the ugliness, were it only truthful, carefully studied, heightened by some splendid effect of colour... Here there is nothing, we are sorry to say it, but the desire to attract attention at any price.' Others tried to come to Manet's rescue, such as the critic Gonzague Privat, who noted that the young woman was rendered in 'a flat tone, her flesh is of an exquisite delicacy, a nicety, in a perfect relationship with the white draperies. The background is charming, the green curtains which enclose the bed are of a light and airy colour. But the public, the crude public that finds it easier to laugh than to look, understands nothing at all of this art which is too abstract for its intelligence.' A few years later, in 1867, Manet's great friend and admirer Émile Zola described his Olympia in *Mon Salon* thus: 'This canvas is the veritable flesh and the blood of the painter, the most characteristic example of his talent, his greatest achievement.'

ST FRANCIS OF STILL LIFE

Below left: Peonies, *1864–5.*
Below right: Vase of Peonies, *1864.*
The majority of Manet's still lifes of the 1860s show peonies, and yet each work is remarkably individual and different, both in size and technique. These two examples show peonies arranged in formal ceramic vases, but he painted others in a beer mug and an Italian wine bottle, all in 1864. They were clearly Manet's favourite flowers – peonies are associated with romance, prosperity and good fortune and even a happy marriage.

In both *Dejeuner sur l'herbe* and *Olympia* there are beautifully observed still-life details – in the former, a basket and fruit on the grass, and the woman's discarded clothing; in the latter, the splendid bouquet of flowers. Manet was an accomplished painter of still lifes and once said: 'Still life is the touchstone of the painter' and later that 'A painter can say all he want to with fruit or flowers'. He apparently once expressed the wish to be known as St Francis of Still Life. Manet had included purely still life paintings in his Martinet exhibition in 1863 and, indeed, the critic Ernest Chesenau had purchased one of them. The artist told Baudelaire, 'Chesenau bought a painting from me, two flowers in a vase, a little nothing. Perhaps he will bring me good luck.' In fact, that particular critic was then to be scathing of both *Dejeuneur sur l'herbe* and *Olympia*. Yet throughout the period that Manet was painting works which created such outraged public reaction, he was also creating carefully observed still lifes.

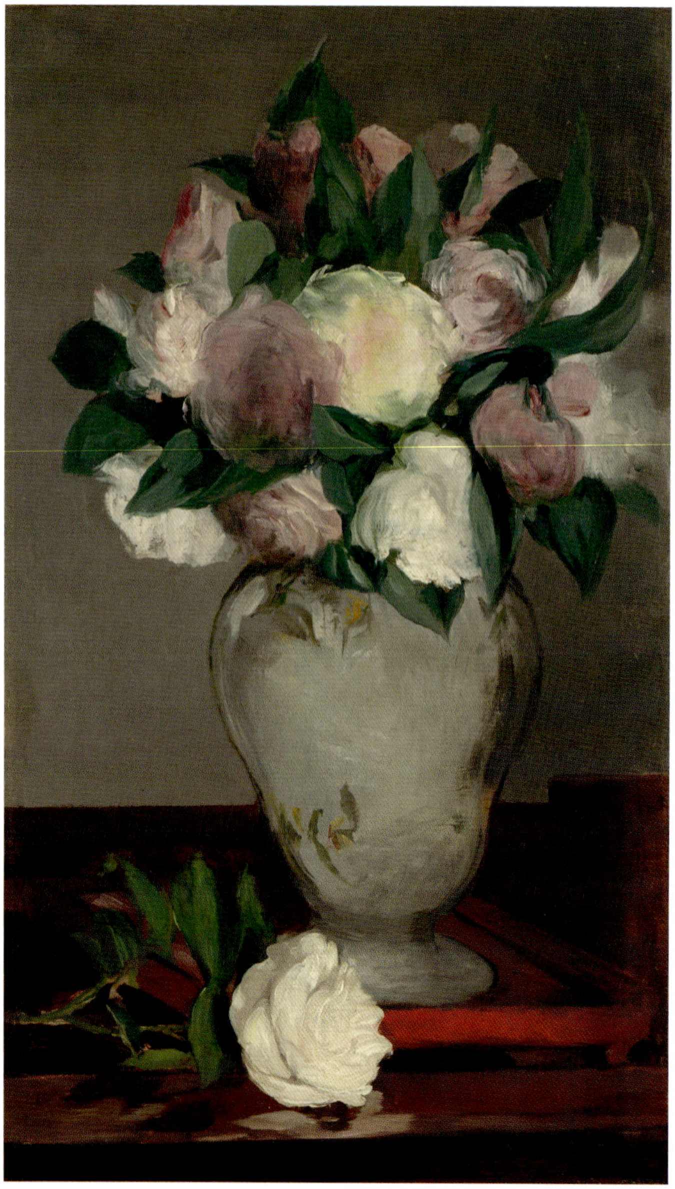

During the 1860s, he painted eight flower still lifes, particularly in 1864, often being drawn to the observation of what appear to be his favourite flowers, peonies. While the variety of flower may have been the same, he varied their presentation compositionally. Sometimes he showed them arranged in a vase, such as *Peonies* (1864) and *Vase of*

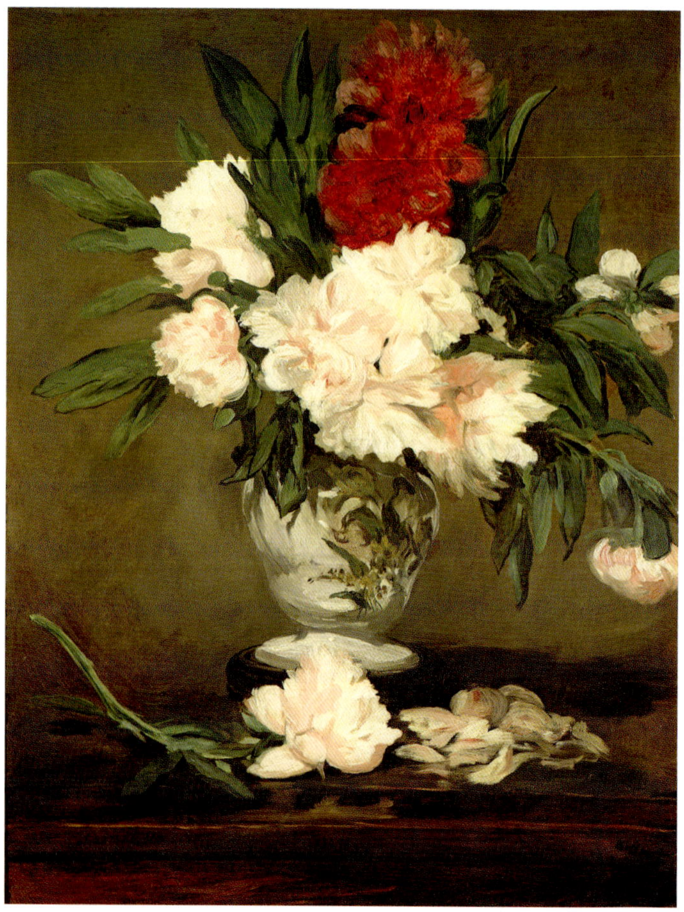

Peonies (1864); sometimes he included other objects in more informal works illustrating the recent cutting of flowers for arrangement, *Peony Stems and Pruning Shears* and *Peonies and Pruning Shears* (both 1864). He also painted accomplished observations of fruit, such as *Basket of Fruit* (*c.* 1864) and the beautifully rendered *Still Life with Melon and Peaches* (1866), and he made a number of related studies of melons.

He had undoubtedly observed the still lives of the Spanish and Dutch schools and paid tribute to these, with works such as *Guitar and Hat* (1862) and *Still Life with a Salmon*, (1866) respectively. The latter shows the arrangement set off by a white tablecloth with the large cooked fish cut through, and the serving knife and fork poised for use. The half-peeled lemons and a Delft-like bowl, as well as a glass reflecting the light, all suggest the influence of Dutch still life masters such as Jan Davidszoon de Heem (1606–84) and Willem Kalf (1619–93), whose work he could have observed in the Louvre. The semi-peeled lemon allowed artists to demonstrate their skills in still life observation and could also be interpreted as a symbol of time passing or even bitterness. *Still Life with a Salmon* is the same size as *Still Life with Melon and Peaches* and they may have been painted as a pendant. *The Rabbit* (1866) appears more of a homage to Jean-Baptiste-Siméon Chardin (1699–1779), who was enjoying a revival of interest. The small size of this work suggests that Manet had been studying Chardin's *Dead Rabbit with game bag and powder flask*, and it was successful enough for him

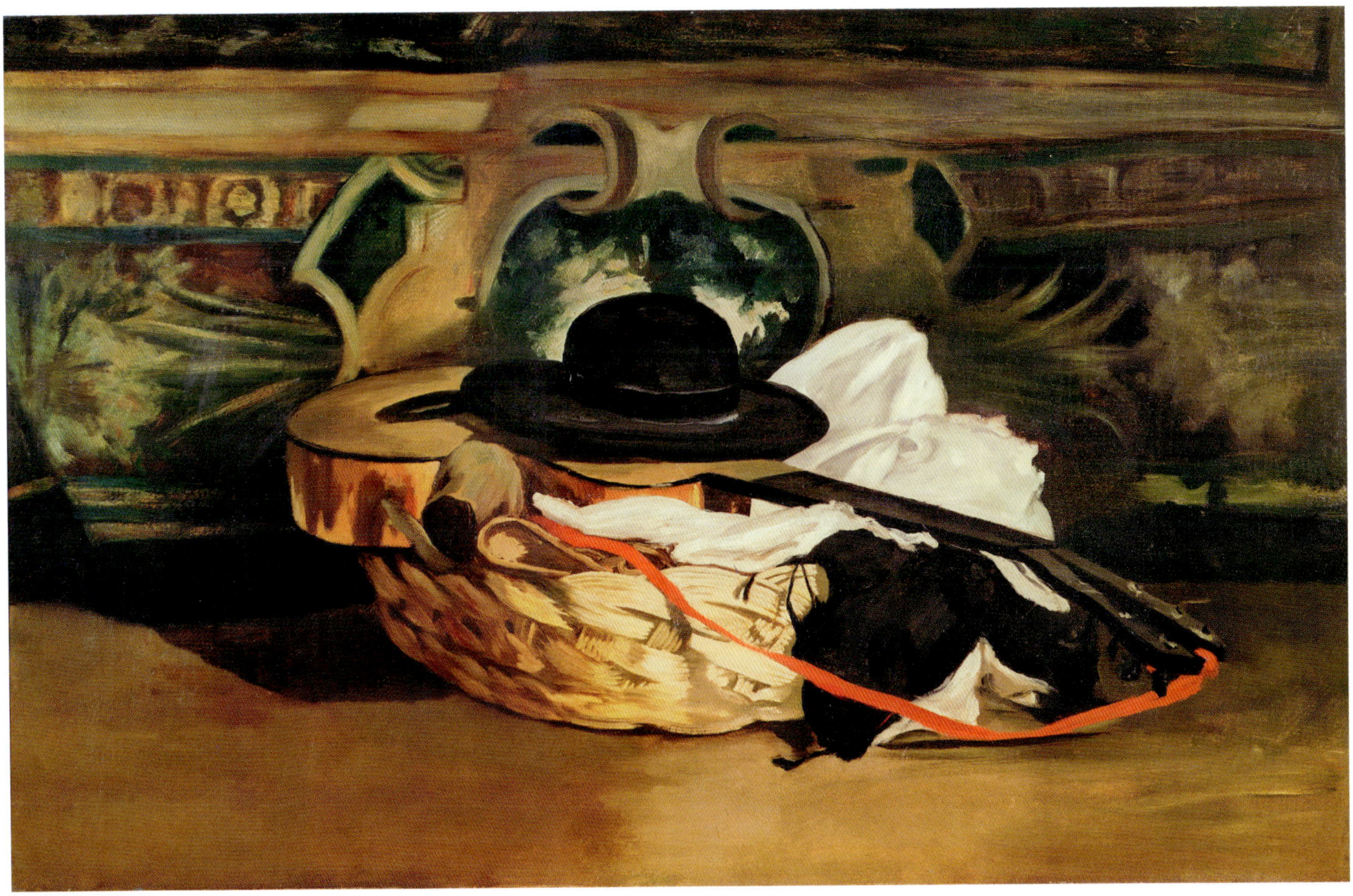

Guitar and Hat, *1862. Manet kept a number of props in his studio for his paintings and it is entirely possible that the ones depicted in this still life were used for his work* The Spanish Singer.

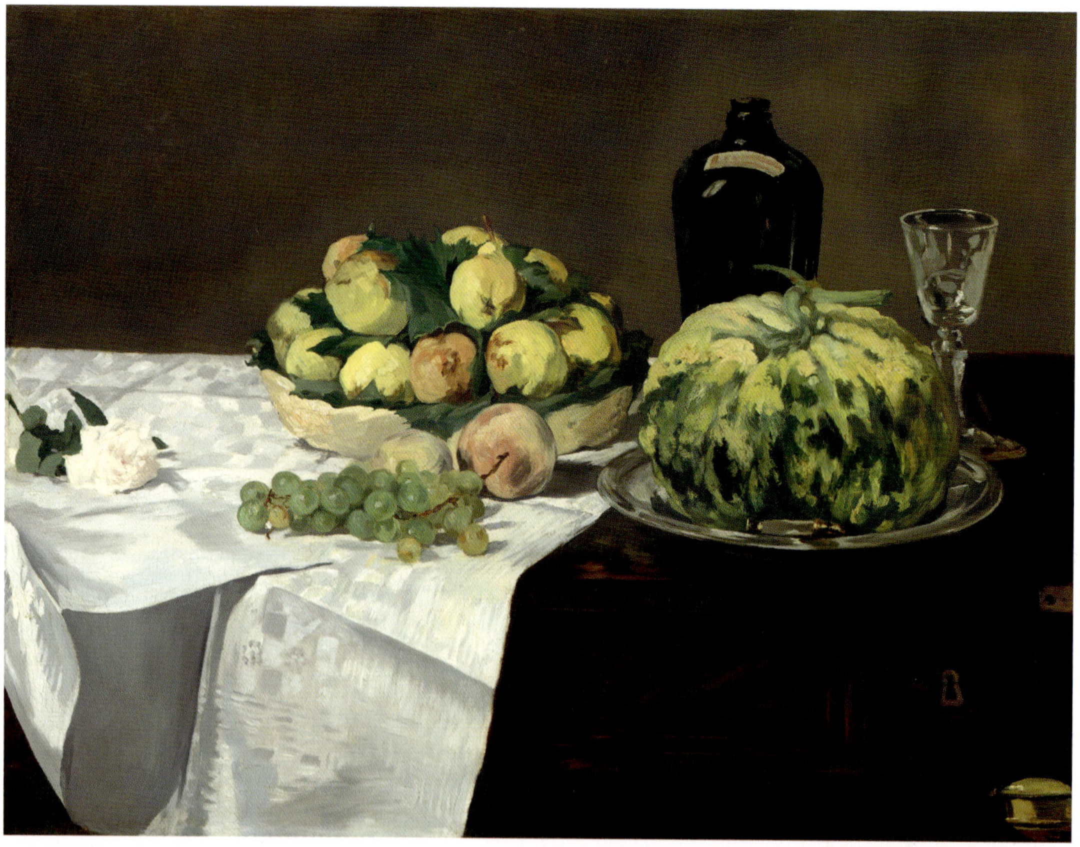

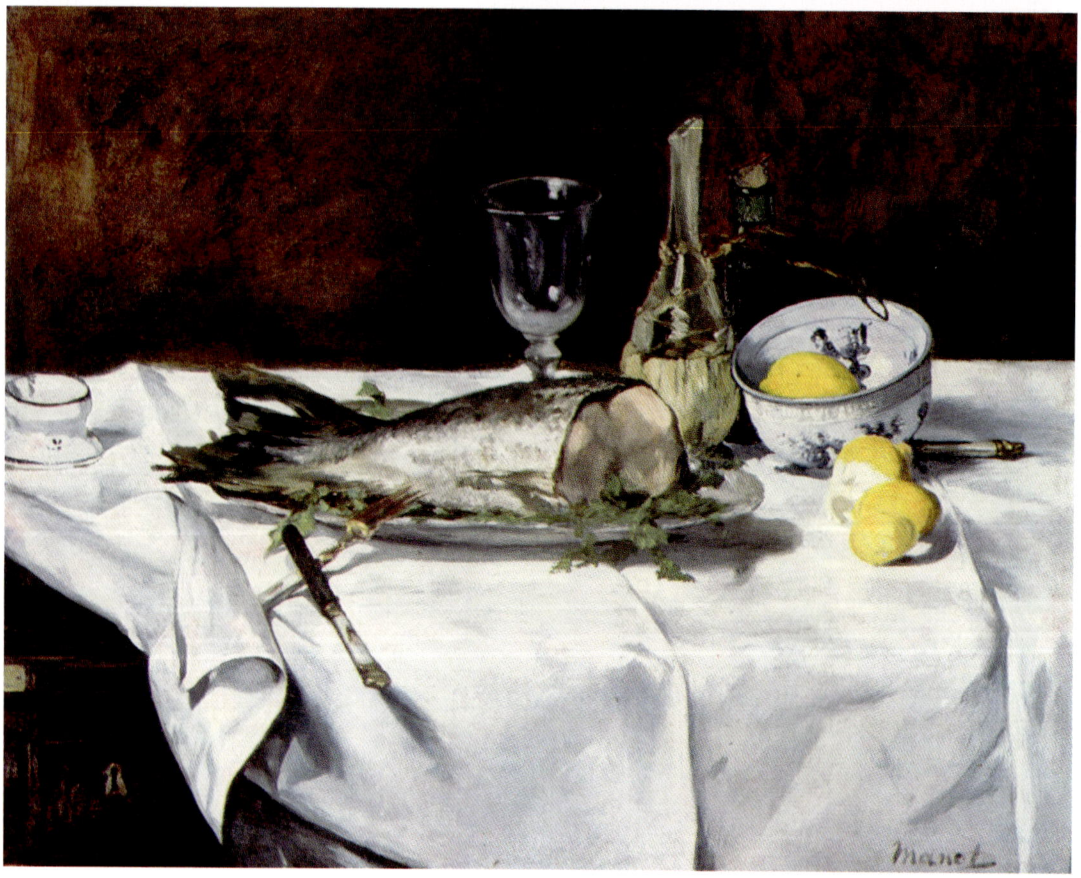

Left: Still Life with Melon and Peaches, c. *1866.*
Below left: Still Life with a Salmon, c. *1868.*
Both compositions make use of a crisp white tablecloth as a contrast to the still life observations. The tablecloth in Still Life with Melon and Peaches *is the same as that which appears in* The Luncheon in the Studio *of 1868 (see page 50). Meanwhile,* Still Life with a Salmon *includes a large cooked fish cut through, half-peeled lemons and a Delft-style bowl, as well as a glass reflecting the light, all suggesting the influence of Dutch still life masters such as Jan Davidszoon de Heem and Willem Kalf, whose work Manet could have observed in the Louvre, as well as the impact of works such as Jean-Baptiste-Siméon Chardin's* The Ray *(1728) on the artist.*

to produce an etching of it. Other artists at the time, such as Eugène Boudin (1824–98), were also drawn to Chardin's still lifes, and Manet would return to the theme of a dead rabbit again later in his career. Still life observations are included in a number of portraits of the critics who supported Manet during this period: *Zacharie Astruc* (1864) is shown seated by a table of books, a glass and peeled lemon; *Théodore Duret* (1868) is depicted full length against another plain background, with a stool on which stands a tray with a lemon, a glass and a water decanter; and *Emile Zola* (1868) sits on an elaborately observed chair, with numerous still life details depicted on his desk, as well as a Japanese print on the wall, an engraving after Velázquez's *Bacchus* and a reproduction of Manet's famous *Olympia*, which he had defended.

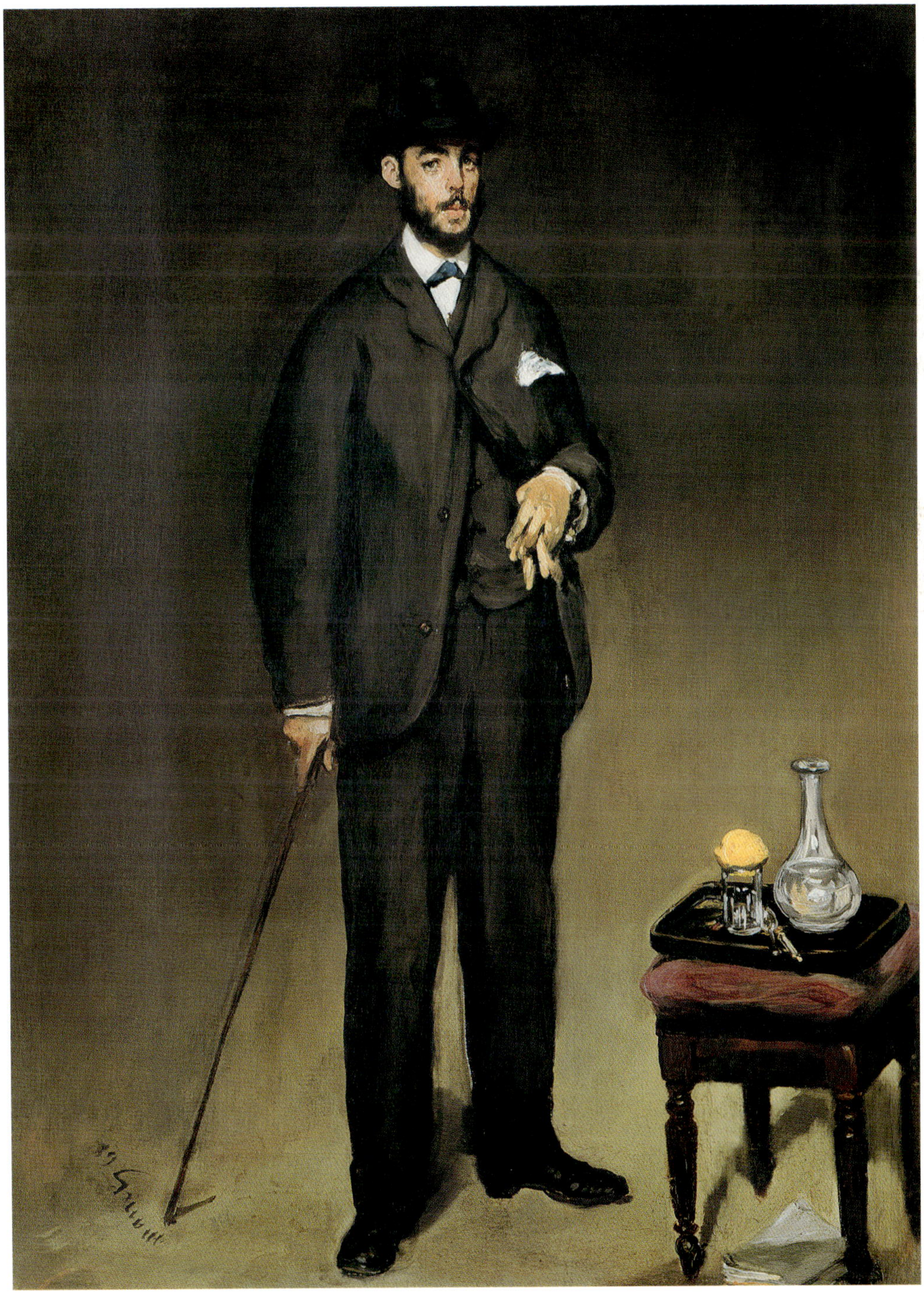

Portrait of Théodore Duret, *1868. Manet first encountered Duret in Madrid in 1865, where they visited the Prado and studied Velázquez together and the journalist and critic included Manet's work in his* Les Peintres français en 1867. *This full length portrait shows Duret against a plain background with still life details on a stool including a glass, peeled lemon and a decanter on a black tray.*

RELIGIOUS WORKS

Manet, the observer of Parisian modern life, may have been somewhat overlooked until recently as a painter of still lifes, but he is rarely associated with religious painting either. However, in his early career he was drawn to biblical subjects that had inspired the Old Masters he had studied, and he painted two important works. It seems likely that there was a connection between his interest in biblical subjects in the early 1860s and the publication of the popular 1863 biography *Vie de Jésus (Life of Jesus)* by the French philosopher and historian Joseph-Ernest Renan. This was a controversial work that emphasized Christ's humanity and attempted to reconstruct Jesus' biography using only historical documents and verifiable facts. Two key religious works of these years are known. The first, painted in 1864, was *The Dead Christ with Angels*, in which Manet portrayed Jesus as realistic and vulnerable. The pose may have been inspired by Mantegna's *Christ as the Suffering Redeemer*. However, his knowledge of the Bible does not seem to have been as thorough as it might have been. For instance, the Gospel according to St John in fact describes Christ's tomb as empty except for two angels; Christ himself is missing. Manet submitted the canvas to the 1864 Salon, but then realized that he had made a further error, depicting Christ's wound on the wrong side. Despite Charles Baudelaire's warning that he would

The Dead Christ with Angels, *1864. Manet inscribed the subject of this painting on the rock: St John's Gospel (20:12). Mary Magdalene arrives at Jesus' tomb and sees two angels, but Jesus' body is missing. Manet shows Christ's body with the angels.*

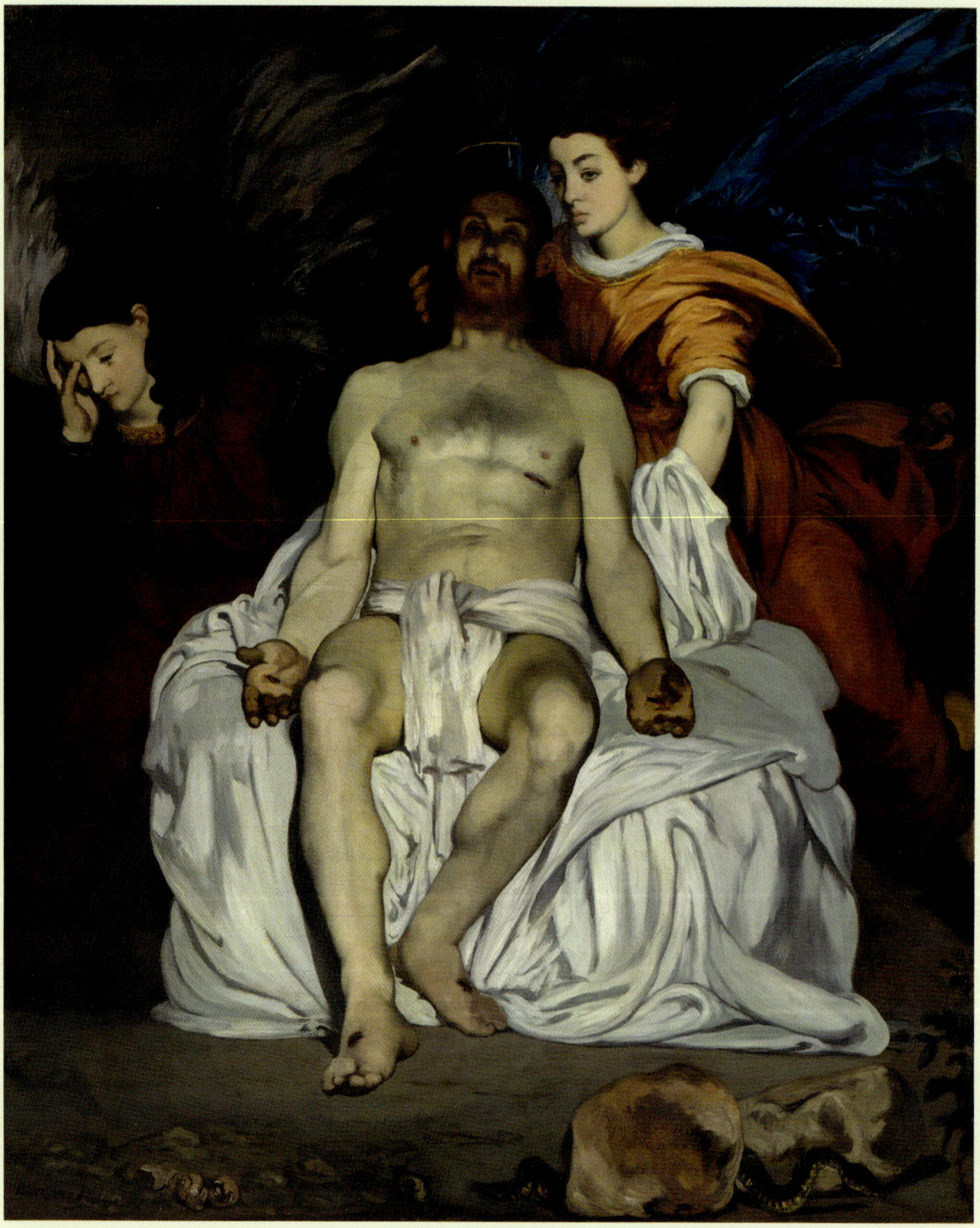

'give the malicious something to laugh at', the artist did not correct his mistake. Critics indeed denounced the picture as 'incomprehensible, provocative, crudely drawn, hastily painted'.

Another religious work, *Jesus Mocked by the Soldiers* (1865) was painted the following year and accepted along with *Olympia* for the official Salon in 1865. Again, Manet shows Jesus as human and vulnerable by presenting him frontally, his pale body seeming passive and limp. The model was not professional but someone employed by Manet to help with odd jobs, named Janvier. The work depicts the moment when Jesus's captors mock the 'King of the Jews' by crowning him with thorns and covering him with a robe. Overall, the work is steeped in Spanish influences and a preparatory drawing in pen and brown wash shows an original composition without the outward-gazing figure. The kneeling soldier seems to derive from Velázquez's *Adoration of the Magi* and the figure holding the robe appears to derive from a type in Velázquez's *Vulcan's Forge*. The visible brushstrokes and Manet's almost monochromatic tonality did not appeal to the public or critics, who again ridiculed the work. Stung by the criticism he received, Manet did not return to religious subjects again.

Jesus Mocked by the Soldiers, *1865. Manet called on all his knowledge of great Spanish art in the composition of the figures in this work.*

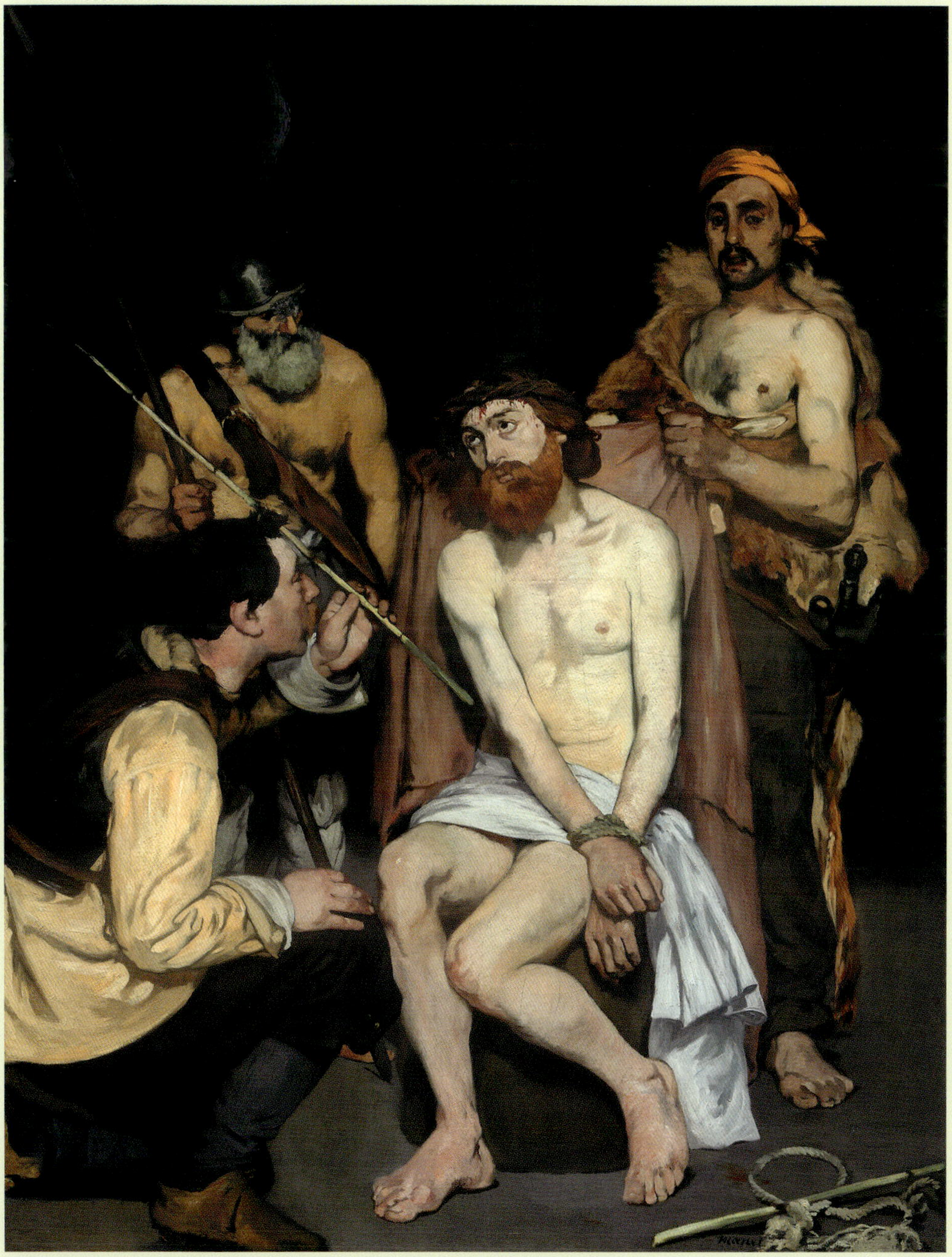

Disillusioned by his lack of critical success, Manet went on holiday to Boulogne-sur-Mer as soon as the exhibition closed and then in August he left for Spain. Despite his great admiration for Spanish art, he had not actually gone to Spain before. There, he visited Burgos, Valladolid, Toledo and Madrid, where he spent time in the Museo del Prado and met the collector and critic Théodore Duret, who would become a long-term friend.

INDIVIDUAL MALE FIGURES

In 1866, Manet began work on one of his most charming and familiar pictures, *The Fifer*. The sitter is a young military bandsman and mascot of the Garde Impériale, who was sent to Manet to paint by his friend Commander Lejosne. The young boy is captured against a completely plain background. This work undoubtedly suggests Manet has been looking at Japanese art in the flat rendering and sylized approach but it is also another homage to Velázquez, whose *Portrait of Pablo de Valladolid*, an actor and jester at the Court of Philip IV (*c.* 1635), had particularly impressed him in the Prado. He wrote to his friend Fantin-Latour that the portrait was 'the most astonishing piece of painting ever done... the background disappears: it is air which surrounds the fellow, dressed all in black and full of life'.

In just the same way, Manet's young fifer floats in the middle of the painting, as he plays his instrument, wide-eyed – though, unlike the actor, his uniform is not entirely black. Indeed, it is his striking red trousers that stand out, and the black stripe on each trouser leg is particularly bold, defining the boy from the neutral background surrounding him. Manet employs solid areas of colour, with only some modelling effects for the flesh and the instrument case. It has also been noted that the pose of the fifer has some possible relationship with a popular contemporary French tarot card representing the Fool (Joker) in the pack – which may itself

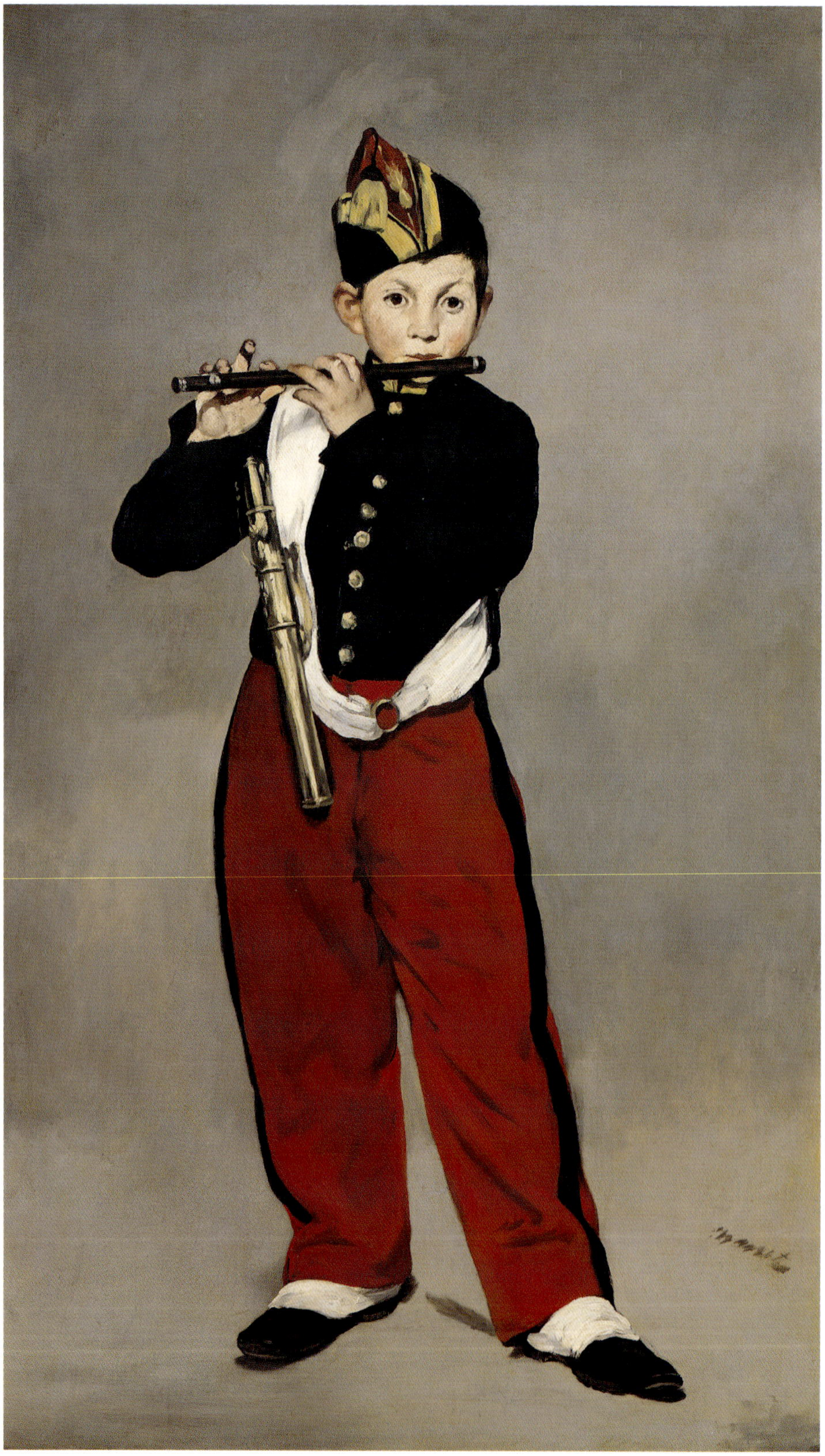

The Fifer, *1866. A masterpiece in simplicity, the figure is lit from the front and sharply defined against a plain grey background, with the distinctive black stripe of the red trouser legs providing bold lines to contour the legs. The painting was rejected by the Salon jury of 1866.*

reference the original Velázquez. Manet's close friend Edmond Bazire wrote the first biography of the artist, published only nine months after his death, in which he said: 'This urchin, so jauntily painted, lively and gay, detaches himself from the dark background as if he were about to walk out of it.' The simplicity Manet adopted in this work has an enduring appeal. Recognized today as one of his most striking and memorable works, it was not considered suitable by the judging committee for the Salon of 1866.

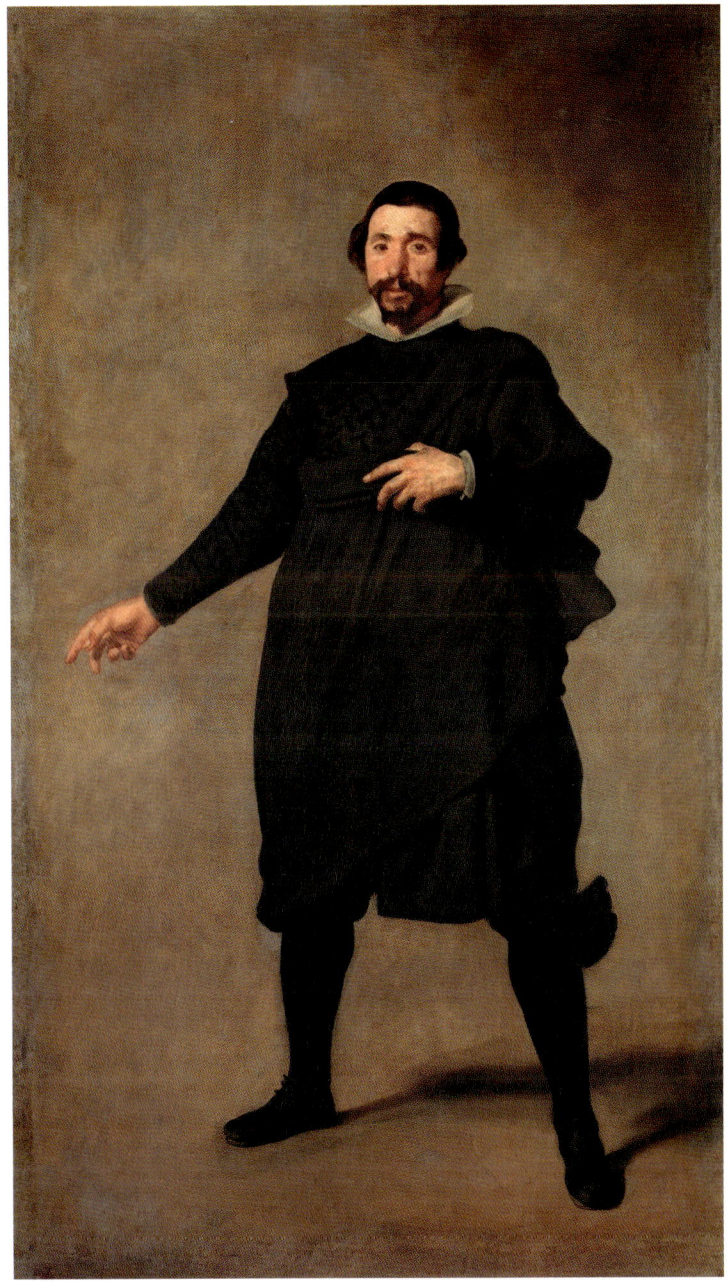

Portrait of Pablo de Valladolid, *Diego Velázquez,* c. *1635. The sitter was an actor and jester at the Court of Philip IV, born in Vallecas in 1587, and dying in December 1648, having served Philip since 1632. The work particularly impressed Manet when he visited the Prado.*

Émile Zola entirely recognized the significance of the work and praised the painting highly along with *The Tragic Actor (Rouvière as Hamlet)* (1865–6 – *see* page 46), another work that also has a blank background and shadows similar to the portrait by Velázquez. The renowned French actor Philibert Rouvière, who died in 1865, stands isolated by theatrical lighting. His role as Hamlet was renowned and thought to have been inspired by a series of lithographs by Delacroix. It was also submitted by Manet to the Salon, but again rejected despite being a tribute to one of France's greatest actors and an extraordinary exercise in painting the colour black, capturing every shade of the colour in the classic leggings, a textured and possibly velvet cloak and a feather-plumed hat. The entire costume is relieved only by a barely visible white ruffled shirt. The extraordinary brushwork also reflects Manet's study of Frans Hals, and Manet was stung by the rejection. His new friend Zola felt the Salon without him was 'dismal nullity'. Writing in 1866, he explained of his relationship to Manet, 'I liked him right away; since we first met, I've penetrated his talent.' He continued: 'You know what effect Monsieur Manet's canvases produce at the Salon. They punch holes in the wall. Spread all around them are the wares of fashionable confectioners – sugarcane trees and pie-crust houses, gingerbread gents and whipped-cream ladies.' By contrast, Zola felt Manet captured 'his figures alive, he does not shrink from nature's rowdiness, he lets objects assert themselves… What results is a strong solid painting.' Zola was passionate in his praise: 'Since no one else says it, I shall say it, at the top of my voice. I am so certain that Monsieur Manet will be one of the masters of tomorrow, that, were I rich, I should consider it a bargain to buy up his entire works this very day.' Manet wrote in May, to thank him for his support and asked to meet him at the Café de Bade where, he explained, he could be found every day between 5.30 and 7.00 p.m.

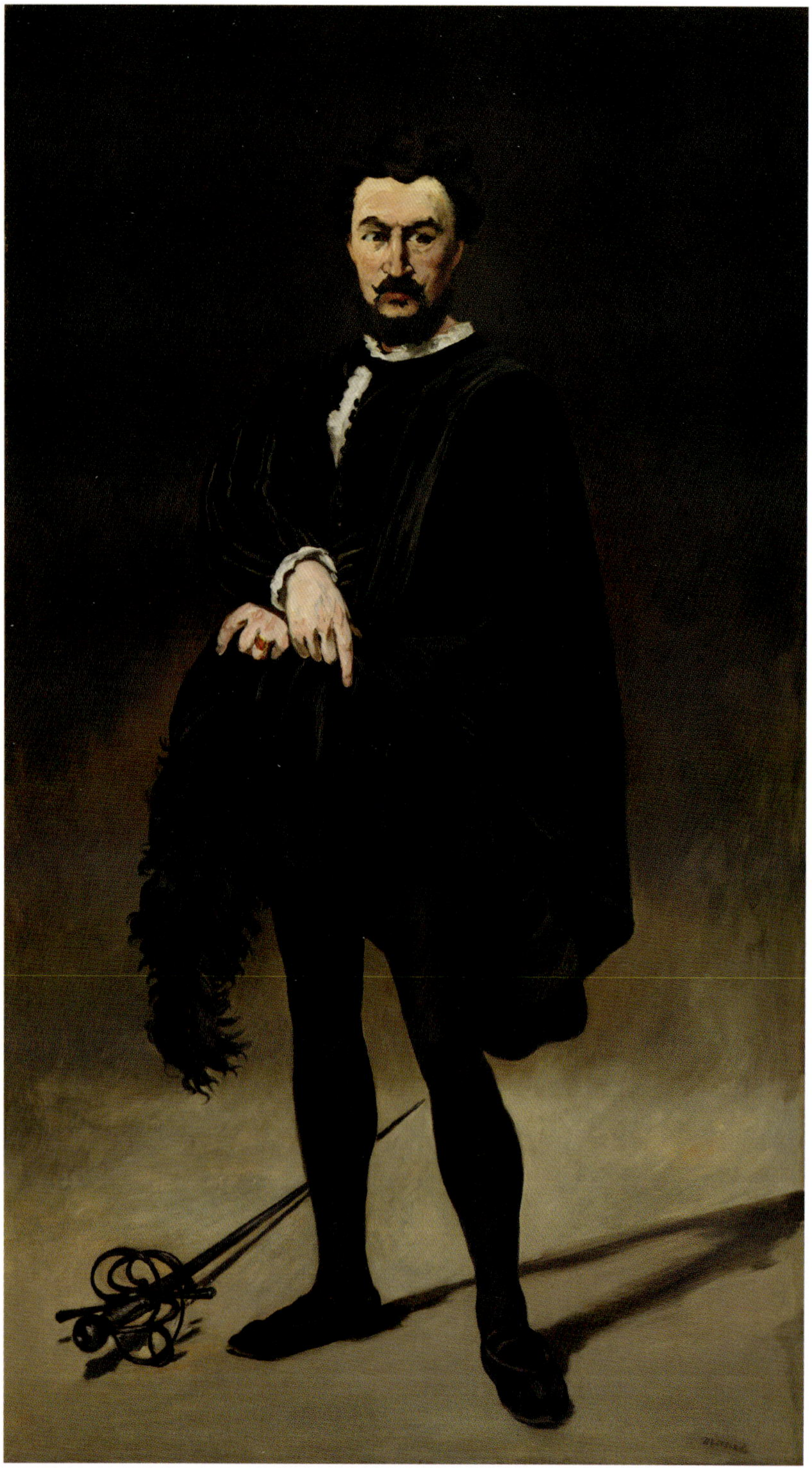

The Tragic Actor (Rouvière as Hamlet), *1866. Using once more a completely plain background, this is a tribute to the famous French actor Philibert Rouvière, who died in 1865. He stands isolated by theatrical lighting, shown in one of his most famous roles as Hamlet. It was rejected by the Salon jury even though it honoured one of France's greatest actors.*

Both *The Fifer* and *The Tragic Actor* were included in a solo independent exhibition: 'Tableaux de Edouard Manet'. He mounted this himself the following year in a pavilion in the Marquis de Pomereux garden, after securing funding from his mother of more than 18,000 francs. His exhibition opened on 24 May with an admission fee of 50 centimes and a catalogue with an introduction written jointly with Astruc. Fifty-six paintings, from well-known works to never previously exhibited still lifes, were displayed, but it was again a critical failure. Either the exhibition was overlooked entirely, or caricatured – as Randon's mocking cartoon series, published in May 1867.

Manet did not submit any works that year to the official Salon, though he did have a presence, as the sitter in Fantin-Latour's accomplished portrait of him, dated 1867. Fantin-Latour portrayed Manet as a fashionable and sophisticated man about town, rather than a modern artist at his easel. The blank background is inscribed: 'To my friend Manet', ensuring that all visitors to the Salon recognized the sitter and the affection in which he was held. One critic admitted, however, that for him the portrait was a complete surprise, having assumed the infamous Manet to be a long-haired unkempt bohemian. In fact, of course, Manet was always beautifully attired and presented. The artist Pierre-Georges Jeanniot noted that, one evening when he was walking down rue Pigalle, he 'saw approaching me a man of youthful appearance, and distinguished in carriage, dressed with elegant simplicity', and as the figure approach he realized he was a 'blond wearing a fine silky beard, he had grey eyes, a straight nose, mobile nostrils, gloved hands, with a gait both alert and jaunty. It was Manet.' Fantin-Latour, it was agreed, had captured the likeness of his friend perfectly.

A POLITICALLY INSPIRED MASTERPIECE

Portrait of Édouard Manet, *Henri Fantin-Latour, 1867. Fantin-Latour was an admirer of Manet and exhibited his portrait of him at the 1867 Salon, dedicating the portrait 'To my friend Manet'. Fantin-Latour does not portray Manet as an artist but as a suave, elegant man about town.*

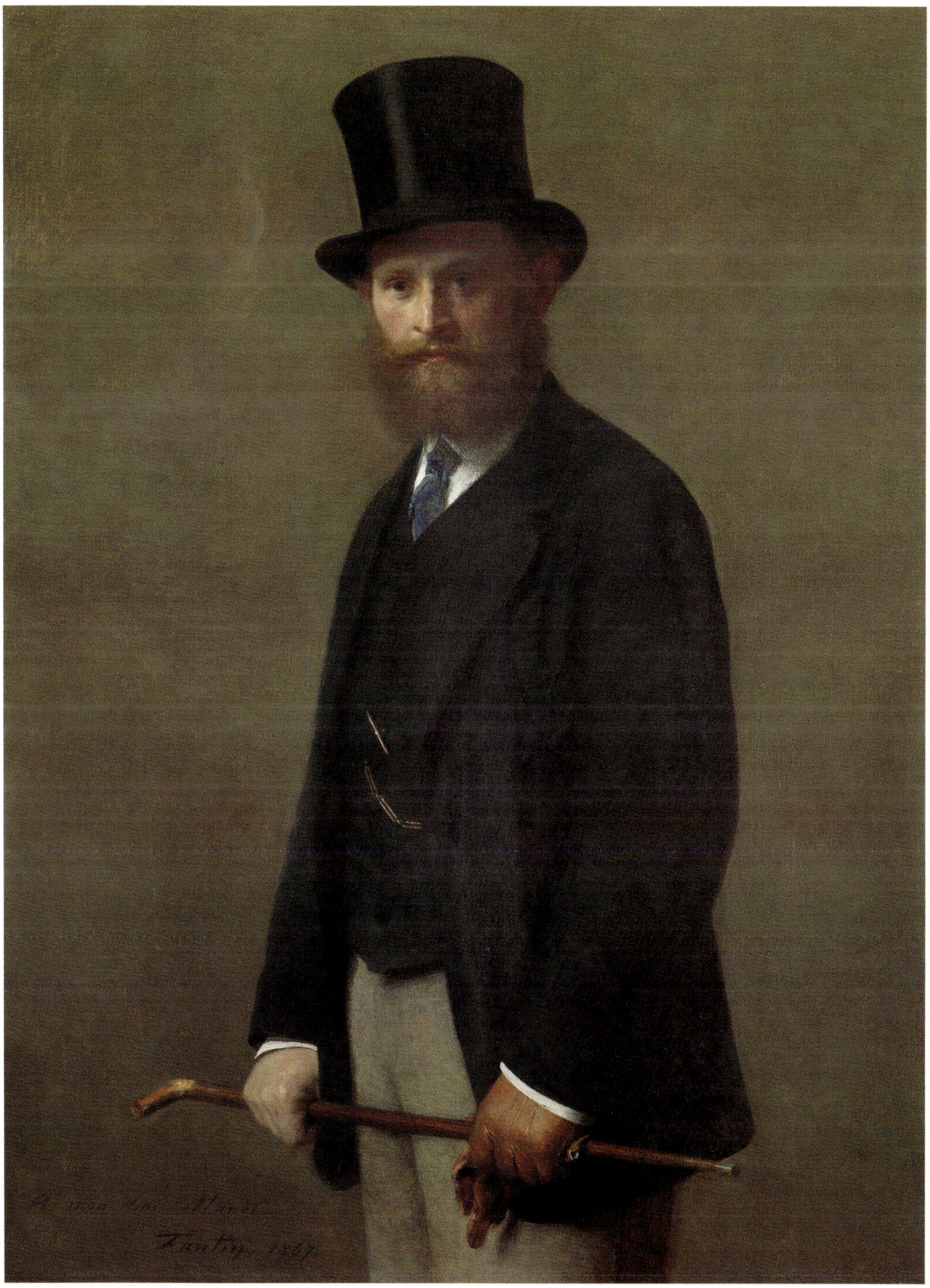

By the late summer of 1867, Manet was already working on a new, large-scale controversial work. In July that year, the newspaper *Le Figaro* published a graphic account of the execution of the Emperor Maximilian in Mexico, who had been installed three years earlier by Napoleon III. When those French troops were withdrawn, despite earlier reasurrances to the contrary, the unpopular Emperor was left vulnerable and was quickly captured by the deposed president Benito Juarez's guerrilla fighters. Tried for treason and aged just 35, he was executed by a firing squad of Mexican Army riflemen. Maximilian's end was agonizing since the first round of fire failed to kill him outright and had to be repeated. France was horrified by the turn of events. Manet was, like many of his friends and his brothers, a staunch republican and anti-Bonapartist, and against French colonial expansion. This painting clearly expressed such political leanings. In September that year, he also experienced personal grief with the death of his great friend Charles Baudelaire, a loss that added to a sense of doom and gloom.

In his first attempt at the subject, with few hard facts to hand and believing the Emperor to have been shot by peasants, Manet created a work featuring Mexicans wearing sombreros. Only two featureless figures to the left, almost hidden by gun smoke, are being executed. The work was clearly inspired by Goya's famous

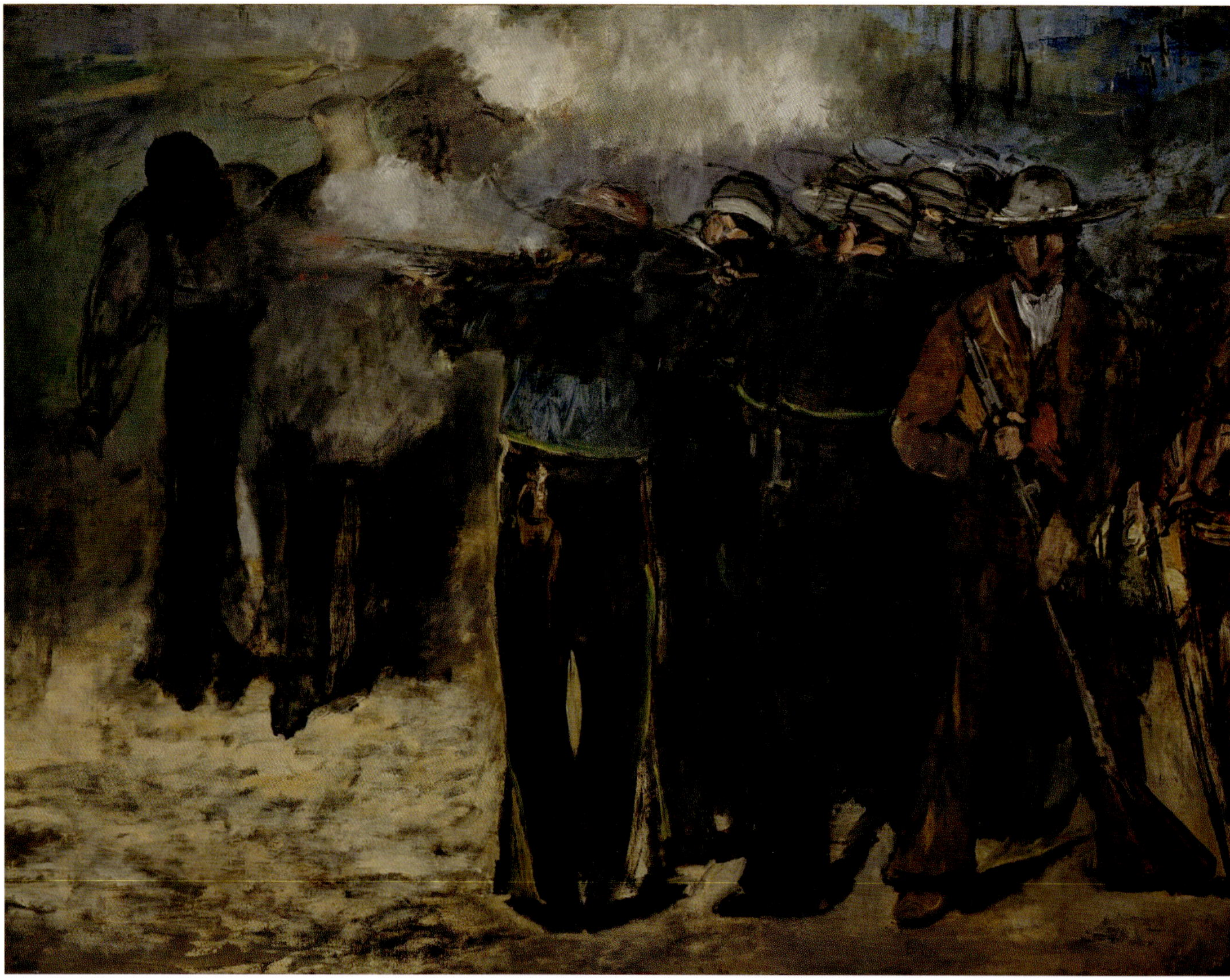

The Execution of the Emperor Maximilian of Mexico, *1867. Manet created a series of compositions showing the shocking execution of Emperor Maximilian, a member of the Hapsburg family of Austria, who had been installed in Mexico by Napoleon III of France during the French-Mexican War. His government spectacularly failed, when Napoleon III withdrew French troops, ending in Maximilian's death, with two of his generals, at the hands of Benito Juárez's guerillas. This is Manet's first attempt at the subject before he had the full facts available to him.*

3 May 1808, although his response is far less dramatic. By the autumn he had begun another variation, now set against open ground and sky, with a uniformed firing squad. The resulting picture was politically explosive and therefore Manet put it into storage, where it suffered damage. Now only four fragments survive, which are in the National Gallery, London. The final version of *The Execution of the Emperor Maximilian of Mexico* (now in the Städtische Kunsthalle, Mannheim) dates from 1867–8, by which time Manet had been able to fully research the incident. This is an electrifying, powerful work capturing, in bold strokes, the execution in front of a high wall, with spectators trying to get a glimpse over the top, and with soldiers who wear uniforms very close to those of the French army. The Emperor Maximilian is shown incorrectly in the centre with his two generals Miguel Miramón and Tomás Mejía on either side of him. It was a truly dramatic, shocking composition; the gunpowder explosion as the soldiers let off their rifles is brilliantly depicted. It, too, was politically sensitive and could not be exhibited in France. Indeed, it was not shown in public until 1879, and even then only in New York.

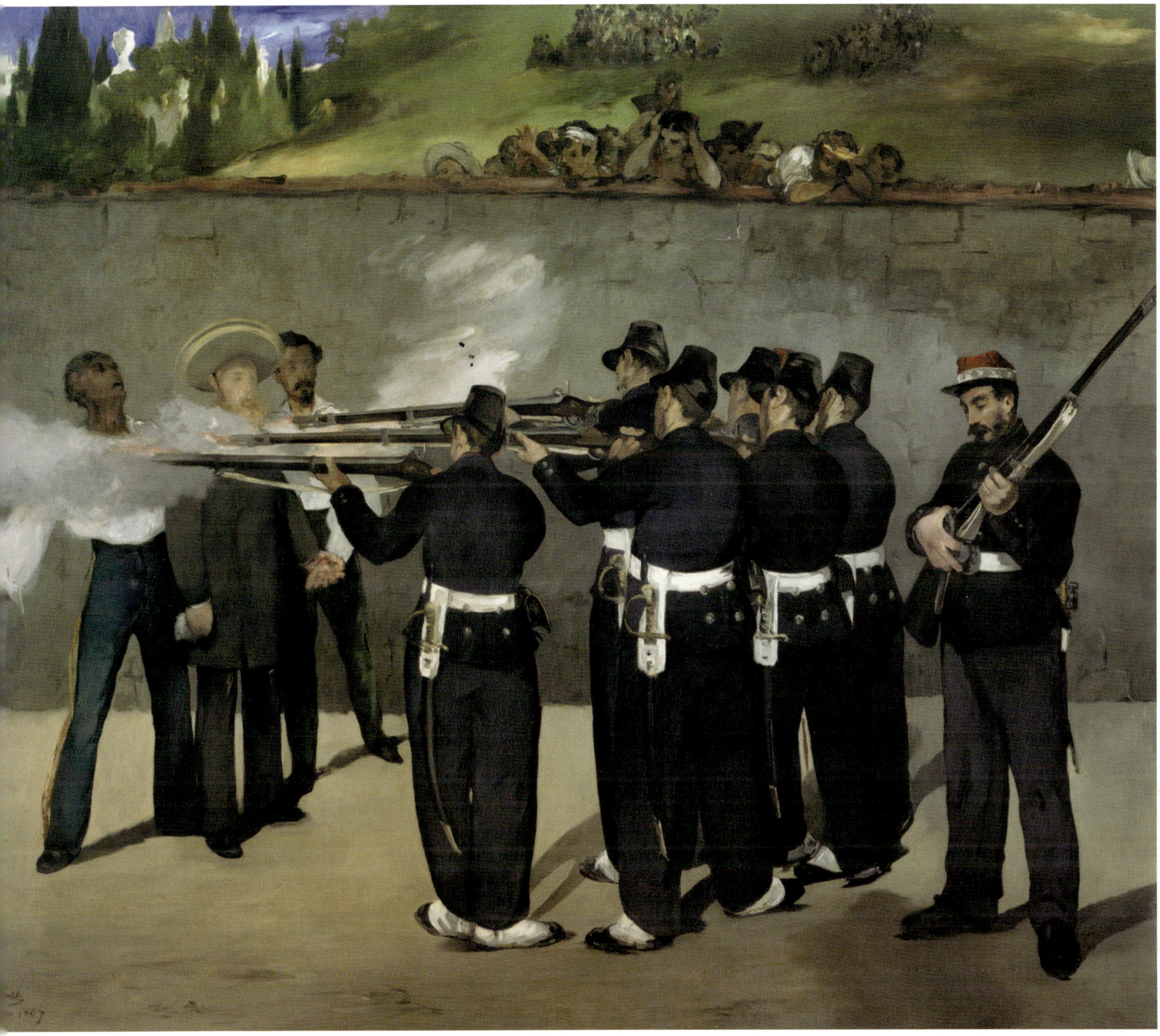

The Execution of the Emperor Maximilian of Mexico, *1868. This is the final version of the final moments of Maximilian's life. The execution took place on 19 June 1867. That date is inscribed by Manet on his canvas. He also produced a lithograph of the subject (1868–9).*

CONTEMPORARY MODERN LIFE PAINTINGS

In 1868, Manet began work on two paintings which seem to mark a new departure in his art and which are once more inspired by contemporary life in Paris. His mood seems to lighten with *Luncheon in the Studio*, which he began to paint over the summer at Boulogne-sur-Mer, and *The Balcony*. *Luncheon in the Studio* is undoubtedly a mysterious painting full of ambiguities. The central figure is based upon his possible son Léon Koëlla, who appears frequently as a model in his paintings (no less than 17 times). The 16-year-old gazes out beyond us, wearing a straw boater and oblivious of the bearded man smoking at the table behind him, who may well have been modelled by Auguste Rousselin, a painter and collector, whom Manet had known since his days in Couture's studio. The female figure appears to be a servant carrying a coffee pot. All appear oddly detached from each other. The familiar still life detail on the table includes the half-peeled lemon that is so common in Manet's still lifes, set on a familiar white tablecloth. Again, this could also be interpreted as a symbol of time passing; Léon is becoming a young man and reaching maturity.

The painting was begun in the dining room of the rented house the family had taken at Boulogne-sur-Mer but finished in Manet's Paris studio. In this contemporary setting the presence of a sword, helmet and musket, objects presumably intended as studio props, seem incongruous, but they too may be interpreted as referencing his son's coming of age. Manet simply exhibited it initially as *Le Déjeuner*, leading to ambiguity about the setting; the later title suggests it was a depiction of an artist's studio. The painting was accepted for the 1869 Salon, as was *The Balcony*, for which Léon also modelled, although here he is a distant figure in the background. The critic Jules-Antoine Castagnary criticized both works, writing of *Le Dejeuner*,

'In the *Luncheon*, for example, I see on a table where coffee is served a half-peeled lemon and fresh oysters, but these objects don't go together. Why have they been put there then?... And just as Manet brings together, solely for the pleasure of striking the eyes, still-life elements that belong apart, he also distributes his personages haphazardly, without anything necessary and forced in their composition. Whence the uncertainty and often the obscurity of his thought? What is the young man doing in the *Luncheon*, seated in the foreground and seeming to look out at the public?'

It was at Boulogne-sur-Mer, where Manet was staying with his family over the summer 1868, that he also first thought about a painting a work showing a contemporary group on a balcony, as a homage to Goya's *Majas on a Balcony*, and he made an initial sketch there. The painting itself

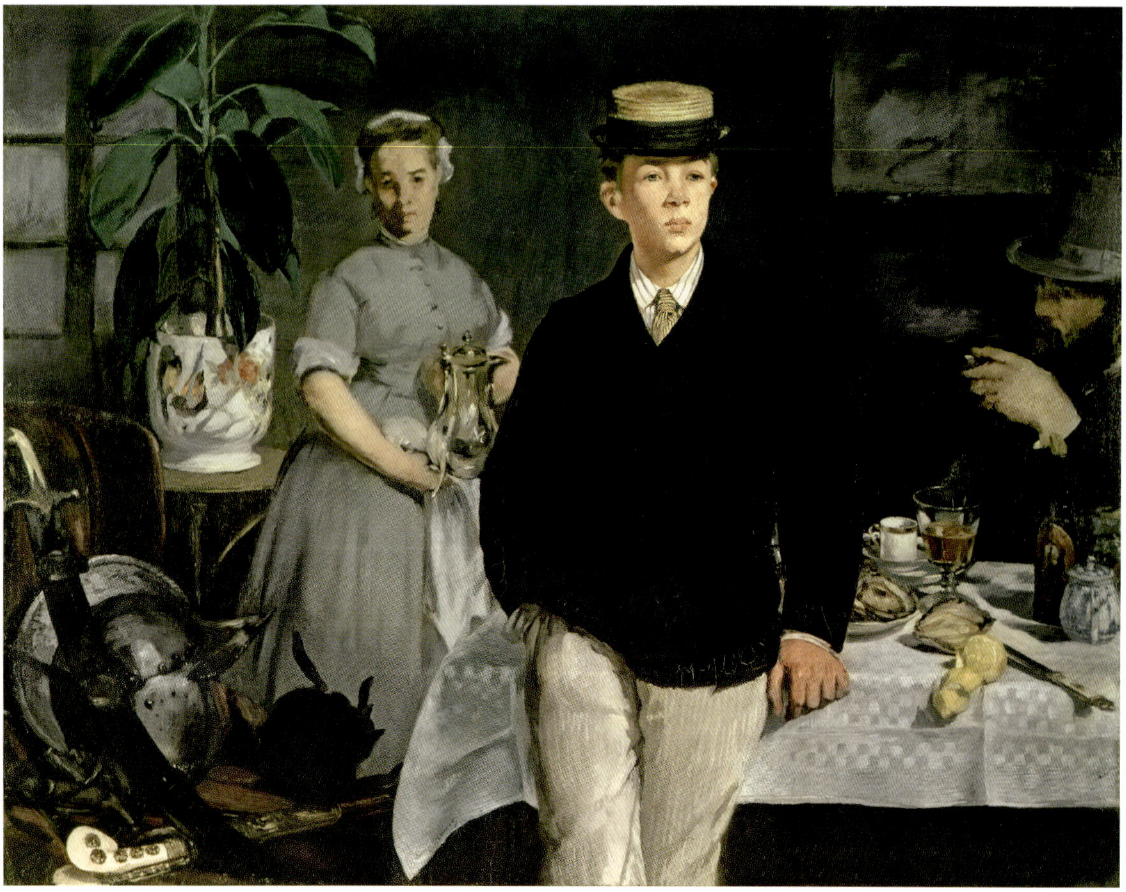

Luncheon in the Studio, *1868. Painted while Manet was on holiday in Boulogne-sur-Mer, the central figure is based upon Léon Koëlla. Manet again observes many still life details, referencing his admiration for Dutch still life painting.*

Opposite above: Majas on a Balcony, *Francisco de Goya,* c. *1800–12.*
Opposite below: The Balcony, *1868–9. Berth Morisot posed for Manet for this painting, seated on a stool, with the violinist Fanny Claus beside her. The standing central figure is Antoine Guillemet with Léon Koëlla just visible in the dark.*

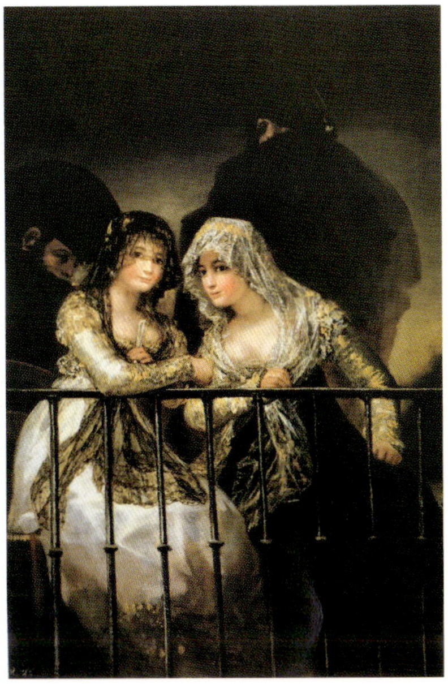

was completed back in Paris and and the principal model is the attractive young Impressionist painter Berthe Morisot. The two had been introduced by Fantin-Latour in the Louvre, where she sat copying a Rubens painting. Her dark hair, eyes and dazzling beauty immediately attracted him and she was invited with her mother and sister Edma to one of his own mother's soirées, which were often attended by the critic Zola, the sculptor Astruc and the painters Edgar Degas (1834–1917) and Alfred Stevens (1823–1906). On such occasions Manet held court, with his wife Suzanne playing the piano to entertain the illustrious company. The Manet and Morisot families were soon to become firm friends. Both the Morisot sisters made an impression on Manet and he observed to Fantin-Latour that it was a shame that as painters they were not men, but pondered if each married an academician they would 'sow the seeds of discord in the ranks of that rotten lot.'

Berthe was 27 years old and appears in *The Balcony* seated at the front, wearing a white dress, with a fan in her hand and a small dog at her feet. Standing beside her is concert violinist Fanny Claus (1846–1877), a close friend of Manet's wife Suzanne and a member of the first all-women string quartet in Paris. Fanny also wears white and is shown holding her parasol, adjusting her gloves and staring directly out at the viewer. Berthe looks in another direction to the side, glancing downwards, apparently watching the street below. Behind, and looking to the other side, is Antoine Guillemet (1843–1918), the young ambitious landscape painter who was a pupil of Corot. It was he who had introduced Manet to Émile Zola and his family friend Cézanne (1809–1936). In the dark background, a young boy can just be seen, carrying food on to the balcony, said to be modelled by Léon. Beside Berthe is a beautifully observed lily planted in an ornate pot. The figures are harshly frontally lit and are again, as in *Luncheon in the Studio*, apparently detached from each other, framed by the green shutters and enclosed by the matching ironwork of the balcony itself.

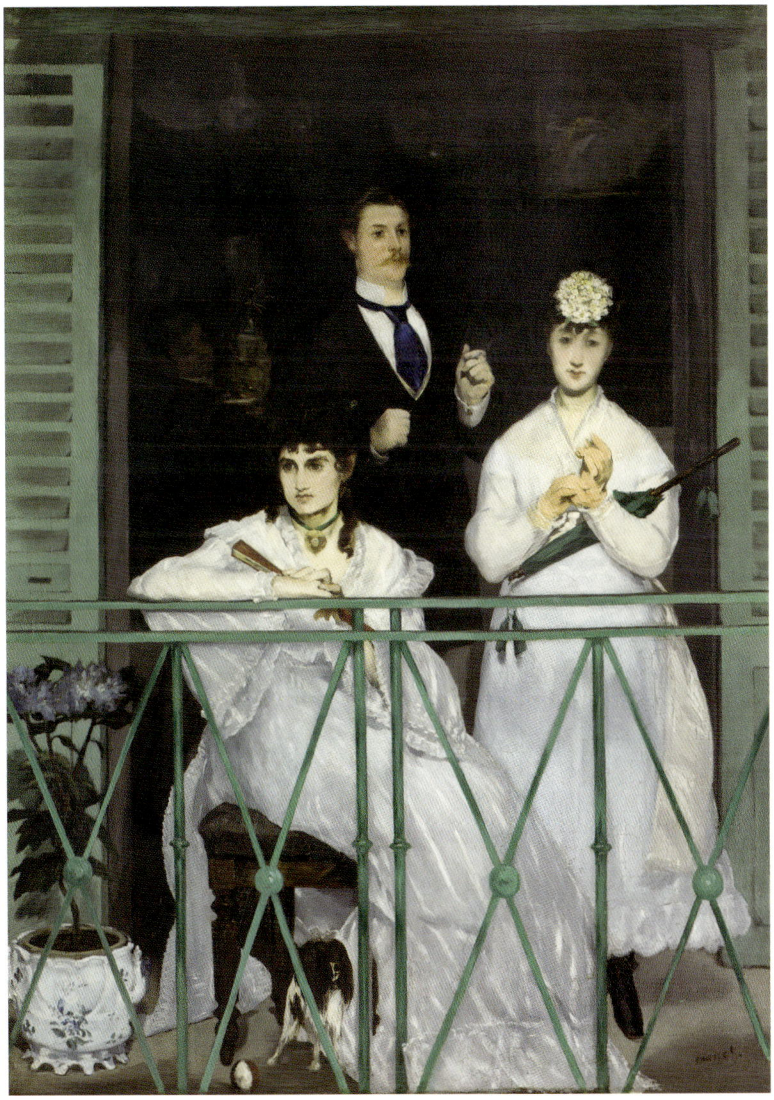

Following numerous sittings, the models prepared to view the finished work. Berthe's mother wrote to her other daughter Edma, 'Tomorrow we are going to see Manet's painting. Antoine says that he made him pose fifteen times to no effect and that Mademoiselle Claus is atrocious. Both of them, tired of posing on their feet, say to him: "It's perfect – there is nothing more to be done."' Manet clearly laboured long and hard over the work and must have been delighted when it was accepted at the Salon – as was a landscape by Guillemet – but it was a good reception from the critics he craved and he was clearly anxious about how it would be received. Again writing to her sister Edma, Berthe reveals, 'I found Manet with his hat on the back of his head and looking demented. He begged me to go and see his picture because he did not dare to do so himself. He laughed, looked worried, swearing all the time both that *The Balcony* was a very bad picture and that it would be very successful.' As to her own appearance in the painting and its reception at the Salon, she informed her sister, 'I appear strange rather than ugly. I hear that those looking at me have murmured the words Femme fatale'.

The critics were contemptuous, the caricaturist Cham declaring sarcastically, 'Close the shutters!'. It was the ambiguity of the composition that particularly offended – just as in *Luncheon in the Studio*, the relationship between the three figures was unclear. Jules Castagnary, writing in *Le Siècle* in June 1869, asked 'are they sisters? Are they mother and daughter? I do not know.' Edmond Duranty in *Paris Journal* felt that 'The background is too opaque' while another critic wrote harshly that Manet had 'lowered himself to the point of being in competition with the painters of the building trade'. The stark contrast between the green shutters and white dresses also caused offence. The traditional hierarchy applied to the depiction of human figures and objects had been overturned: the flowers were observed in more detail than some of the faces. The effect of this criticism on Manet was noted by Berthe, who informed her sister philosophically: 'Poor Manet is sad. His exhibits are, as usual, not to the taste of the public – a perpetual source of surprise to him.' She was to become a favourite model of Manet and later married his brother Eugène.

ENCOUNTERING THE IMPRESSIONISTS

Manet could not please the critics, expect Zola, but he had an increasing number of close followers from a younger generation of artists, as well as his own circle, who often joined him for animated discussion at the Café de Bade. Manet had known Degas since 1859 and first encountered Monet (1840–1926) in 1866, when confusion arose over their names. While Manet's art had been rejected at the Salon that year, the young Monet had had two works accepted and the signature on one, *The Road to Chailly* (a village near Fontainebleau), had caused considerable comment as the public pored over the signature, wondering whether this could be a work by Manet. The popular cartoonist André Gill picked up on this confusion, and published a caricature with the caption 'Monet or Manet? Monet, but we owe Monet to Manet. Bravo Monet! Thanks Manet!'

Édouard Manet was not thrilled by such comparison and a new name so similar to his own, with a signature just like his too! However, he decided to investigate and invited the young man to the Café de Bade. Monet, of course, knew all about Manet, and the reception given to works such as *Olympia*. After clearing up the initial misunderstanding, the two became friends and Monet introduced him to his friends Pierre-Auguste Renoir (1841–1919), Frédéric Bazille (1841–70) and Alfred Sisley (1839–99). In that same year Zola introduced him to Paul Cézanne (1839–1906), who in turn brought Camille Pissarro (1830–1903) along. Manet had already known Degas since 1859. Gradually, this disparate group of artists came to meet more in the small Café Guerbois, where Manet held court, sitting around small tables and discussing artistic influences, such as Delacroix and Ingres, plein-air painting and the state's influence on art in France at the time. Sometimes, particularly when Zola was in attendance, the subject turned to politics when Manet expressed his republicanism. The stage was now set for the development of Impressionism in the next decade. Before then, however, the Franco-Prussian War was to break out, with differing impacts on all these artists but most especially for Manet. He stayed to defend Paris and in 1870 painted what is arguably the first truly Impressionist painting.

Portrait of Émile Zola, *1868. Manet met the playwright, journalist and critic Zola in 1866, and Zola was soon an enthusiastic admirer of the artist's work. This portrait was shown at the 1868 Salon. Shown seated at his crowded desk, a phamplet by Zola on Manet is visible, while on the wall an aquantint version of* Olympia *is displayed and to the left there is a Japanese screen. Manet presented Zola with the work, which he was said not to be entirely flattered by, hanging it in a back room at his home.*

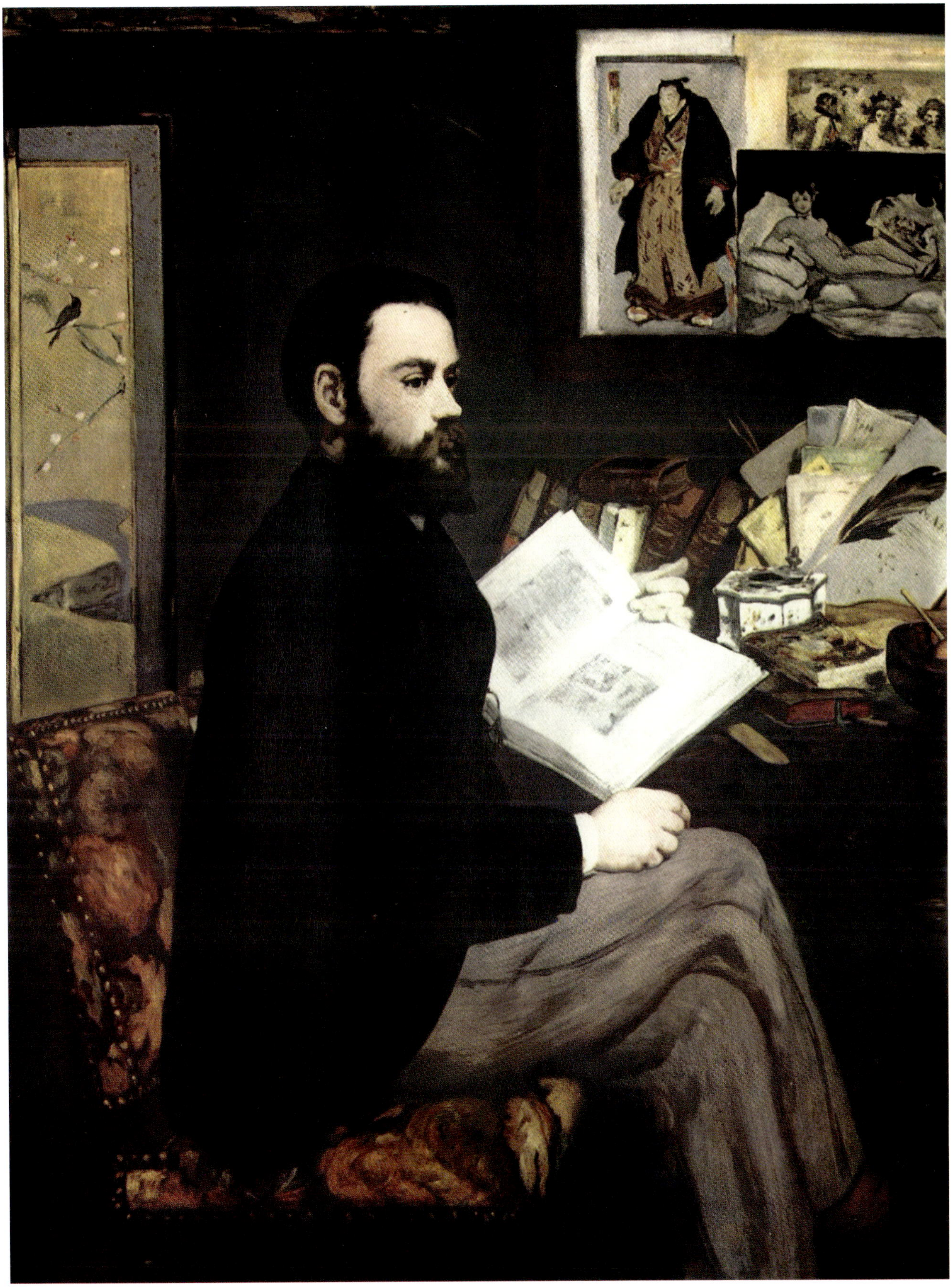

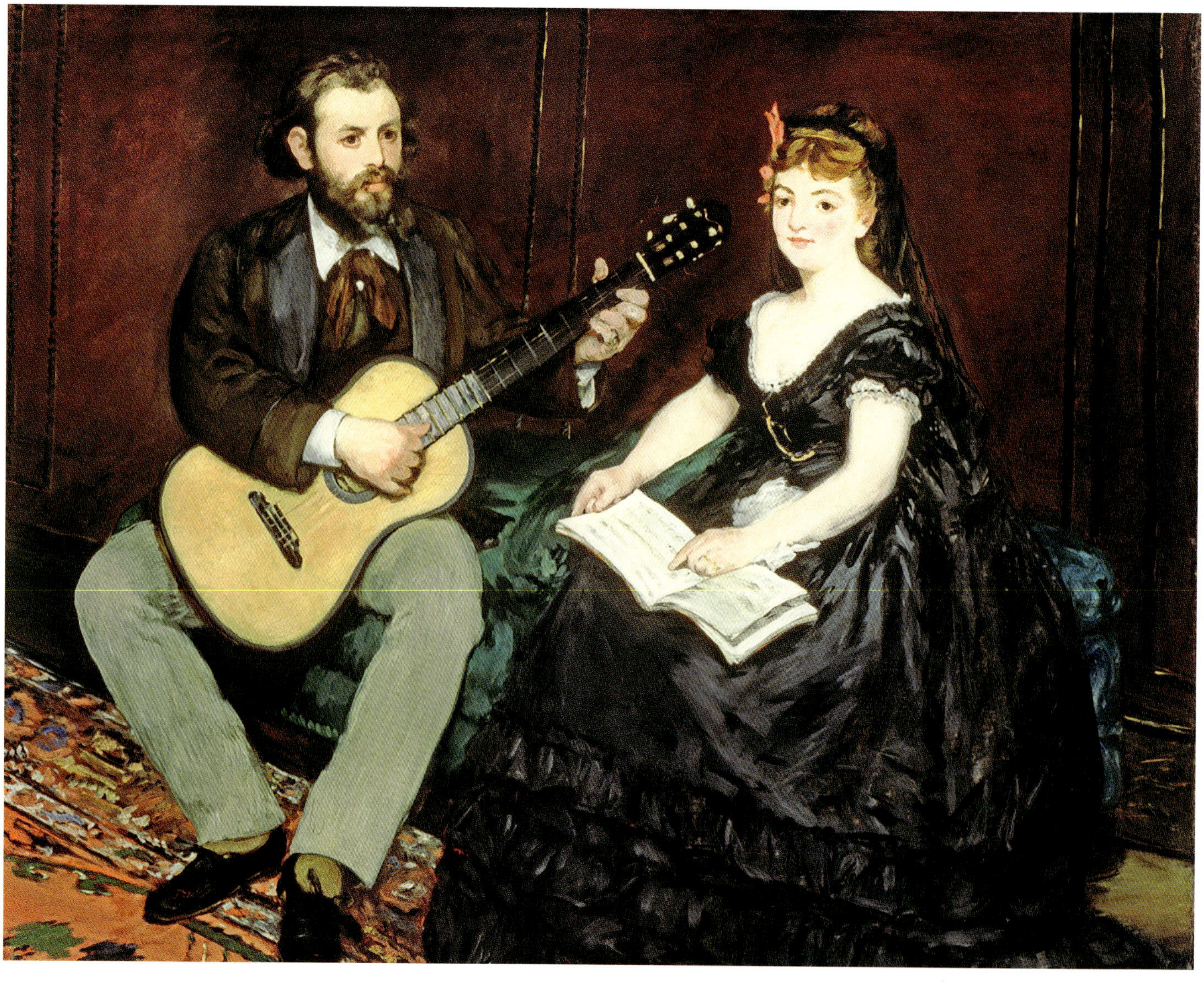

The Music Lesson, c. *1868. Music was important to Manet and his wife, Suzanne Leenhoff, an accomplished pianist. Together, they held regular musical soirées in their home. Music was also a constant theme in Manet's art, and he captured many musicians playing and performing in theatres and café concerts as well as designing cover illustrations for sheet music by composer friends. This is, however, a personal glimpse of him with his wife, enjoying their passion for music. It was accepted by the Salon in the spring of 1870 and remained in the artist's collection until the sale of Manet's estate in 1884.*

CHAPTER 4
Inspiring Impressionism

PORTRAITS AND OBSERVATIONS

Manet's paintings *The Music Lesson* (*c*. 1868), a somewhat stilted portrait of himself and his wife, and his striking portrait *Eva Gonzalès at the easel* (1870) were both accepted by the Salon in the spring of 1870, receiving a mixed critical reception. Berthe Morisot was not the only young woman artist to benefit from Manet's mentoring. Eva was the daughter of a well-known novelist and journalist and initially trained with the French painter Charles Chaplin. Manet had a wide circle of artist friends as well as the young Impressionists and it was Alfred Stevens who introduced Gonzalès to Manet. She became his only formal pupil and a successful artist in her own right, exhibiting at the Salon. Shown here apparently painting at her easel in his studio, she finishes an already framed painting of peonies. On the floor, a rolled canvas bearing her master's signature testifies to their professional relationship. Her pose and fluidly painted white dress are a homage to Goya, reflecting her Spanish heritage.

His latest reviews left Manet disappointed, and he retreated, spending the summer at Saint-Germain-en-Laye with the Italian artist Giuseppe de Nittis, who would exhibit at the first Impressionist exhibition in 1874. It may be the de Nittis family who

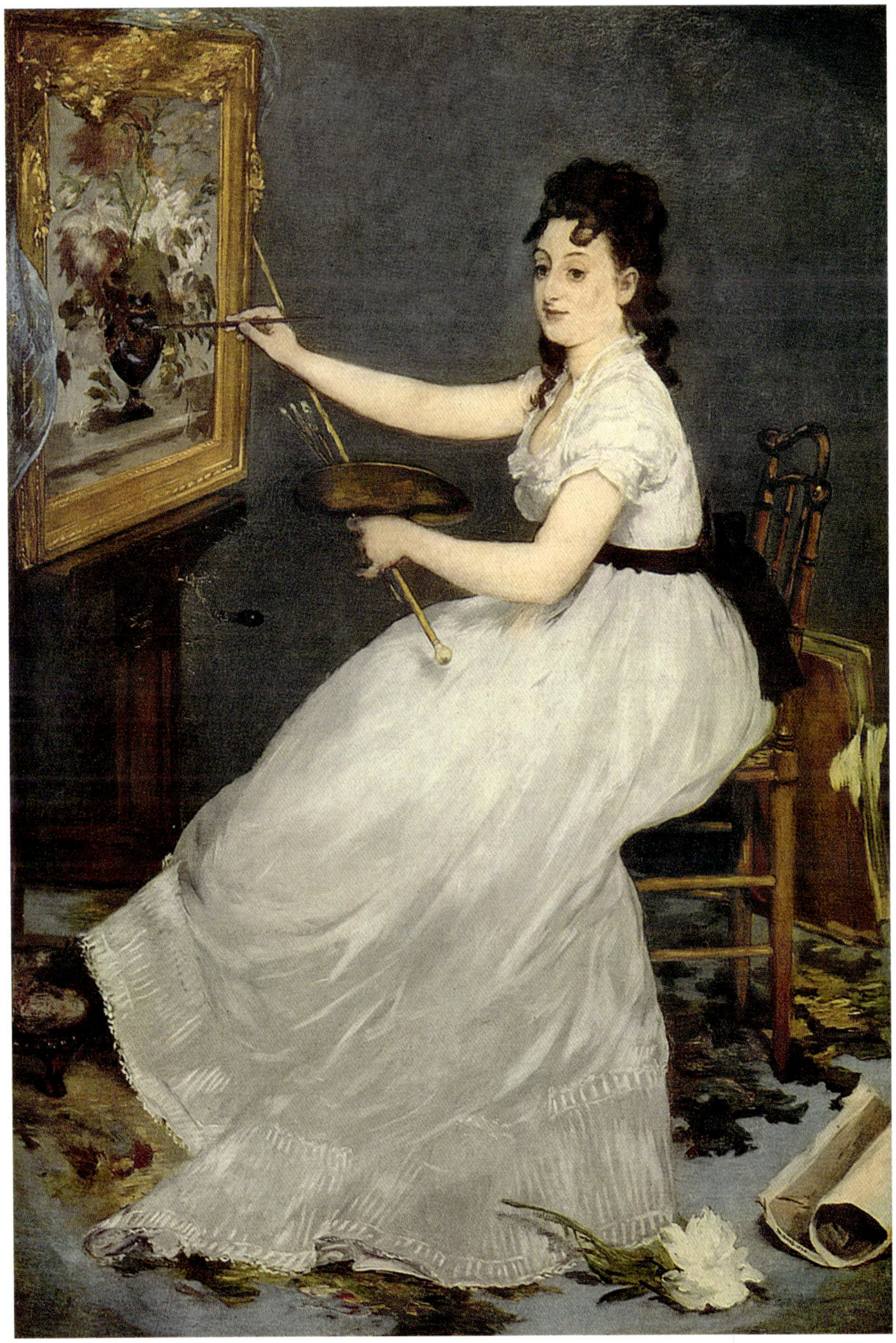

Eva Gonzalès at the Easel, c. *1870. She was the daughter of the novelist Emmanuel Gonzalès.*

are the sitters in his informal *In the Garden*, 1870, which Manet gave to the artist, who greatly appreciated it and gave him one of his own works in return. In contrast to Eva at her easel, the artist is shown relaxing with his Parisian wife, whom he had married the previous year, and their young baby, in the beautiful grounds of his villa between Reuil and Saint-Germain-en-Laye. It may represent an early example of Manet experimenting with *plein air* painting. There is a relaxed sense of immediacy, enhanced by the apparently random cropping of the composition at the edges, which looks forward to works such as *On the Beach* (1873) and *Boating* (1874) and which may be influenced by photography. It is a marked contrast to Manet's submission to the Salon of *The Music Lesson*, in which the figures of himself and his wife seem wooden and stiff. His enjoyable stay with the Italian artist de Nittis was rudely interrupted, however, on 19 July by the news that France had declared war on Prussia. Life was going to change pretty swiftly for Manet and his friends.

In the Garden, *1870. Manet spent the summer at Saint-Germain-en-Laye with the Italian artist Giuseppe de Nittis, who would exhibit at the first Impressionist exhibition in 1874. It may be the de Nittis family who are shown in relaxed pose here, with Léontine de Nittis, Giuseppe's wife, being the main focus, with her direct gaze, in this informal observation of a young family enjoying the sunshine in their garden.*

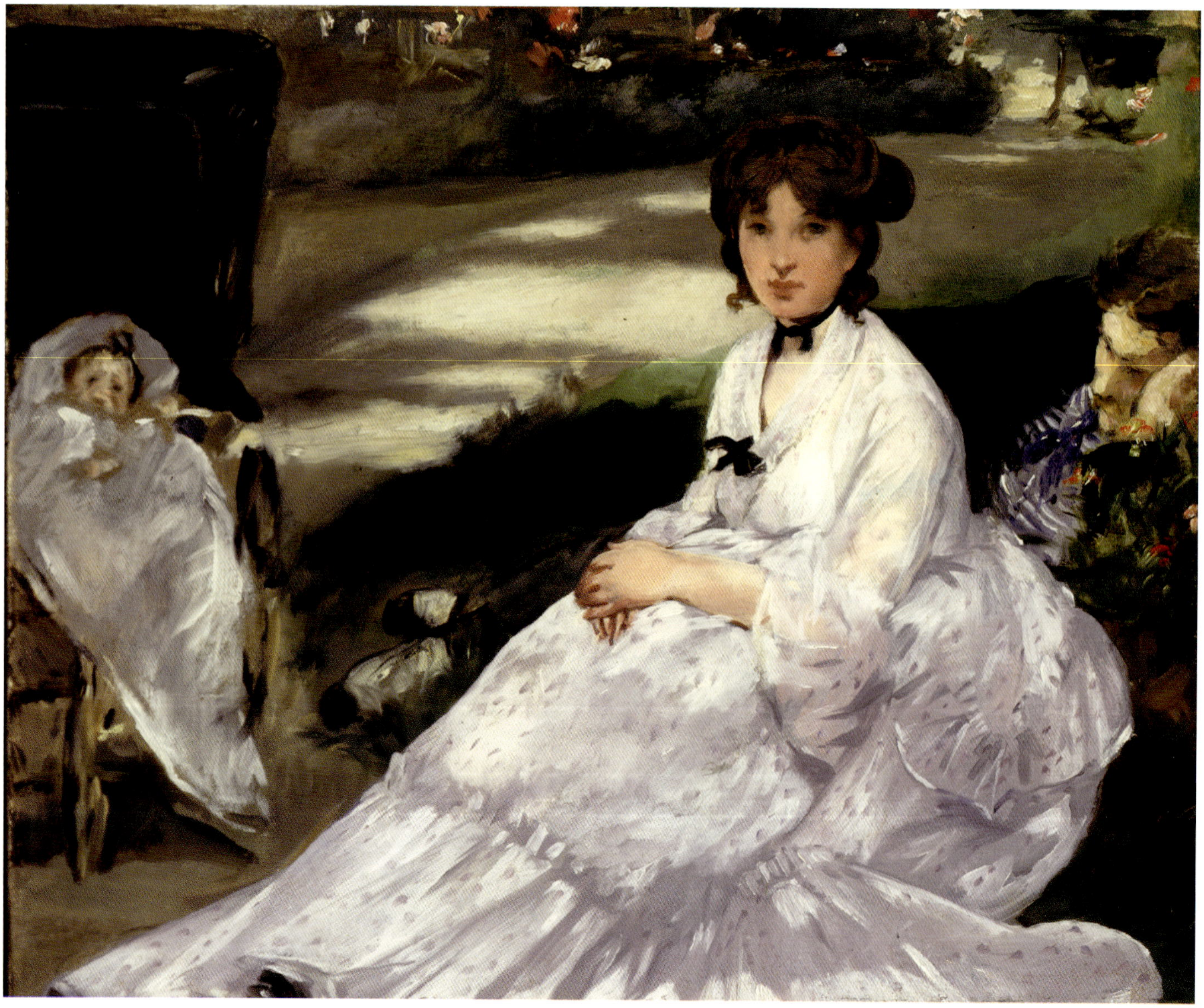

MANET AND THE FRANCO-PRUSSIAN WAR

By 4 September, following major defeats for the French army and the fall of Napoleon III, the Third Republic was established. Later in September when the Prussians threatened the capital itself, Manet, who was a proud Parisian, did not flee. He organized for his family to go to the safety of Oloron-Sainte-Marie in the Pyrennees, but by November had enlisted with the National Guard, first in the artillery and then the General Staff. While his younger friends Monet and Pissarro worked in very different circumstances in exile in England, Manet experienced first-hand the horrors of a siege. Within a matter of a few months his life had changed out of all recognition. He closed up his studio at rue Guyot, put some paintings for safe keeping in the cellar of his friend, the critic and journalist Duret, and rather optimistically took a smaller studio. But by the end of September, the city was completely surrounded by Prussian forces and the siege had begun.

His letters to his wife provide a valuable record of his life in Paris during this time. He wrote to Suzanne on 24 September, 'Paris is determined to defend itself to the last.' His letters were sent out via balloon and so were at risk of being shot down, and initially Manet was unsure if his reports were reaching her. By the end of the month he was telling her that food supplies were running low, especially of milk and meat. As autumn set in, the temperature dropped and there was little food to eat, and despite daily drilling, he and his fellow soldiers were bored. 'You have no idea how dreary it is,' he wrote later in November, 'our state of boredom is such that we don't want to see anyone – always the same conversation, the same illusions. The evenings are hard to bear.' The queues for food lengthened, smallpox began to spread and gas and salt ran out. Manet himself developed a problem with his foot, which swelled up and was increasingly painful. At times, he regretted sending the family away but as the situation deteriorated he was glad he had done so. He missed his wife, writing that he had found a photograph of her 'so I can look at your comforting face from time to time. I woke in the night thinking I heard you calling out to me.' But during daylight hours there was still time for painting. In another letter to his wife he explained, 'My soldier's knapsack serves… to hold everything necessary for painting. I shall soon start some sketches from life. They will be souvenirs that one day will have value.' Although he appears to have produced a number of such works, only two survive.

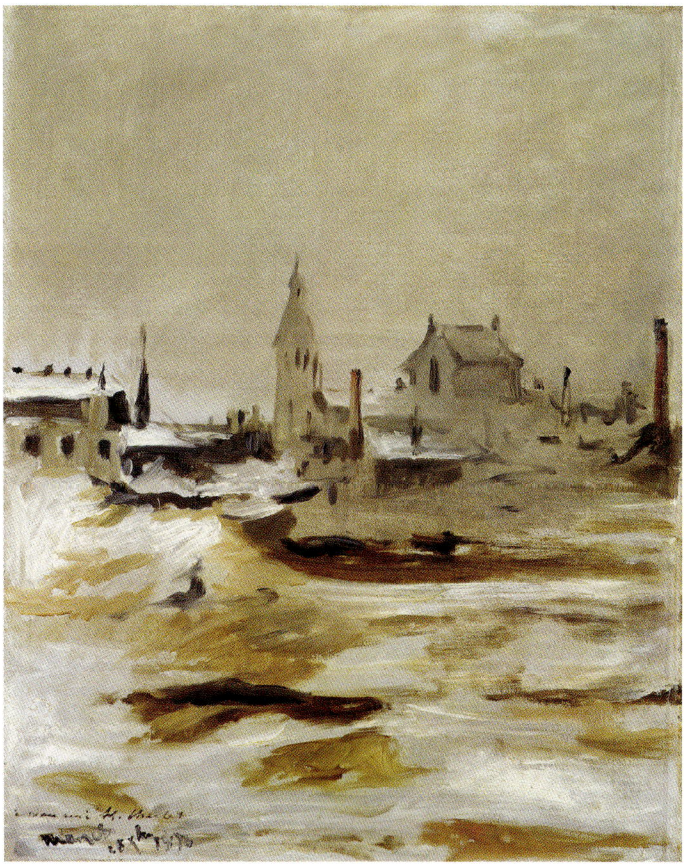

Effect of Snow at Petit-Montrouge, *1870. Manet produced one of his first truly Impressionist paintings, while serving in the National Guard during the Franco-Prussian War.*

In late December 1870, Manet found himself in a part of Paris he would not usually frequent, Petit-Montrouge, a quartier in the south of the 14th arrondissement. He was there on 22 December to see his brother Eugène, also in the Guard, and according to the inscription on this small painting Manet returned again on 28 December 1870. In the extreme cold, Manet and his fellow soldiers were awaiting the Prussians' inevitable attack, and it seems that the artist painted to relieve his boredom. The small picture *Effect of Snow at Petit-Montrouge*, 1870 is executed in greys, browns, beiges and dirty white highlights and was probably dashed off in one swift sitting; no under-drawing is discernible. This is not freshly fallen snow in a picturesque landscape but snow that has been there lying in the city for days, during one of the coldest winters on record. In the foreground is an empty wasteland, and the Church of St Pierre de Montrouge with its exceptionally tall bell tower dominates the distance. It was a relatively new building, completed only seven years earlier in 1863, and now this symbol of more prosperous times was being used as a field hospital, with the tower employed as a lookout station. On this fine linen canvas Manet, who was ill and suffering from sores, captures the dreary half-light of a late December, snow-laden day. The absence of under-drawing suggests that this is an on-the-spot sketch dashed off between duties and many now consider this to be his first truly Impressionist painting. He inscribed the work there and then, while the paint was still wet, and dedicated it to H. Charlet, presumably a fellow soldier. He dated it '28 Xbre 1870'.

Another work painted on the same day, of exactly the same dimensions, *La Gare du Chemin de Fer de Sceaux* (Private Collection), was thought to be lost, but came to light in 2005 and was sold more recently at Sothebys. It too has the same spontaneous brushwork and cool palette of greys, browns and beiges, capturing the haunting quality of a small, snowbound train station in a city under siege. Despite the name, mystery surrounds the actual location: while Sceaux is only 8 km (5 miles) from Petit-Montrouge, it was beyond the Prussian lines on that date and would have been inaccessible to Manet. In this case, the artist presented his sketch to a fellow soldier named Lambert in the National Guard, with whom he was serving as a lieutenant, and it passed down in his family.

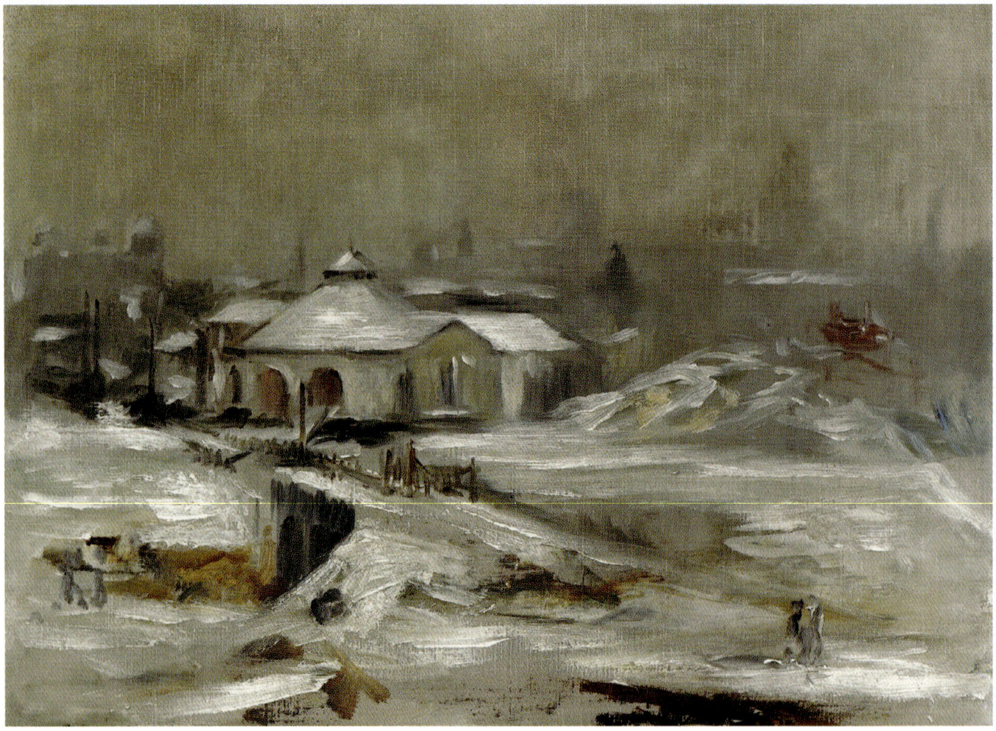

La Gare du Chemin de Fer de Sceaux, *1870. This was one of the first works Manet painted* en plein air.

Within a month of these two paintings being executed, the Siege of Paris was over. On 28 January 1871, the French surrendered to the Prussians. A treaty followed in which France lost Alsace and Lorraine. In February, Manet left the city and headed to the Pyrenees, to be reunited with his family. With the situation still so unstable in Paris itself, they moved to Bordeaux in March and then Arachon, returning to Paris only in late May after the *semaine sanglante* (bloody week) of 21–28 May, during which thousands of Communards in the city were killed. Exhausted and demoralized, Manet was instructed by his doctor to rest and went to his family home at Boulogne-sur-Mer.

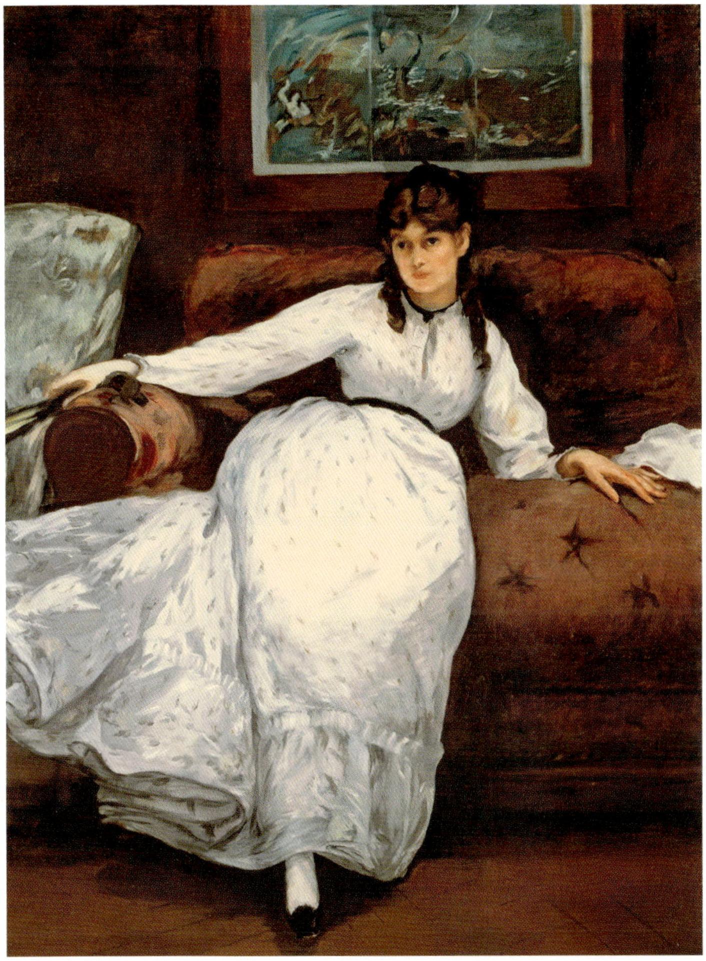

Above: The Repose *1870. The model was Berthe Morisot again. This time she is shown relaxing on a sofa. Hanging on the wall behind her is a well-known Japanese print, identifiable as being by Utagawa Kuniyoshi. The reception of* Repose *was not encouraging. The art critics and public found her dress too informal and her pose and distracted gaze too casual.*

TOWARDS IMPRESSIONISM

In the summer of 1872, Manet and Suzanne visited Holland again, including Haarlem and the new Frans Hals museum. His old studio in rue Guyot had been destroyed in the siege of Paris and on his return from Holland, he moved to a new studio, near the Gare Saint-Lazare, to return to painting again. He would work there until 1878. Manet had long admired Frans Hals, and the influence of the Dutch seventeenth-century master can be seen in his painting *Le Bon Bock*, 1873, which was a success at the 1873 Salon. By contrast, his other entry *Repose*, 1870, with its broad, tactile paint-handling received negative criticism for its apparent lack of resolution. This striking work was obviously a portrait of the artist Berthe Morrisot, to whom he was so close. Manet used his typical contrasts of light and dark tones, creating a sense of shallow space, but critics and public thought her dress was too informal and her pose and distracted gaze too casual. Manet could not comprehend the issues and was clear that it was intended to be not a simple portrait but – as the title suggests – an observation of physical and pychological repose, 'not at all in the character of a portrait'.

Tired of controversy, Manet spent the summer of 1873 on holiday with his family in the little coastal town of Berck-sur-Mer. There his wife Suzanne and his brother Eugène posed for him on the beach. This painting was executed out of doors, as is demonstrated by the grains of sand mixed with the paint, demonstrating the increasingly influence of the young Impressionists on his style, though his palette is still relatively dark. The sketchy, fluid *On the Beach*, 1873, shows Suzanne, well protected against the sun and the wind by a muslin veil and large dress. She is reading a book while his brother gazes out to sea, where a few boats can be seen in the distance. The relationship between the figures is unresolved, as is

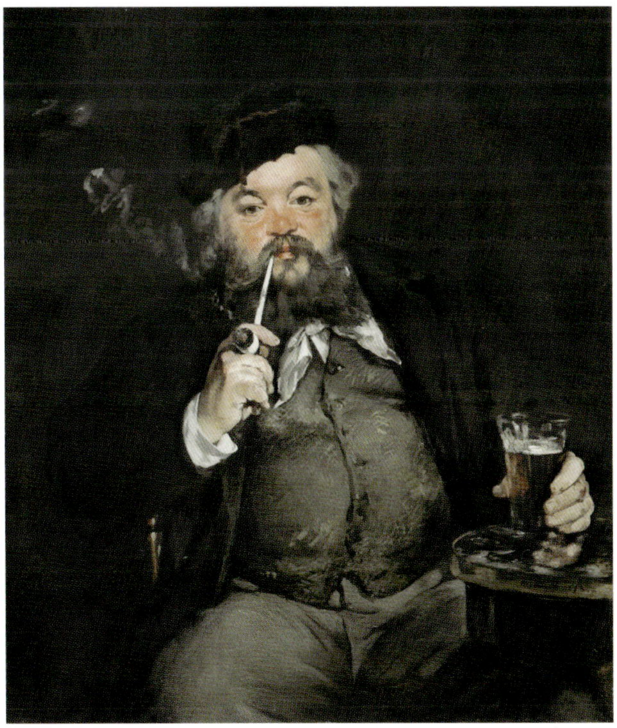

Right: Le Bon Bock, c. *1868. At one level, this appears to be a vivid depiction of a portly Dutch drinker enjoying Bock, a rich beer brewed in the spring. The sitter was actually the art dealer and print maker, Emile Bellot, who later set up the Bon Bock Society, a beer-drinking society for artists, writers and performers.*

often the case in his compositions.

Manet continued to struggle to have his works accepted by the Salon. In 1874 his painting *The Railway* (1873) was accepted, but *Swallows* (1873) and the *Masked Ball at the Opera* (1873) were rejected. The faux liberalism of Napoleon III had now been replaced by a new regime that was both politically and culturally repressive. The Salon reflected this shift in emphasis, making it an even more unlikely vehicle for the exposure of Manet and his followers' new style of painting.

Most critics at the Salon were dismissive of *The Railway* and what they considered to be Manet's trivial and unresolved subject matter at the 1874 Salon, and found fault with his usual strident colours, loose brush work and flatly painted forms. Today, the painting is considered to be one of his great masterpieces, and is so familiar that it is hard to perceive how remarkably modern it seemed at the time. One of the first paintings he completed in his new studio, near the busiest railway station in Paris, the Gare Saint-Lazare on rue de Saint-Pétersbourg, *The Railway* reflects modern life in the city. It shows not a train but a young woman, with a small beagle puppy in her lap and an open book. She looks directly at us and beside her stands a young girl, her back to us, gazing through the railings at the smoke from the trains, which were now an everyday part of life in the city. Visitors to Manet's studio often remarked that his floors and windows shook as trains went in and out of the nearby station.

This scene is actually set in the garden of the home of his friend the artist Alphonse

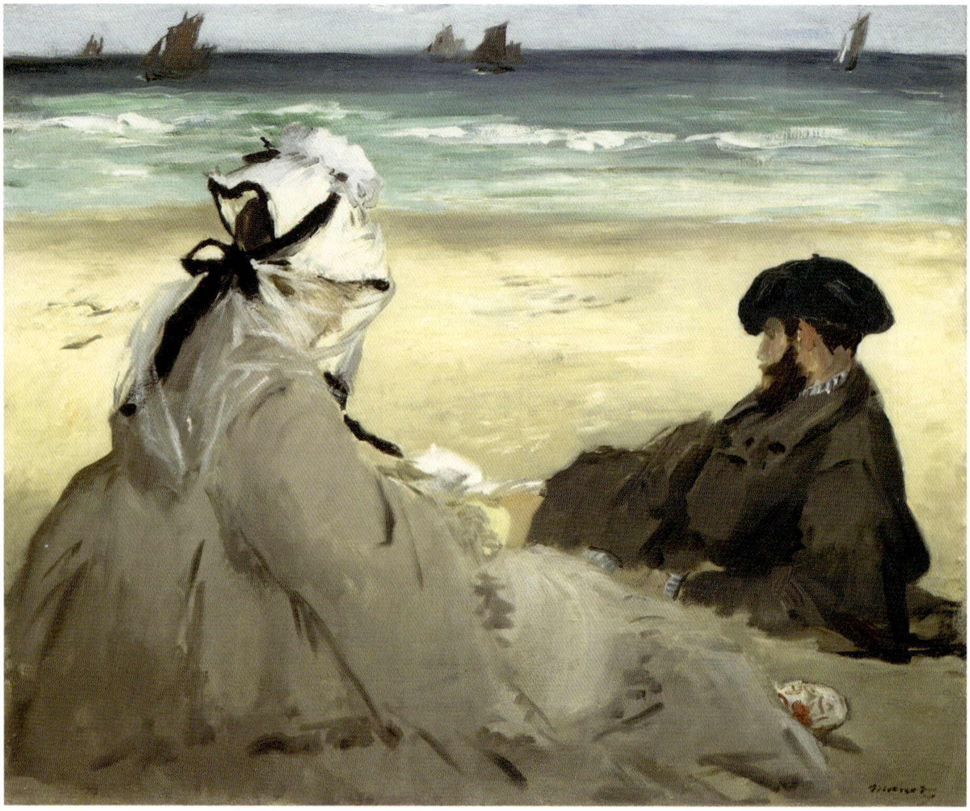

On the Beach, *1873. Manet painted during the summer of 1873 at Berck-sur-Mer, on the northern coast of France, renowned for its spa treatment and vast sandy beach.*

Swallows, *1873. The artist's mother, reading a book, and his wife appear in this loosely painted work, depicting the spring, with swallows swooping low to the ground.*

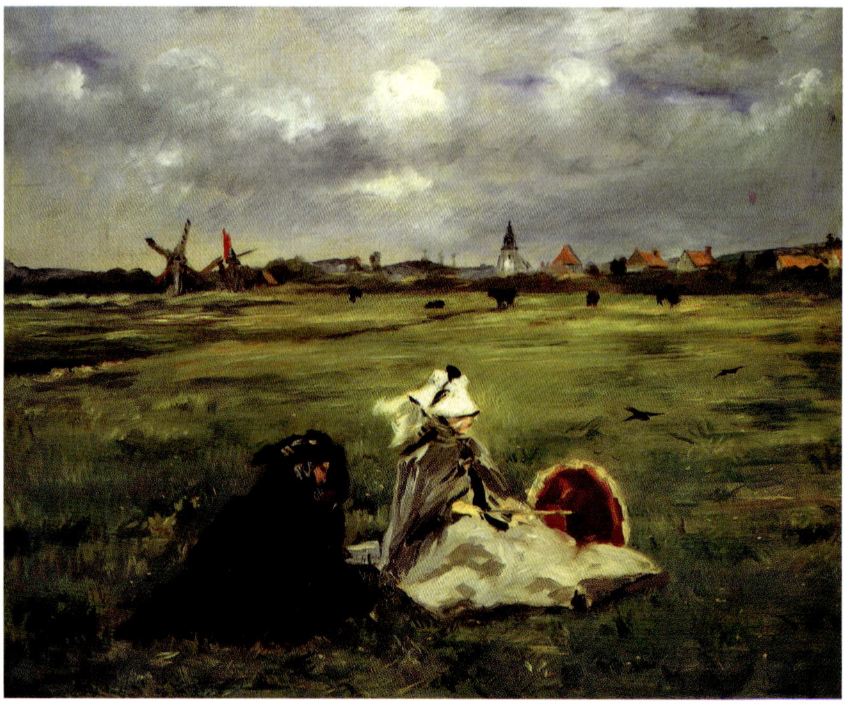

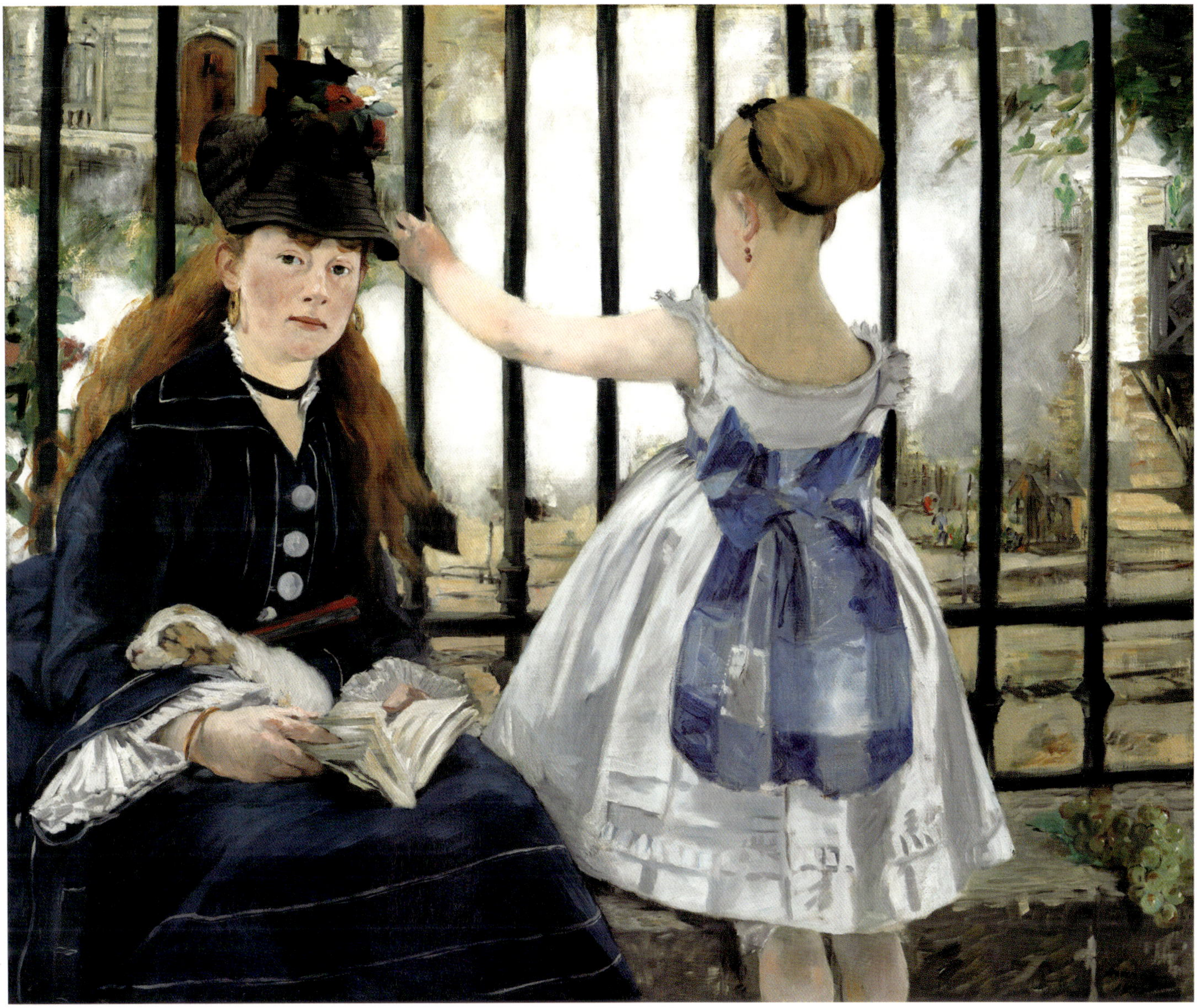

The Railway, 1873. *This work shows two figures – a young girl in a beautifully observed white dress, with her back to the onlooker, gazing through railings at the billowing smoke from an unseen train below at the Gare Saint-Lazare, Paris' busiest train station. Looking directly out at the spectator is a young fashionably dressed woman. The model is Victorine Meurent, who also sat for* Olympia. *Manet gives no hint of the relationship between the woman and child. At the Salon, many critics dismissed the work finding the subject trivial and disliked his usual strident colours and loose brush work.*

Hirsch, whose own studio was in a building directly across from Manet's on the rue de Rome. There Victorine Meurent, one of his favourite models who had sat for *Olympia*, posed for him with Hirsch's young daughter. Manet's love of still life is reflected in a bunch of grapes depicted by the railings, presumably about to be consumed by the two figures. The relationship of the sitters is not clear – are they mother and child, an older sister with her sibling, or perhaps even a governess with her young pupil taking a break from studies? Their clothing is sumptuous: the young women wears a deep blue dress with big, fashionable buttons, her red hair streaming from beneath a large black hat, and the young girl wears earrings, a black ribbon in her hair, a white dress and a blue satin bow tied at the back around her waist. This is modern life in the city: a railway station and the billowing smoke of a train.

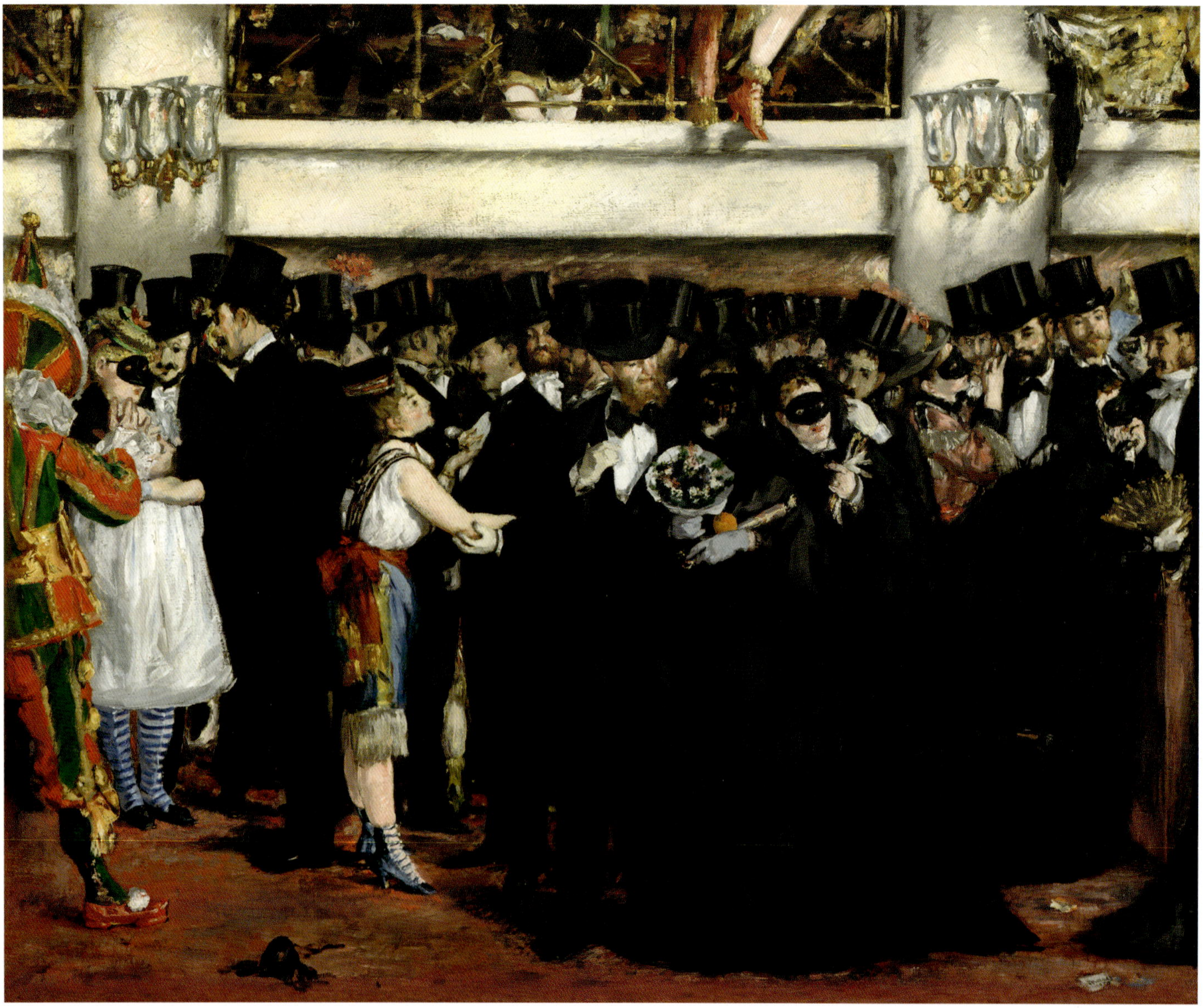

Masked Ball at the Opera, *1873. Manet depicts a well-known masked ball held each year during Lent, where young women were masked. Manet made observational sketches at the ball but finished the work in his studio. He included several of his artistic and musical friends and even represented himself, bearded on the right with a direct gaze outwards. At his feet, a fallen dance card bears his signature. At the top of the painting, a pair of female legs dangles over a railing, suggesting the somewhat risqué nature of the celebrated evening. The painting was rejected by the Salon jury that year.*

Opposite: Moonlight at the Port of Boulogne, *1868. This work would appear to have been painted in August 1868 from a window of the Hôtel Folkestone on the quay at Boulogne-sur-Mer. Manet observes by moonlight the return of a fishing boat to harbour and the fishermen's wives waiting on the quay. Such moonlit shipping scenes reflect his interest in Dutch seventeenth-century art by artists such as Cuyp and van der Neer.*

Despite his continued disappointment at the reception of his work, Manet's artistic fortunes seemed to be turning. In early 1872 the art dealer Paul Durand-Ruel had seen two of his paintings in the studio of another of his friends, the successful artist Alfred Stevens.

Manet had asked his friend to hang *The Salmon* (1868) and *Moonlight at the Port of Bolougne* (1868) in his smart studio in case they appealed to collectors. The dealer saw them and purchased both for 1,600 francs. He swiftly went around to Manet's new studio and acquired a further 23 canvases for 35,000 francs, returning a few days later to buy still more. As Manet's work was controversial, this was undoubtedly an act of speculation on the part of the dealer who would go on to be a major supporter of the young emerging Impressionists. In March 1872, Durand-Ruel organized an exhibition in London which included another work by Manet, *The Balcony*, although this was never part of his stock and was presumably lent by the artist directly to the exhibition. Although Durand-Ruel was very slow to pay the artist, his intervention meant that Manet's work was now being viewed much more broadly. The dealer was also the means by which he began to get to know Monet better too. Manet even assisted Monet in his wish to move with his family to the small suburban town of Argenteuil on the Seine, putting him in contact there with a friend who would rent them a house. Because of his own family property nearby, Manet was well connected in the area.

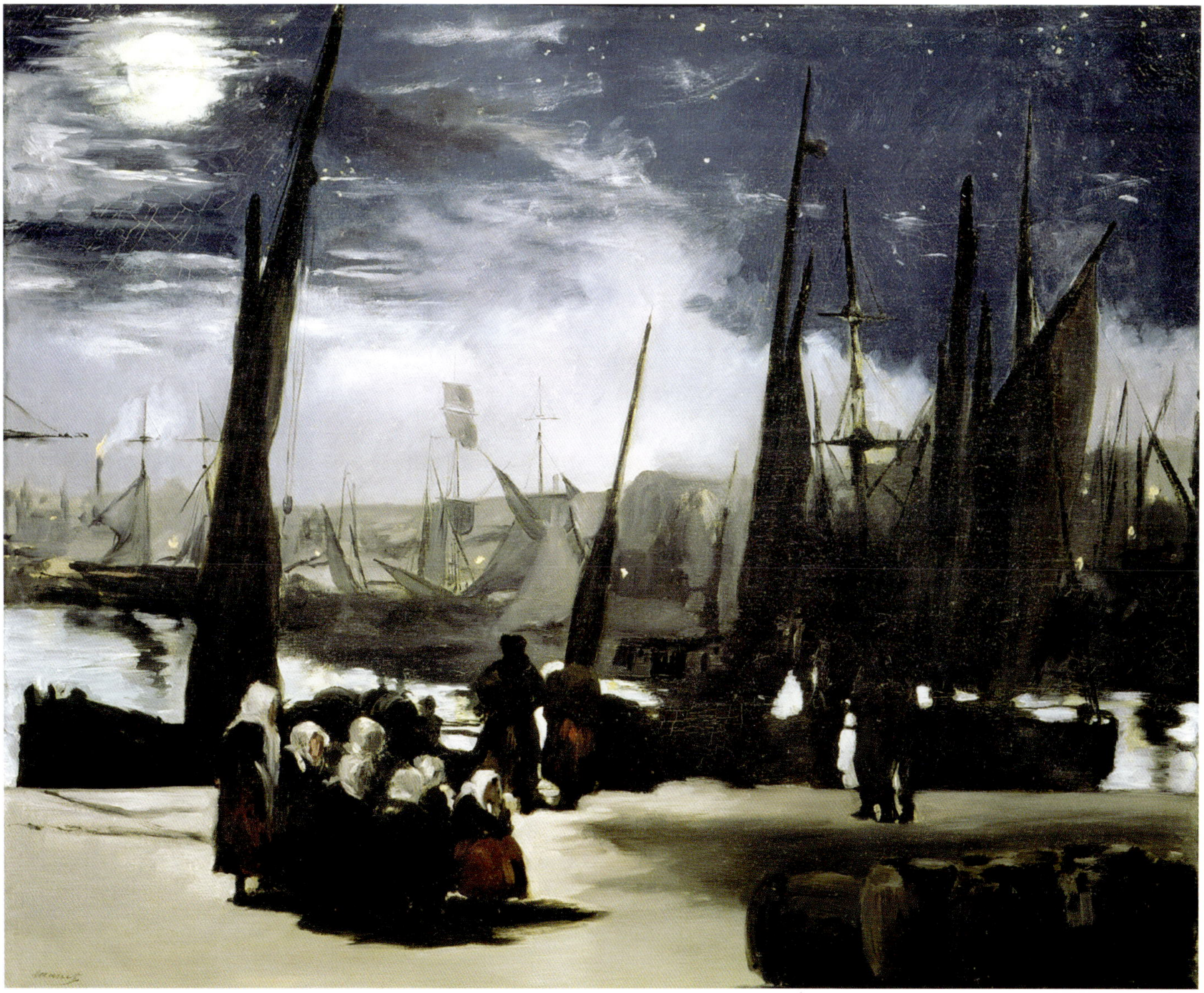

DEVELOPING IMPRESSIONISM AT ARGENTEUIL

Argenteuil, a small town 16 km (10 miles) north-west of Paris on the Seine, was known for its tanneries, silk mills, ironworks and gypsum mines as well as its renowned boating club, annual races and festivals on the river with its popular tree-lined promenade. It would prove to be a key site for the development of Impressionism: a group of artists with shared interests and stylistic similarities were inspired by the river, the bridges that spanned it, the boating and by Monet's house and garden, where they painted portraits of each other as their friendships deepened.

By 1874 the future Impressionists had, unlike Manet, lost patience with the Salon and decided to organize an independent exhibition at Nadar's studio in Paris on the boulevard des Capucines to reach the public directly. Entitled the Société Annoyme des Artistes, Peintres, Sculpteurs et Graveurs, it opened after much planning in April, and is better known today as the First Impressionist Exhibition. The name 'Impressionism' emerged from here following a derogatory remark about one of Monet's paintings *Impression, Sunrise,* 1873, by the critic Louis. The name was adopted by the group from 1877. Degas, Monet, Morrisot and Renoir were all part of Manet's circle and participated. Only he refused to exhibit, remaining determined to make his reputation at the Salon. He would not participate in any of the following Impressionists exhibitions either, but he did lend works by Morisot and Renoir. While the exhibition in Nadar's studio was ignored by some critics, it did attract over 3,500 visitors. Some critics were even favourable, among them Armand Silvestre. Writing in *L'Opinion Nationale*, he used the term 'impression' in a complimentary manner: 'it is an effect of impression alone that this vision seeks to discover; expression is left to adepts of the line'.

In the summer following the First Impressionist Exhibition, Manet spent time at his family home at Gennevilliers on the Seine, opposite Argenteuil. He visited Monet, who was still living at Argenteuil in the house he had helped him find the previous year. In August, he worked with Monet and also Renoir, who came to stay. Much is made of the influence Manet had on the Impressionists, especially with his modern, bold subjects, his habit of creating form not through a gradual blending of tones but with clear areas of colour side by side, and his use of his vibrant, loose brushstrokes. For his part, he was initially somewhat reluctant to engage with these young painters, but in Argenteuil that summer it is clear that Monet and Renoir began to influence him. Painting side by side with them, Manet began to explore the merits of *plein air* painting, and it was with them that he produced some of his best known Impressionist works. Under their influence,

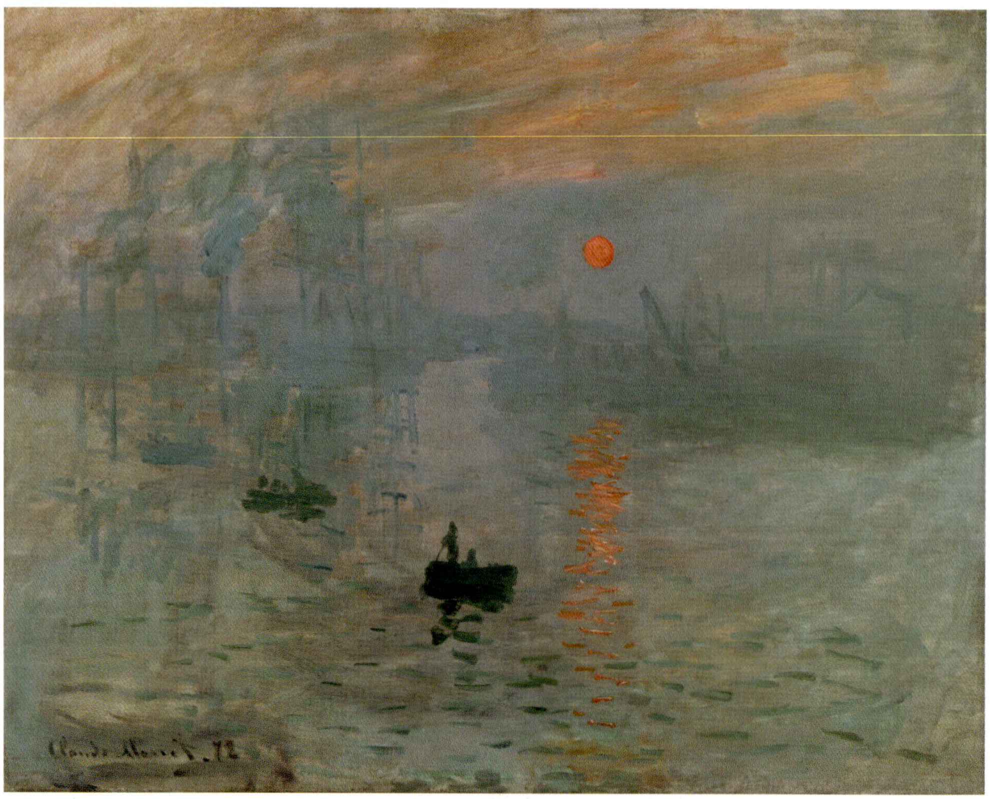

Impression, Sunrise, *Claude Monet, 1872. Depicting Le Havre, this was one of a series of six paintings that Monet produced of the port, showing it at various times of the day and from different viewpoints.*

palette and his brushwork became ever freer. However, he was not always as immediate or spontaneous as they were and held on to a more deliberate process relying much more on careful calculation, drawings and the studio environment.

A painting such as *Argenteuil – Boats*, painted during that summer, shows him observing the activity on the river. Using a fine weave canvas, which he had prepared himself with a pinkish ground that can be seen through the sketchy painting of the sky, he deliberately leaves areas exposed. In this apparently directly observed sketch, with its muted colour combination, he takes a view from the banks of the Seine at Petit Gennevilliers, looking across the water to Argenteuil's floating laundry houses and promenade with the smoke of a factory chimney visible beyond. It appears to be the product of only a few working sessions in front of the motif. The bravura application of paint, especially in the sky where the energetic brushwork is obvious, suggests it is a spontaneous

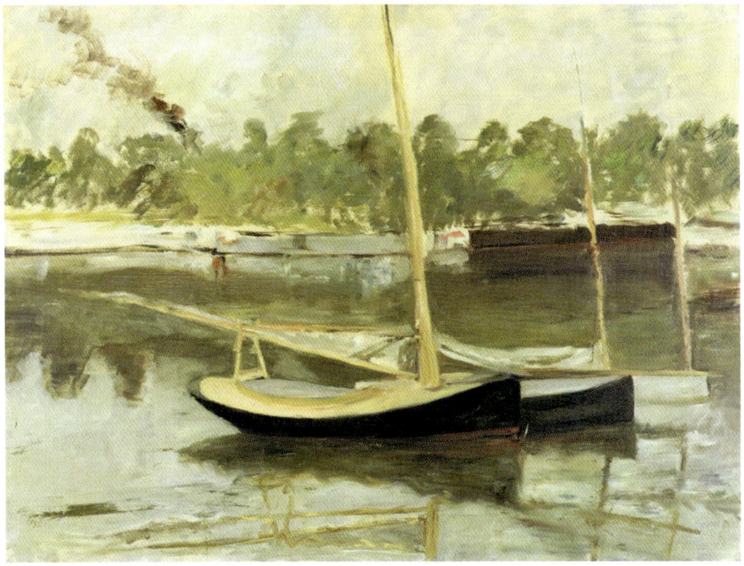

Above: Argenteuil – Boats, *1874. Manet captures three boats on the Seine and in the distance Argenteuil's floating laundry houses and the distant smoke of the factories.*

Below: Banks of the Seine at Argenteuil, *1874. This important work shows Manet experimenting with* plein air *painting, although it was almost certainly finished in the studio. He develops the initial theme explored in the above work.*

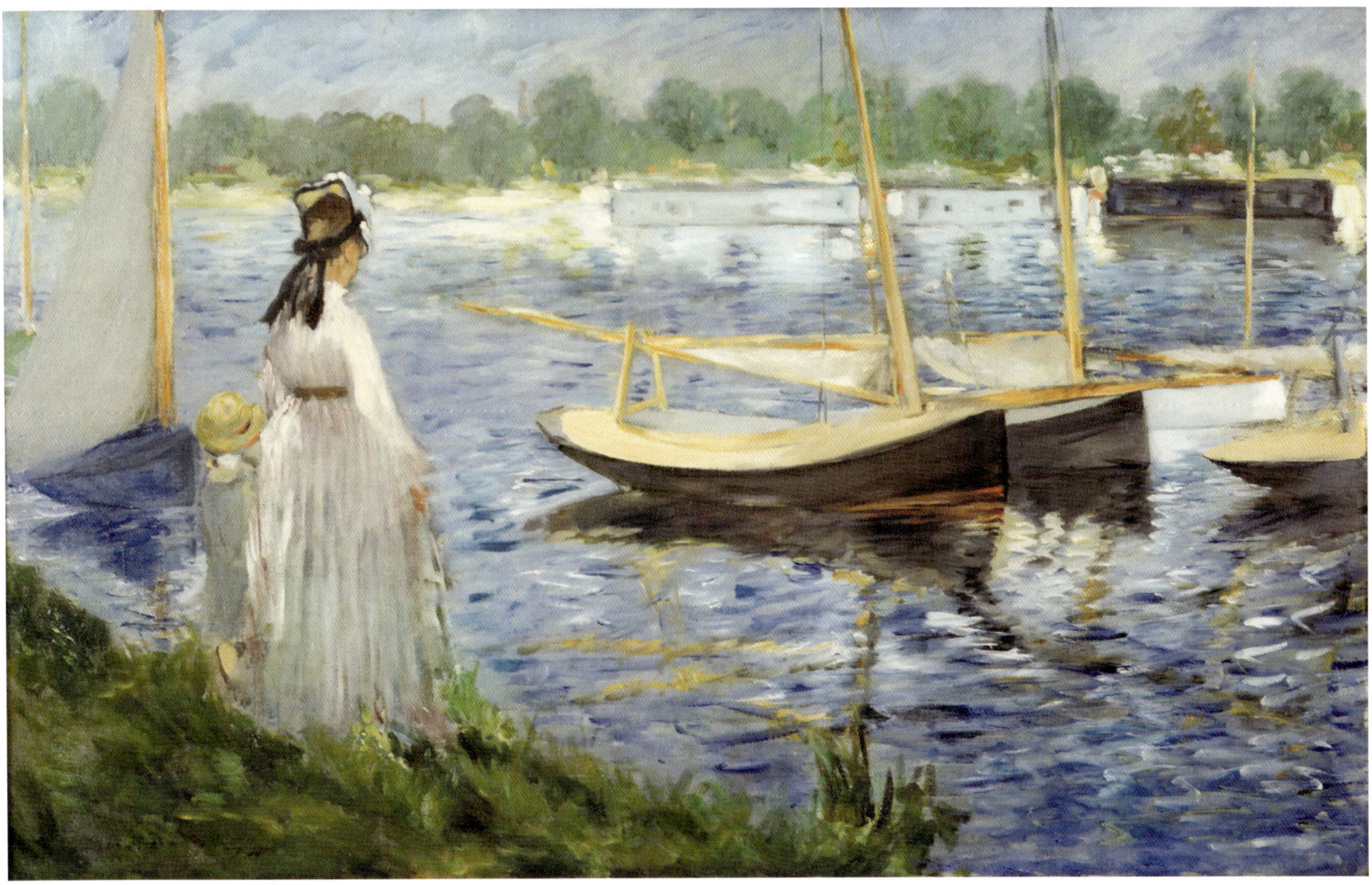

response. In contrast, however, the foreground focus on the three boats, with their bows and masts evenly and precisely arranged, and their relation to the laundry boats behind, suggests it is carefully composed and could actually be a studio work produced indoors rather than spontaneously *en plein air*. Whether painted indoors or out, it demonstrates Manet's masterly talent when balancing apparent spontaneity and considered calculation.

Compositionally this small work relates directly to *Seine at Argenteuil*, 1874. Possibly *Argenteuil – Boats* is a first attempt for the broader composition, in which Manet includes a well-dressed woman and child by the water's edge. In the completed painting, Manet's palette is lighter and he rearranges the boat masts, placing them at more realistic angles which he might have actually observed and creating a more naturalistic relationship to the laundry boats behind. The industrial structures on the far bank are undoubtedly idealized to make them more attractive. The floating laundry appears much more rural, even picturesque, and in maintaining them in his final work, Manet is reflecting that this is a scene from modern life, support for an urban community nearby in the town. The lively brushwork suggests a work observed *en plein air*, but like so many of Manet's paintings it is more calculated and less spontaneous than it might initially appear.

Another striking work completed by Manet at this time was *Boating*, showing a couple enjoying the pleasures of taking a boat out on the Seine. The man and woman are seated at the helm of a boat, which is radically cropped, so only a small proportion is visible to the viewer. The woman is relaxed in a blue dress, white hat and veil while the man, who is dressed in white and wearing a straw boater, holds the rudder and is clearly in charge. It is thought that the male sitter is Rodolphe Leenhoff, the artist's brother-in-law, but the identity of the woman is unknown. Again the influence of the Impressionists is clear in the lighter touch and palette. Manet employs his usual broad planes of colour and the strong diagonals of this unusual composition may be influenced by Japanese prints. It was not shown at the Salon until 1879. The same couple (with Rodolphe, Suzanne's

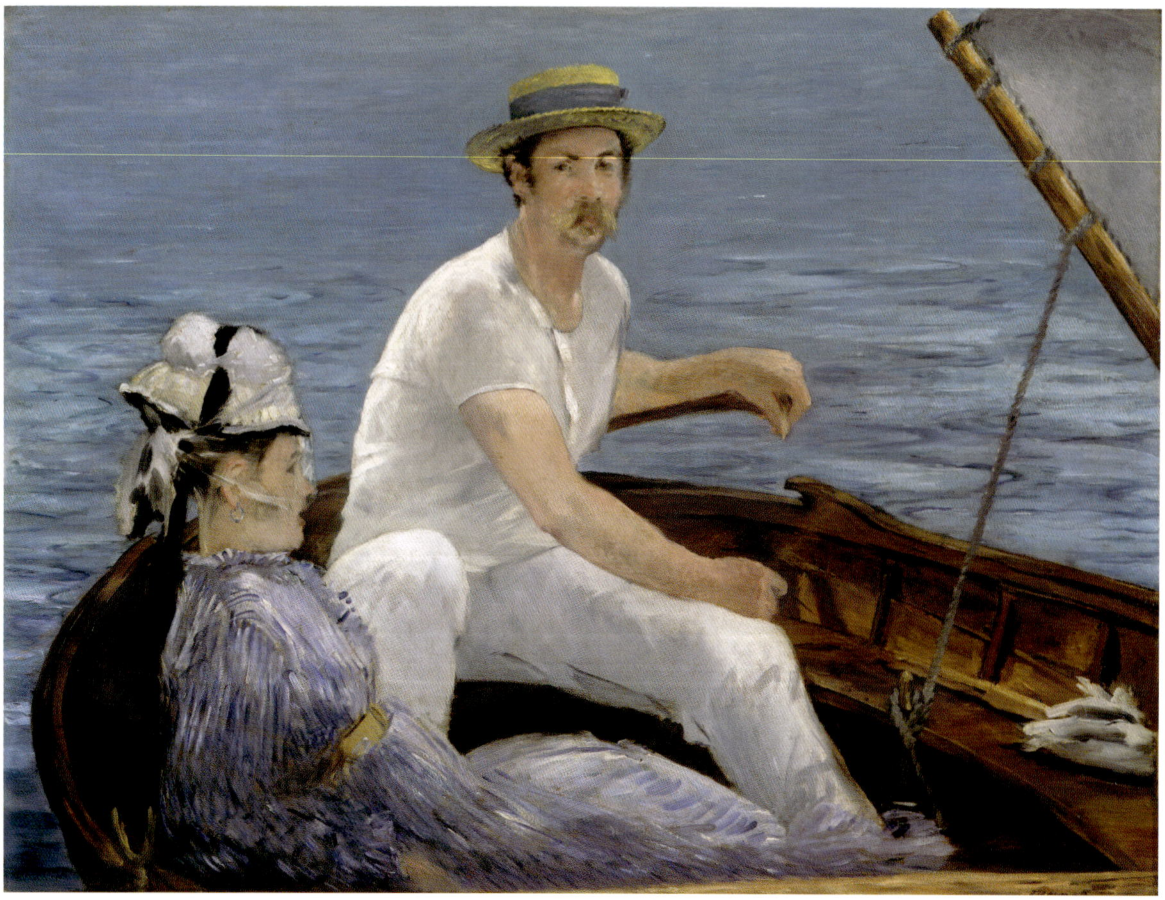

Left: Boating, *1874. This large scale work shows a scene of outdoor leisure, with a couple enjoying boating on the Seine at Argenteuil. The male sitter is probably Rodolphe Leenhoff, the artist's brother-in-law, but the identity of the woman is unknown.*

Opposite: Argenteuil, *1874. The same couple appear again as in* Boating, *and again, Manet uses a brighter, lighter, bold palette, capturing the light of a summer day.*

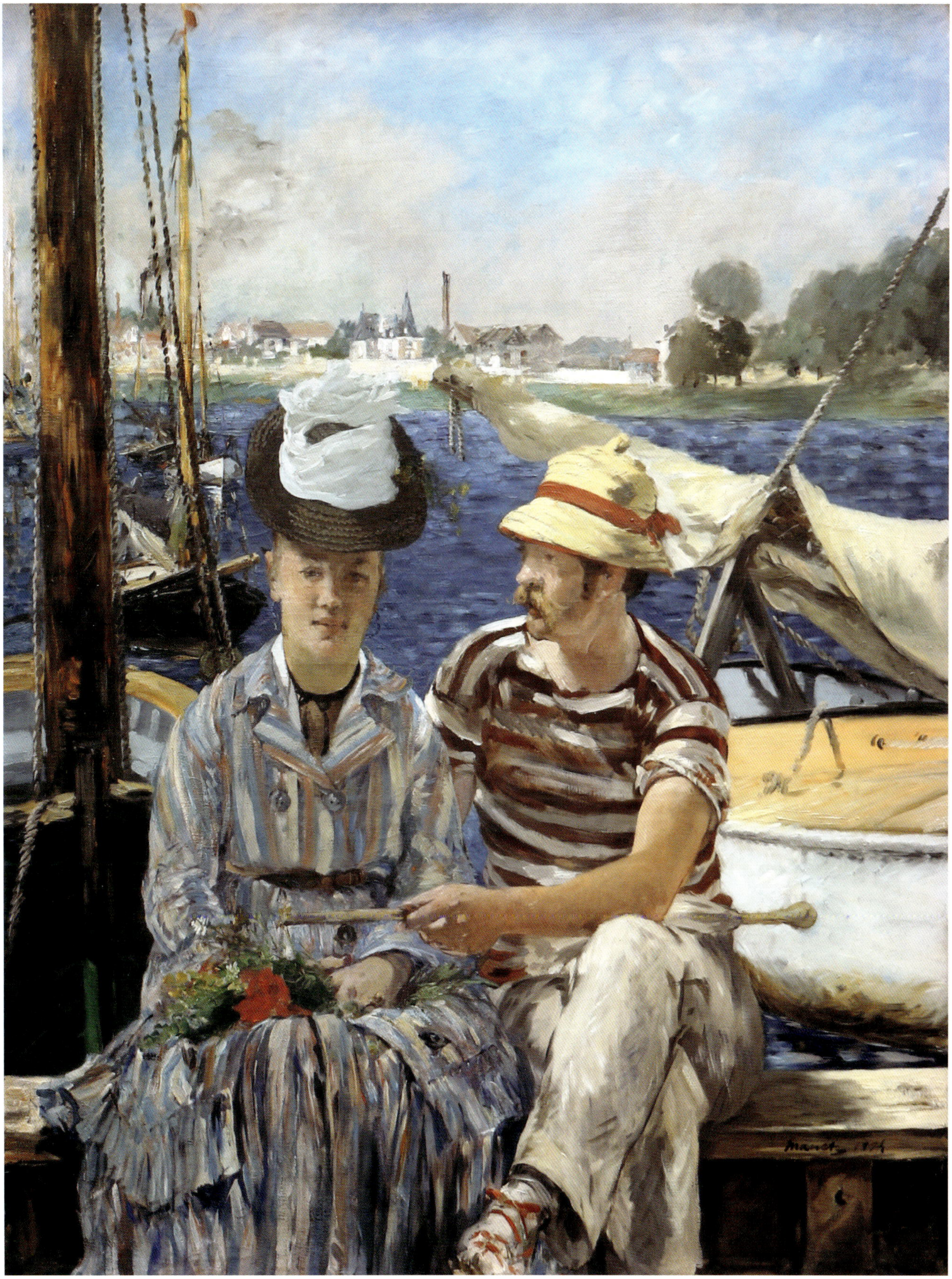

brother probably the male sitter again) appear in another painting, in which they are shown sitting side by side in a more resolved composition, stylistically more finished, with the stripes of the woman's dress more defined. The relationship of this couple was ambiguous in *Boating*, but here in *Argenteuil* they appear to be romantically linked, as the man stares adoringly at his well-dressed companion, who has a bunch of flowers in her lap. Manet submitted *Argenteuil* (1874) to the Salon first of all in 1875, when it was accepted – but still ridiculed by the press.

That summer, Manet also attempted to paint Monet and his wife Camille in the artist's famous studio boat. This old boat had been purchased about 1871 so that Monet could observe the light on the Seine and paint while actually on the water. He may have been influenced by Charles-François Daubigny (1817–78), who also had a studio boat called the *Bottin*. *Claude and Camille Monet in his Studio Boat* (1874) is a thinly painted work with strong black highlights and is unfinished. It is not known why he abandoned such a bold, forthright composition, showing Monet with his palette and his wife sheltering under the canopy, looking directly at the viewer; the Seine lies in the distance. Manet gave the work in its unfinished state to Monet, who kept it until his death in 1924. Manet also completed a different approach to the same subject, in which Monet is more prominent in the foreground, painting on the boat, Camille is in the background under the canopy, and the boat itself is more resolved – *Claude Monet Painting in his Studio Boat* (1874). This painting reflects Monet's influence on Manet's developing style: note the use of sketchy brushstrokes, brighter colours, and the capturing of fractured light reflected from the water broken by the ripples created by the boat.

Below: Claude and Camille Monet in his Studio Boat, *1874. Monet acquired his studio boat in about 1872–3, and used it to make painting trips on the Seine.*

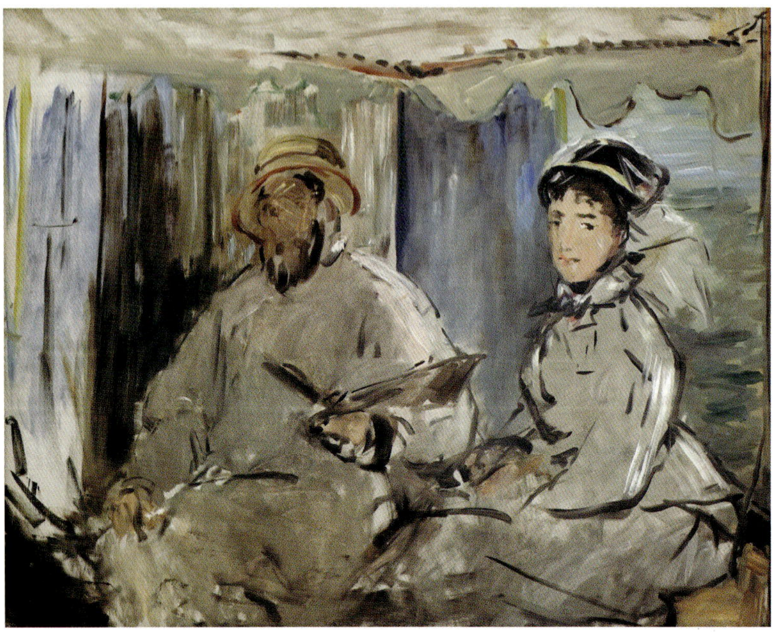

Right: Claude Monet Painting in his Studio Boat, *1874. Manet was clearly intrigued by the boat and make two studies of Monet in the boat with his wife Camille accompanying him.*

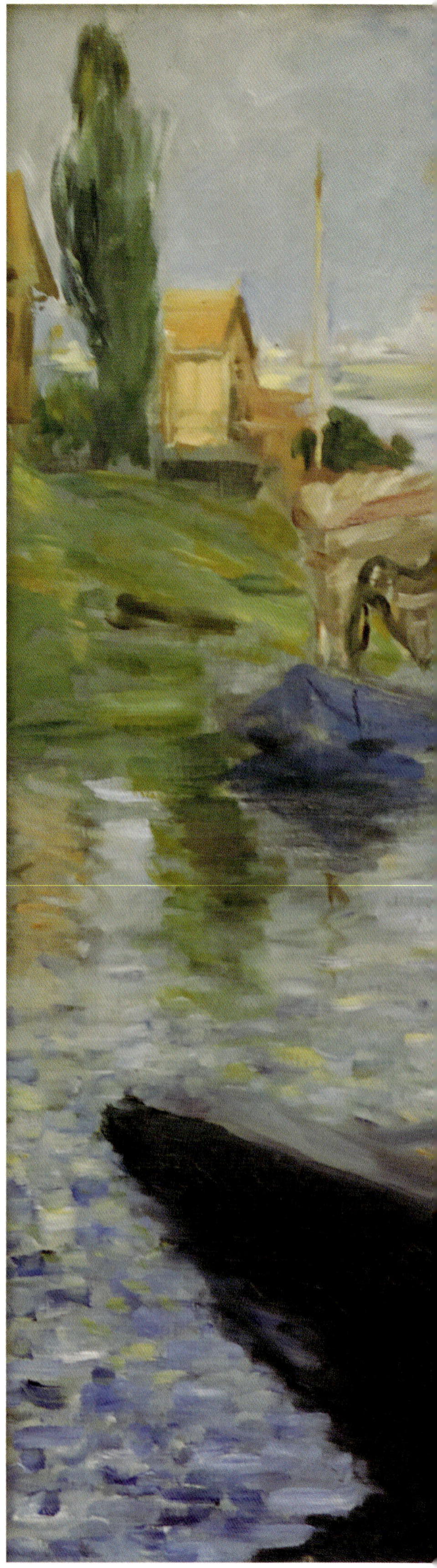

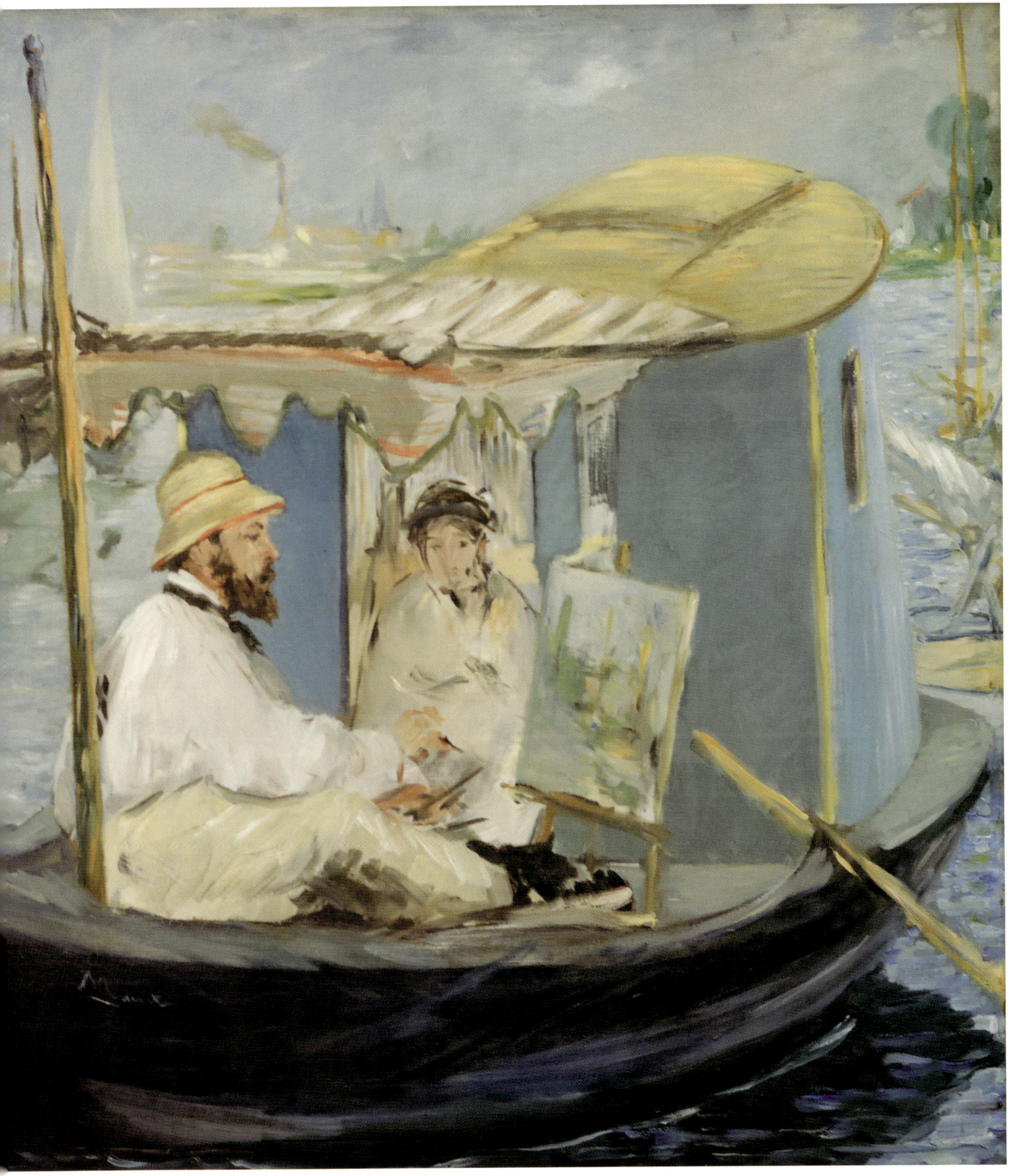

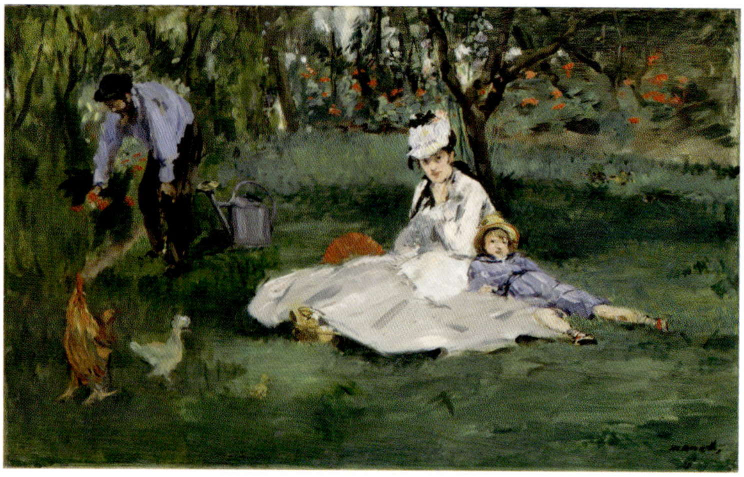

The Monet Family in their Garden at Argenteuil, *1874. Manet further reflects Monet's domestic happiness in this painting and the artist's love of gardening.*

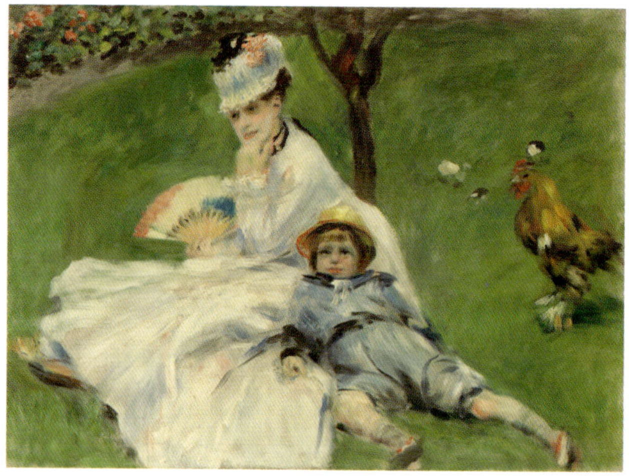

Madame Monet and her Son, *Pierre-Auguste Renoir, 1874. Renoir was also inspired to capture the Monet family at home.*

A further work, *The Monet Family in their Garden at Argenteuil*, 1874, reflects Monet's domestic happiness, as well as the increasingly close relationship of the artists and their related subject matter. Manet captures Camille Monet seated on the lawn, wearing a hat and cooling herself with a fan. Her young son Jean, in a light blue suit, relaxes, lying on her white dress while Monet himself attends to his garden, his watering can by his side and surrounded by chickens. Renoir arrived apparently just as Manet had set up his easel to paint and, positioning himself next to the older artist, borrowed his paints and brushes to paint *Madame Monet and her Son* (1874). He focuses much more closely on Camille and her son, eliminating the details of the garden and representing just one chicken. In Manet's work, Camille's gaze is direct as she looks at the artist; in Renoir's, she is clearly looking away. Apparently, Monet also painted Manet at the easel, but that painting is now lost.

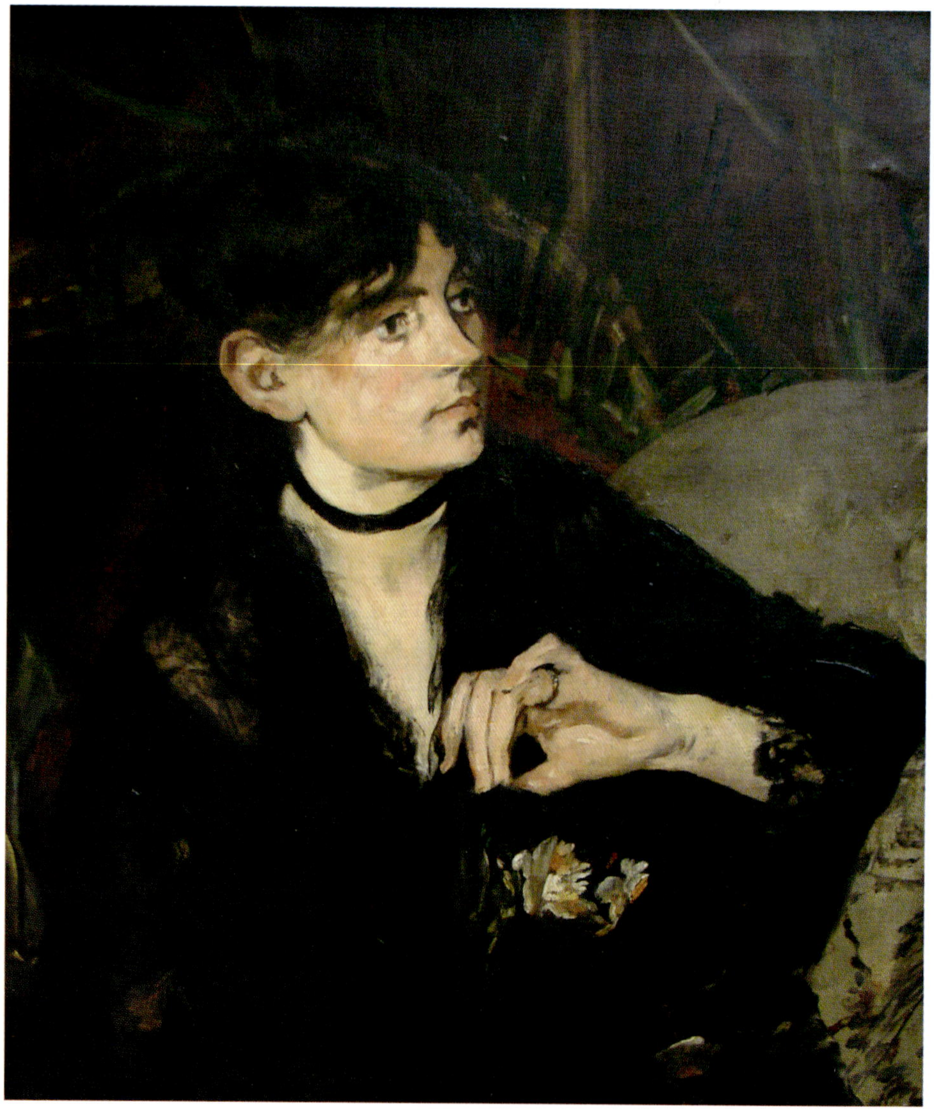

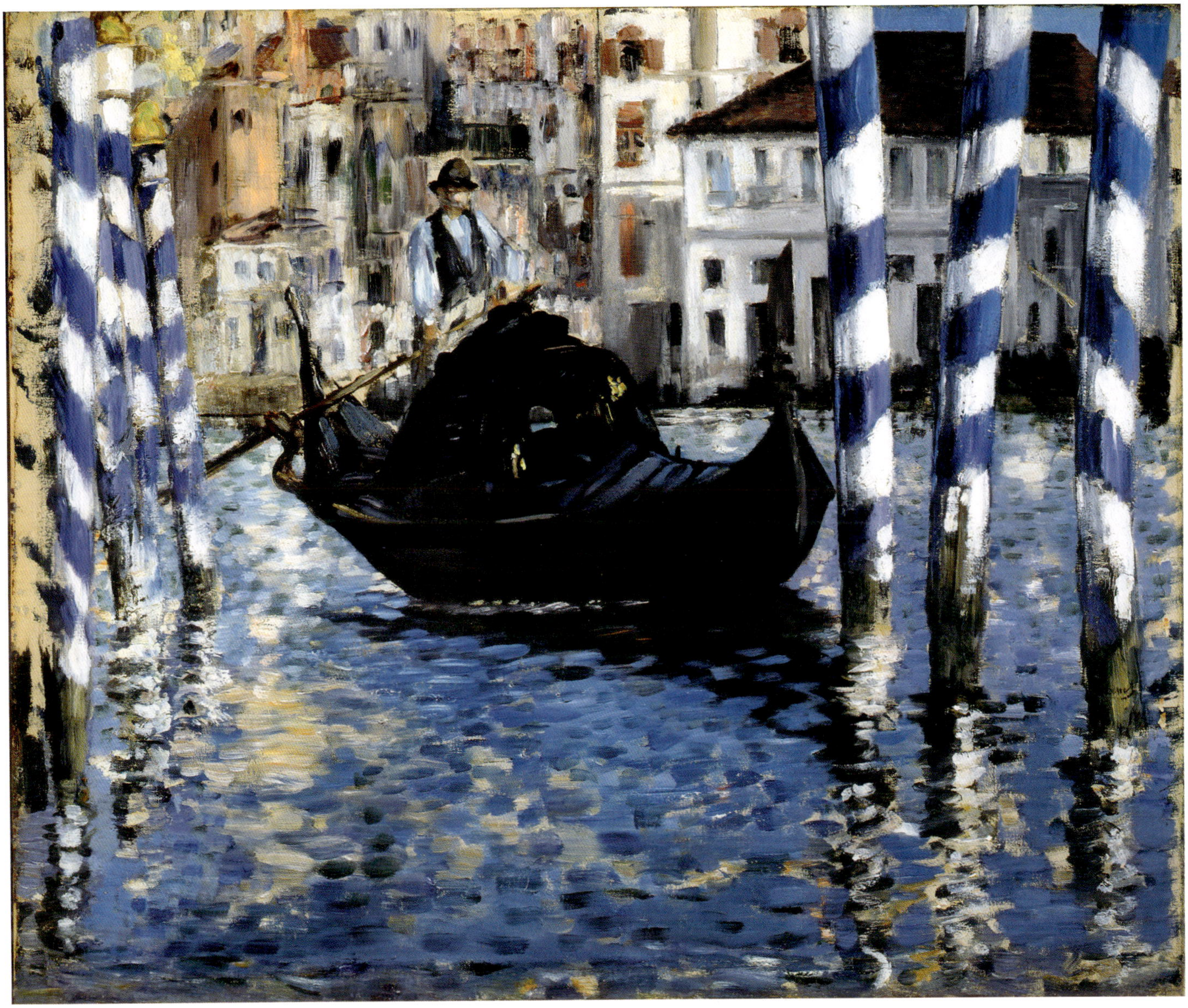

Above: The Grand Canal, Venice (Blue Venice), *1875. Manet visited Venice in September 1875 with his friend, the artist James Tissot. He found the city boring and complained about trying to capture the constantly changing reflections of the canal water. Yet, here, he employs brighter, fresher colours to capture the brilliance of the Venetian canal and gondola, using quick, broken brushstrokes.*

Opposite: Berthe Morisot with a Fan, *1874. Manet depicts his sister-in-law just after her marriage, wearing black in mourning for her father.*

This, then, was a key year for Manet's relationship with Impressionism and with Monet and Renoir. In the September of 1874, he travelled to Venice with Suzanne and the artist James Tissot. There Monet and Renoir's influence continued: Manet employed brighter colours and broken brushstrokes to capture the beauty of the Venetian canals in such works as *The Grand Canal, Venice (Blue Venice)*. Manet also painted the last of his portraits of the artist Berthe Morrisot. In all, he portrayed her on 12 occasions between 1868 and 1874. *Berthe Morisot with a Fan* was actually painted just after her marriage to his brother Eugène, which took place in Passy on 22 December 1874. She is shown in mourning for her recently departed father but wearing an engagement ring. After her marriage, she no longer sat for Manet.

SALON TRIALS AND TRIBULATIONS

When the bright, light and arresting *Argenteuil* was shown at the Salon in 1875, critics and caricaturists were sarcastic about it. Gaillardon noted, 'We had a ray of hope after *Le Bon Bock*, but it is all too obvious that the *Canotiers à Argenteuil* is a disaster. M. Manet is nothing but an eccentric after all.' Rousseau called it 'Marmalade from Argenteuil spread on an indigo river.' On the last day, one caricature by Cham showed the couple stepping out of their frame, with the comment: 'Manet's two canoers aren't sorry to leave since people have been laughing in their faces for almost two months.' Manet's association with the Impressionists seems to have been cemented and from this time onwards, the press began to describe Manet as the leader of the Impressionist group, although he would still not exhibit with them. In the spring of 1876, Mallarmé's article 'The Impressionists and Edouard Manet', published in *Art Monthly Review*, cemented the connection publically and at the third Impressionist Exhibition he lent works from his own collection, two by Monet and one by Sisley. Still determined to succeed at the Salon, Manet submitted works to the 1877 Salon: *Faure as Hamlet* (1877), was accepted and *Nana* (1877), rejected.

Faure as Hamlet, *1877. The baritone Jean-Baptiste Faure is depicted in the title role of the opera* Hamlet, *in 1868. Faure was a great supporter of Manet, but this commission for a portrait was complicated, as Manet struggled with it, destroying two earlier versions. The startled surprise on Faure's face did not please the sitter, who refused to accept the work.*

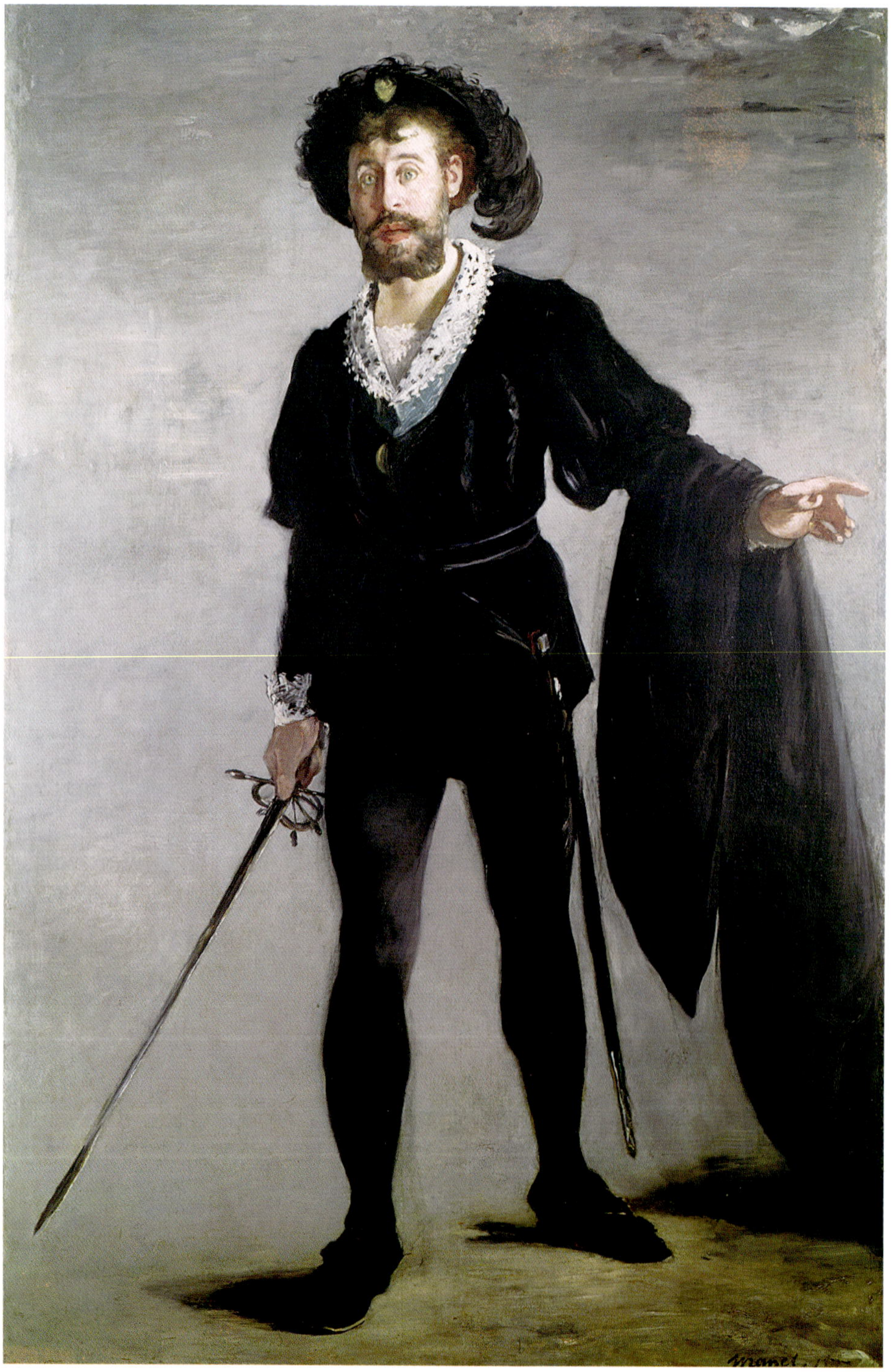

The famous baritone Jean-Baptiste Faure is shown in the title role of the opera *Hamlet* by Ambroise Thomas, at the Paris Opera, which he played in 1868. Faure was of course not only a famous singer but a renowned art collector, who had first acquired Manet's work in 1873. He went on to own nearly 70 works by the artist. So when he required a portrait showing him in one of his best known roles,

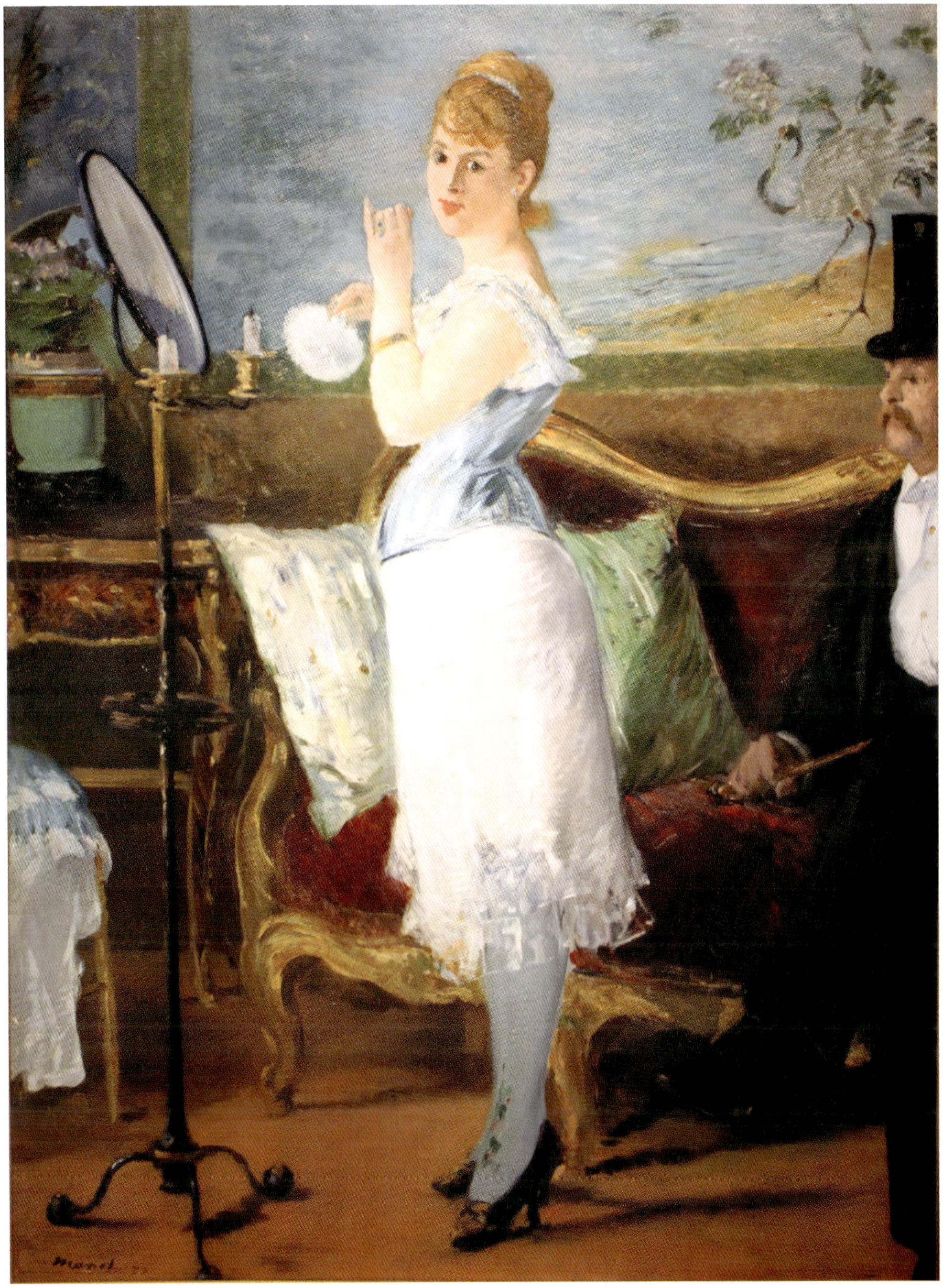

Nana, *1877. Refused at the 1877 Salon, Manet decided to show his brilliantly painted depiction of a young, beautiful and bold prostitute in the window of a trinket shop on the boulevard des Capucines, one of the most popular streets in Paris. It proved popular and the public gathered to view it. At the very edge of the canvas is seated an elegantly dressed man, dramatically cropped. 'Nana' was a popular term for a female prostitute during this period in France.*

it was obvious he would turn to his friend Manet, who was renowned for painting good likenesses, especially of actors and actresses. The artist accepted the commission enthusiastically, but things did not progress smoothly and their friendship was soon under strain. In all, there were 40 sittings during the winter of 1876–7 and Manet restarted the painting a number of times, destroying three versions. Eventually Manet showed the singer sympathetically in the third scene of the first act, when Hamlet, the Prince of Denmark, draws a dagger and swears revenge in front of his father's ghost. Faure's startled gaze is truly unsettling. Once again, Manet looked back to Velázquez's *Pablo de Vallodolid* as inspiration for isolating a single figure against a plain, spatially undefined background as he had done in the 1860s. Faure was not impressed, however, and refused to accept the portrait, but Manet declined to change anything and submitted it to the Salon anyway. There, as the singer had feared, it received adverse criticism. *Nana*, the painting rejected by the Salon that year, depicted an attractive young woman in a state of incomplete dress. She stands before a mirror, powder puff in her hand, gazing out towards the onlooker and wearing only a white chemise, blue corset, silk stockings and high-heeled shoes. She appears to be in her boudoir and seated on the couch behind her, at the very edge of the canvas, is an elegantly dressed man. 'Nana' was a popular term for a female prostitute at the time in France, and this is clearly what Manet intended the subject to be. However brilliantly it was painted, the Salon jury were offended by such a subject, and Manet must have known it would cause shock and outrage. He decided to show the painting anyway, displaying it in the window of a luxury goods shop window, on the boulevard des Capucines, one of Paris's most famous streets. There his controversial work gained much attention, drawing crowds. The critic Huysman announced in his review that Manet's friend Zola intended to write a new novel about Nana, and congratulated the artist on envisaging her 'as she will undoubtedly be'. Zola's novel *Nana* was serialized from October 1879 and published in February 1880, but the link between subject and novel is tenuous.

In 1878, disillusioned by recent reception of his work, Manet did not submit any works to the Salon or the Exposition Universelle. He contemplated mounting another independent, one-man show of 100 paintings but could not secure the funding. He did, however, return that summer to a subject he had been drawn to work on: waitresses. These were a relatively new introduction to Parisian cafés and Manet admired the skill of those at the popular Brasserie de Reichshoffen, on boulevard Rochechouart. For *Corner of a Café-Concert*, 1878–80, which was originally part of a larger canvas, one now agreed to pose for him in his studio, accompanied at her insistence by her young man, apparently the pipe smoker in a blue smock in the foreground. In the background on stage, a double-bass player and a dancer can be seen. Manet's work displays the skill of a waitress serving between the tables, carrying several beers at once, and the social mix of café-goers distinguished by their different attire. A variation of the painting exists in the Louvre. These were begun in a temporary studio and by April 1879 Manet had moved to 77, rue d'Amsterdam, which would be his last studio.

For the Salon in spring of 1879, Manet submitted two works, his earlier Argenteuil painting *Boating* and *In the Conservatory* (1879) a double portrait. Both were accepted. The sitters were Monsieur and Madame Jules Guillemet, the owners of a fashionable clothes boutique on the rue Saint-Honoré. Madame Guillemet was American and a friend of Manet's wife Suzanne. The artist worked on the painting from September 1878 to February 1879. This superb portrait captures the couple relaxing by a bench against a backdrop of dense green foliage and exotic plants. Madame Guillemet is portrayed with great elegance and attention to detail in her dress, which was originally violet blue. Overall, this painting is stylistically highly finished, which is most unusual for Manet, especially in the late 1870s. Possibly this is a result of the portrait being a commission, or the fact that he worked on it so long, or it may be that he had his eye on its acceptance at the Salon that year. By the autumn of 1879, his health was starting to cause concern. And by the summer of 1880, he was staying at Bellevue, where he rented a villa to undertake hydrotherapy for locomotor ataxia, a painful symptom caused by syphilis. The cure was not successful and the last years of his life were marked by a considerable lack of mobility and much pain.

Opposite: Corner of a Café-Concert, *1878–80. Originally the right half of a larger canvas, this remaining image depicts the interior of the Brasserie de Reichshoffen. The work was cut in two by Manet himself.*

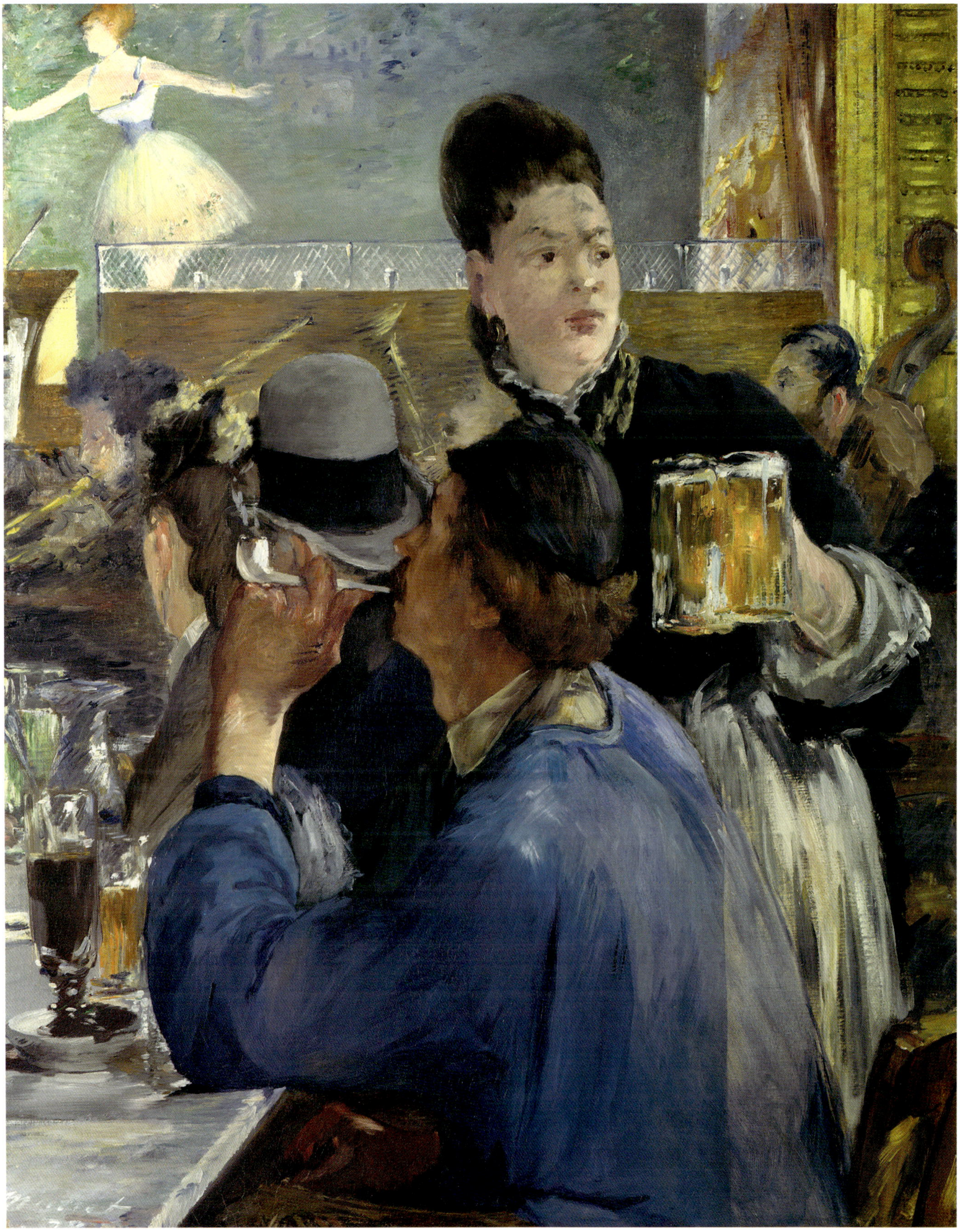

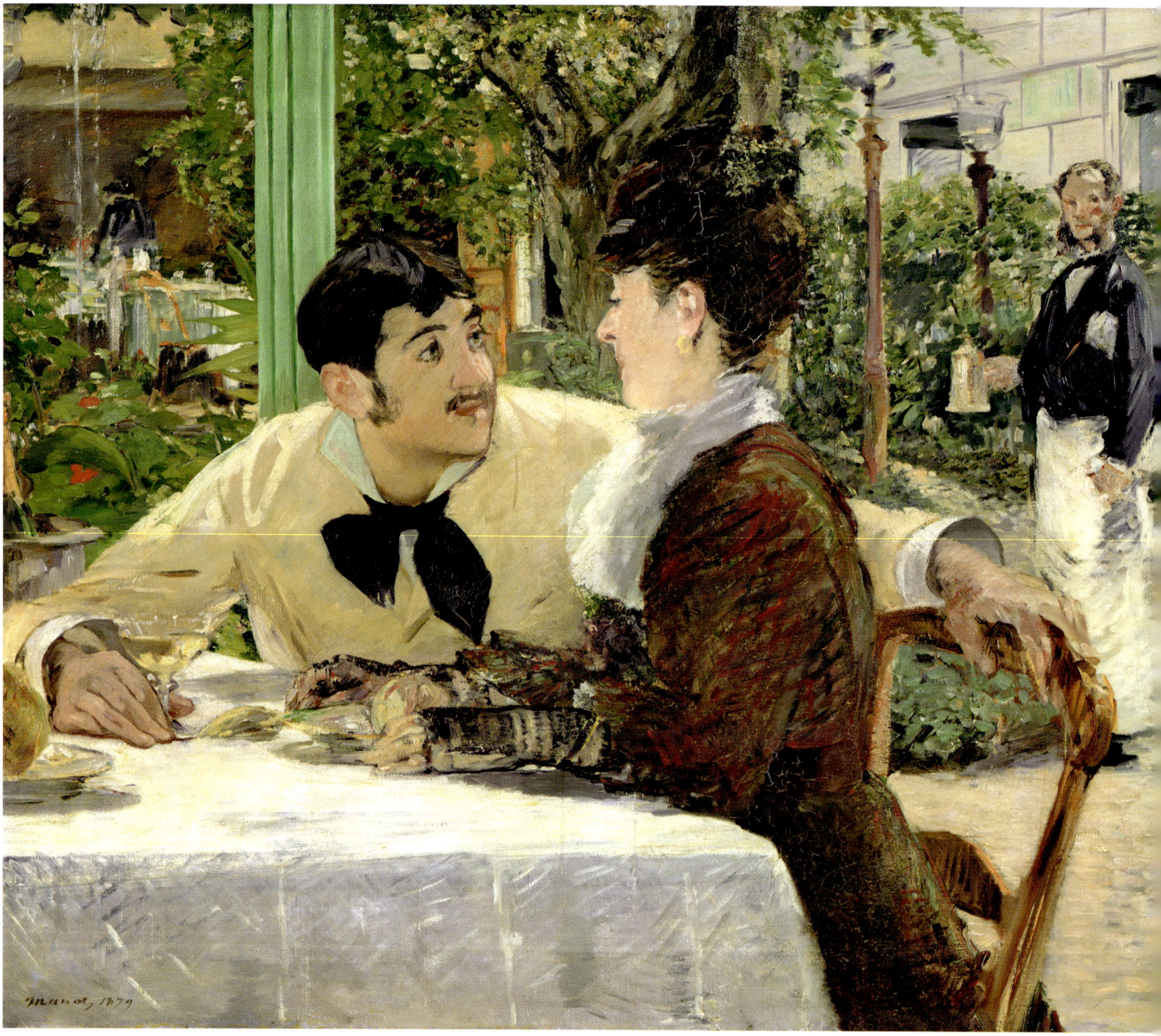

At the Père Lathuille Restaurant, *1879. The models for this romantic couple were posed by the eldest son of the restaurant owner Louis Gauthier-Lathuille (who can himself be seen in the background) and Judith French. The pair gaze into each other's eyes, and are shown on the terrace of the famous café located at 7, avenue de Clinchy in Paris on a summer day.*

CHAPTER 5
Last Years and Legacy

As Manet died relatively young aged only 51, it is not possible to talk about his 'late period' as we can for a long-lived painter such as Monet. Only recently have the last years of his career been studied as a period in detail, and recognized as a personal stylistic development, rather than a period of artistic decline driven by ill health. While his health did deteriorate from 1879 onwards, he never stopped painting even when it was hard to stand before his easel. And while it is his work in the 1860s and '70s that define his career, these last years saw him produce his great late masterpiece reflecting Parisian life, *A Bar at the Folies-Bergere*, as well as a series of sumptuous still lifes and a number of stylish portraits of men and women, focusing increasingly on fashionable details of dress. He also produced delicate pastels and watercolours.

In early 1880, Manet's health was of concern as he increasingly experienced great pain in his left leg and general lack of mobility, but he still managed in April to organize a small solo exhibition in the gallery of the journal *La Vie Moderne*, which included no less than 15 pastels. Manet's new interest in this medium may have been inspired by his student Eva Gonzales, an accomplished pastel painter. He executed them not on paper but on prepared fine weave linen canvas. This was the first exhibition dedicated to his own work since the one he staged at the time of the Exposition Universelle back in 1867. Most of the exhibited paintings were new works and the pastel portraits included one of the emerging Irish writer, poet and playwright George Moore (1852–1933), whom he had met in the spring of 1879. This freely executed pastel was the result of just one sitting, and in it he captures the red hair and fair complexion of the sitter, as well as his artistic temperament. The critics were not kind, though: one suggested the sitter resembled a drowned man fished out of water. The majority of Manet's pastels in his last years were actually of fashionable women – for example Madame Jules Guillemet, who had been the subject of his painting *In the Conservatory*, with her husband and whom he also captured in profile in 1880. More pleasing for the critics at his solo exhibition were works such as *Plum Brandy* (*c.* 1878): they appreciated the greater finish Manet achieved and his acute social observation of the young woman, wearing a pink dress, her plum brandy before her on a café table and an unlit cigarette between her fingers. Leaning forward, she appears isolated and lonely. The model is the actress Ellen Andrée, who was also depicted in *In a Café* by Edgar Degas. Manet sold the painting the following year to the art collector Charles Deudon.

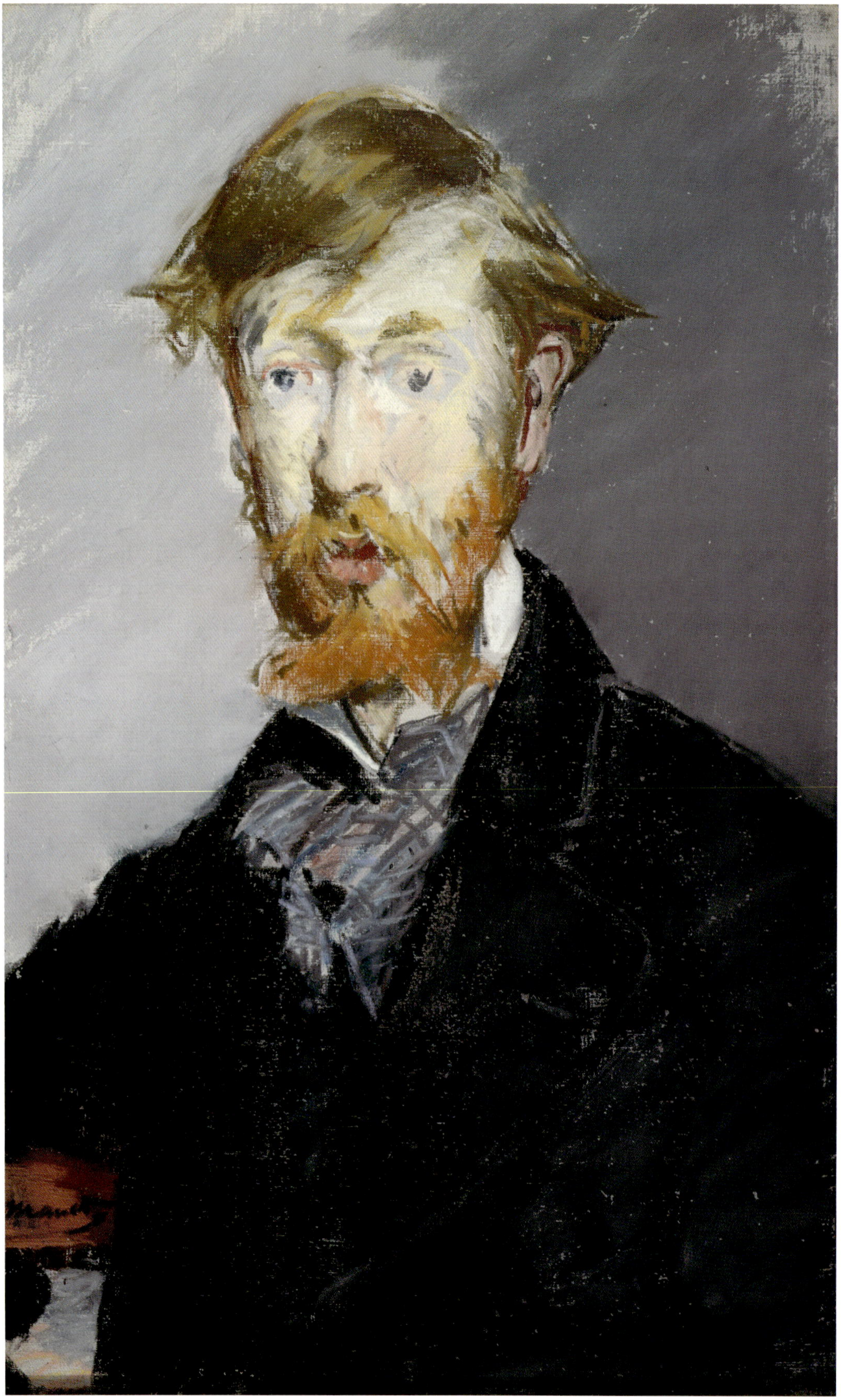

Portrait of George Moore, *1879. Manet met the young Irish writer, poet and playwright in the spring of 1879. This freely executed pastel portrait was the result of just one sitting. He captures the red hair and fair complexion of the sitter, as well as his artistic temperament. Moore used the portrait as the frontispiece for his book* Modern Painting *(1893).*

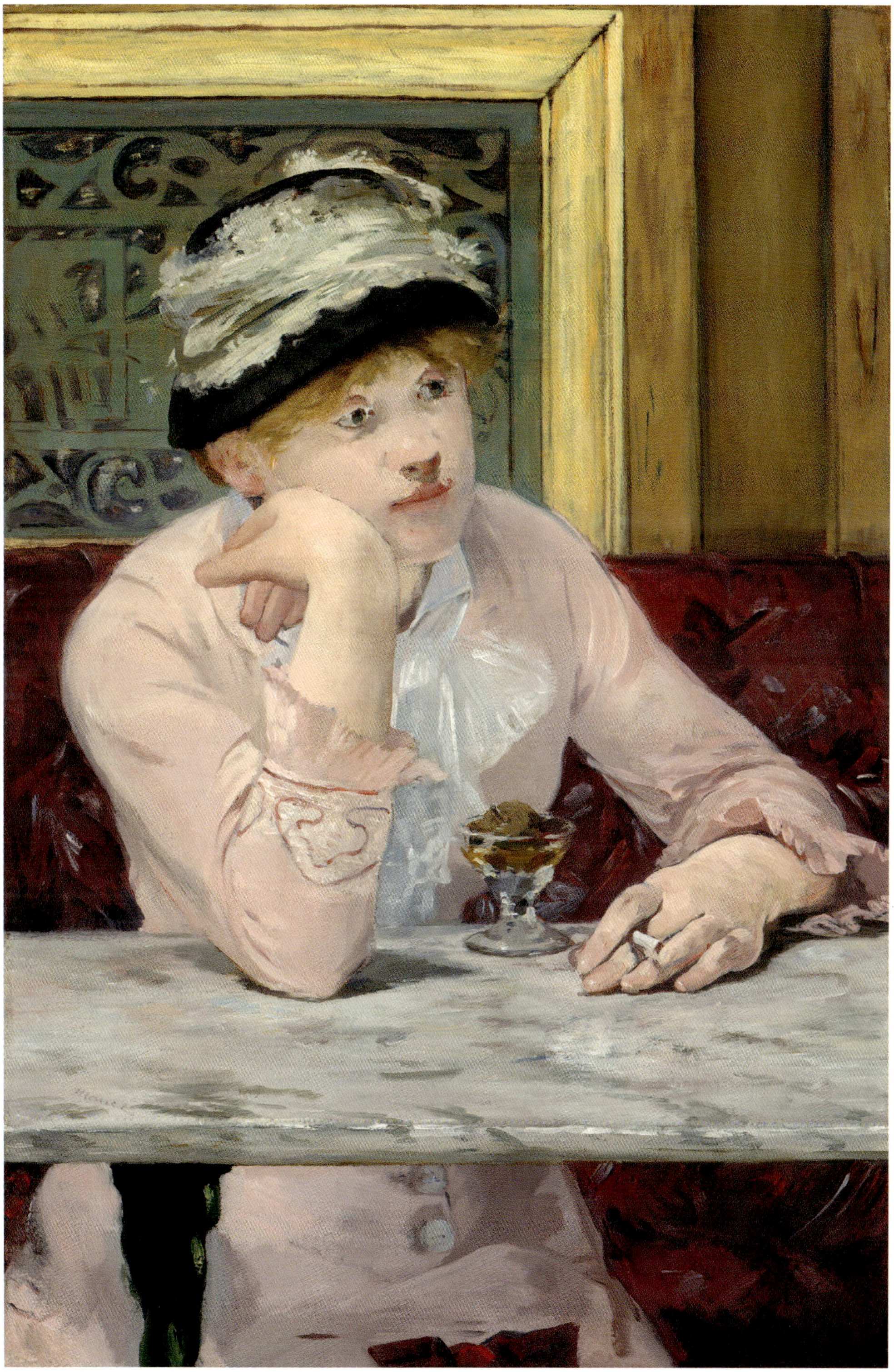

Plum Brandy, *1877. The painting shows a young woman dressed in pink, seated alone at a café table, with a dreamy, distracted expression. Her cigarette is unlit and her plum soaked in brandy is as yet untouched. This sweet was a speciality of Parisian cafés at the time, but originally Manet painted a glass of beer on the table, which would have given the work a very different interpretation.*

In addition to his art being on view in his own exhibition, two works were also accepted for the Salon in 1880, the rather sombre portrait of his childhood friend the critic and journalist Antonin Proust and a modern Parisian scene *At the Père Lathuille Resturant* (1879 – *see* page 76). The romantic couple, who have no time for the onlooker, were posed by the eldest son of the owner Louis Gauthier-Lathuille (who can himself be seen in the background) and Judith French. The young couple are shown on the terrace of the famous café located at 7, avenue de Clinchy, apparently observed on the spot. It is one of the lesser known works to depict a famous Parisian café scene, which not only Manet but Renoir and Degas were drawn towards, and looks forward to the late masterpiece *A Bar at the Folies-Bergère*. Sadly, not all the critics appreciated it, Paul Mantz muttering, 'to lunch with a woman so badly turned out is punishment beyond the horrors of the imagination – let us forget this nightmare.' However, J. K. Huysmans defended Manet's painting in *La Reforme* in July 1880: 'The young man and woman are superb. This canvas catches the eye because it is so clear and bright; it shines among all these official paintings which turn rancid as soon as one sees them. This is the modernism I have spoken about! People

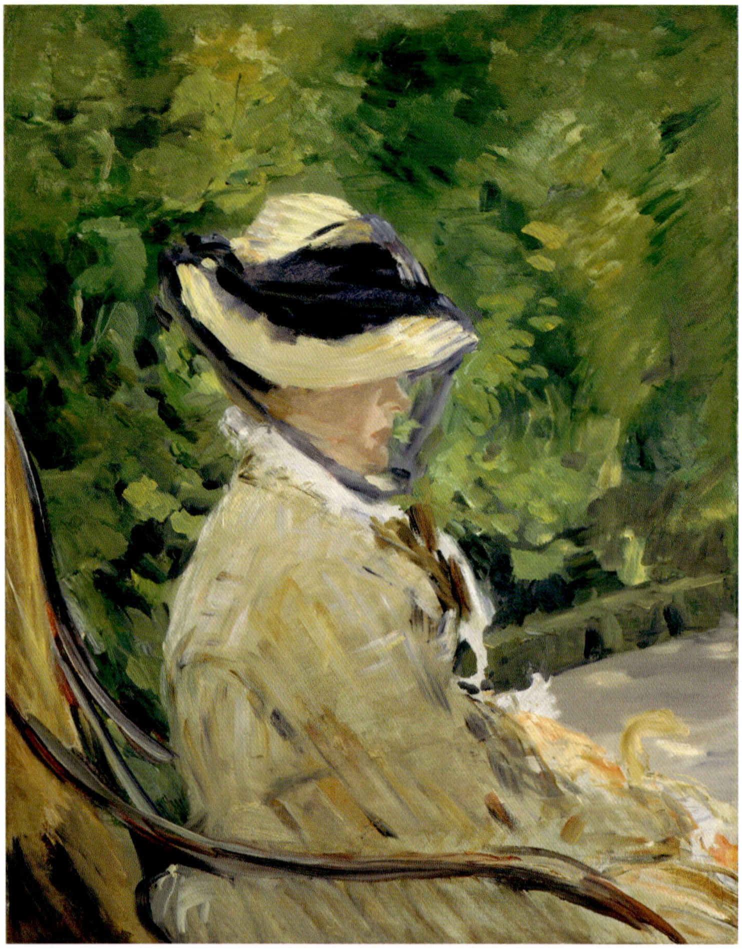

eating lunch in real light, in the open air.'

Manet amused himself in other ways, returning to the medium of watercolours, possibly prompted by the founding of the Society of French Watercolourists, which held its first exhibition in 1879. He produced large watercolours of flowers such as irises and geraniums. Taking the cure at Bellevue during the summer and autumn of 1880, he wrote letters which he often illustrated. At Bellevue that summer Manet had therapeutic showers and lengthy massages to try to revive his health. In the villa's garden, he also painted his last portrait of his beloved and long suffering wife, Suzanne Leenhoff. Despite appearances that this is a rapidly executed Impressionist portrait of her observed *en plein air* with summary brushwork and treatment of detail, two related drawings and an oil sketch are clearly studies for this work, demonstrating that for Manet a sketch was not always as spontaneous as it seemed.

This late period also saw Manet finally gain the public recognition that he had craved so long: in the spring of 1881, he was awarded a second-class medal at the Salon for his portrait of Henri Rochefort. This

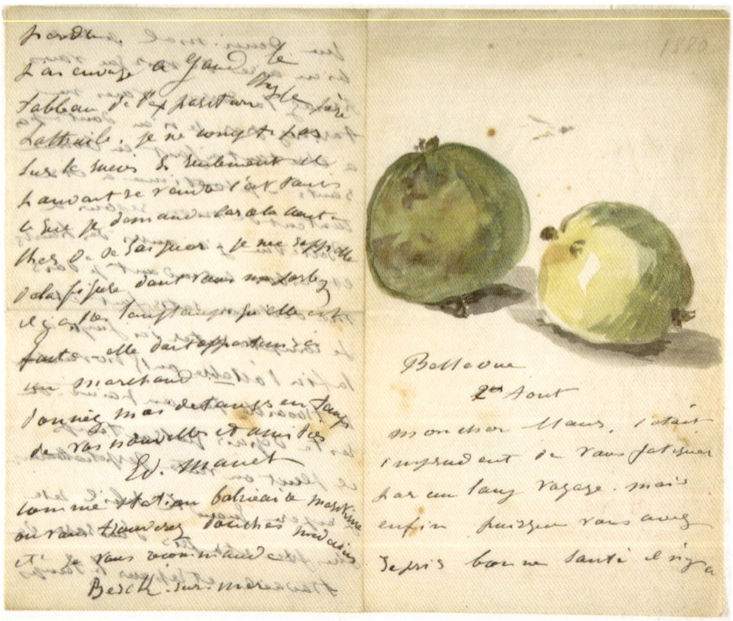

Bellevue
2 Août
mon cher Maus,

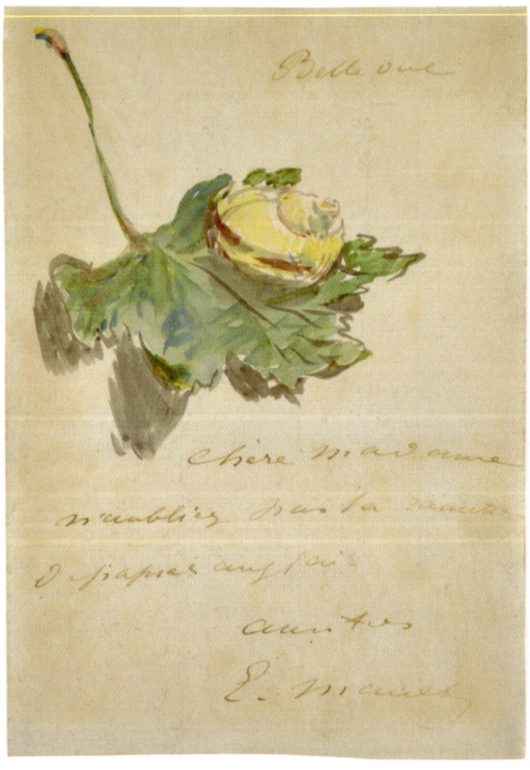

Bellevue
Chère madame
n'oubliez pas la [illegible]
[illegible]
amitiés
E. Manet

Above (top): Madame Manet (Suzanne Leenhoff) at Bellevue, *1880. This is Manet's last portrait of his wife.*
Above: *Letters to Eugène Maus (left) and (possibly) to Madame Jules Guillemet (right), both 1880.*

meant that he would be automatically able to exhibit at subsequent Salons without having to submit his work to the jury – although by this time there were not to be many more Salon submissions for Manet. Over the summer that year, he stayed near Versailles for further medical attention, and then in the December of that year, he was made a Chevalier of the Legion of Honour.

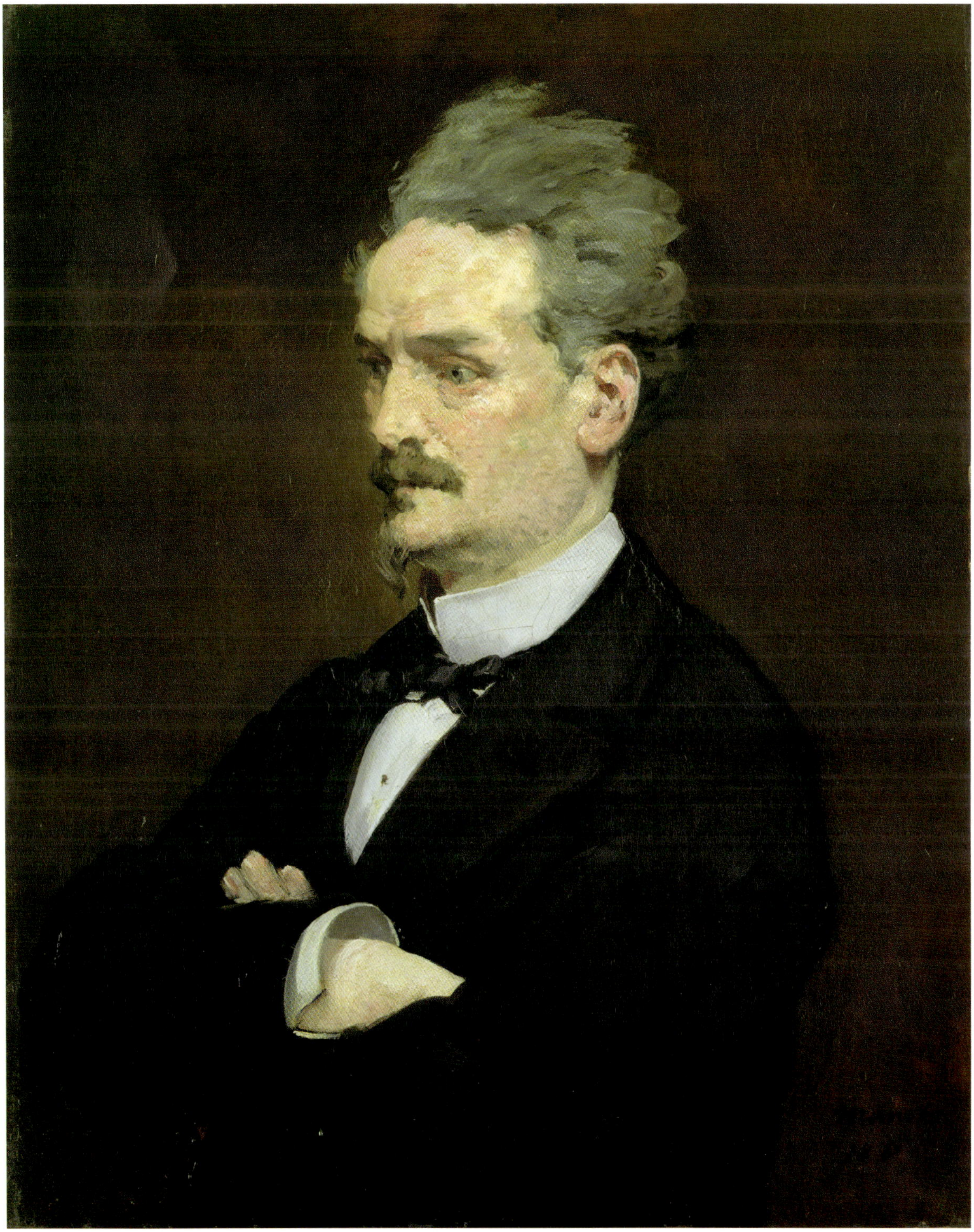

Portrait of Henri Rochefort, *1881. This arresting portrait of Victor Henri Rochefort, Marquis de Rochefort-Luçay, the French writer and politician, won Manet a second-class medal at the Salon of 1881.*

In 1882, 'he was walking with difficulty and came to see me only with huge efforts and accompanied,' his life-long friend Proust remembered, and yet at the Salon that year two of his greatest masterpieces were exhibited: *A Bar at the Folies-Bergère* and *Jeanne (Spring)* (1881). The first work was Manet's last major oil painting and shows one of the best-known music halls in Paris, the Folies-Bergère, notorious as a location frequented by prostitutes; Manet knew it well. The central figure behind the bar was modelled by a woman recorded only as Suzon, who worked at the Folies-Bergère in the early 1880s. Manet persuaded her to pose in his studio and the dish of oranges may indicate that she worked as a prostitute too. The mirror behind reflects not only the packed music hall crowd, but the man she is serving and the green-clad legs of a trapeze artist performing above. The central young woman appears isolated from her setting, detached and somewhat remote. Both the critics and the public found the composition unsettling, particularly the oddity of the barmaid's reflection, which to some appeared too far to the right, and which continues today to be discussed by art historians. Interestingly, the beer bottles display the labels of Bass Pale Ale and it has been suggested that Manet favoured British beer instead of German due to a lingering hostility after the horrors of the Franco-Prussian War. At the 1882 Salon, the critics struggled to appreciate the work and it was *Jeanne (Spring)* which triumphed, the *Courrier de l'Art* of 1882 noting: 'Edouard Manet. *A Bar*

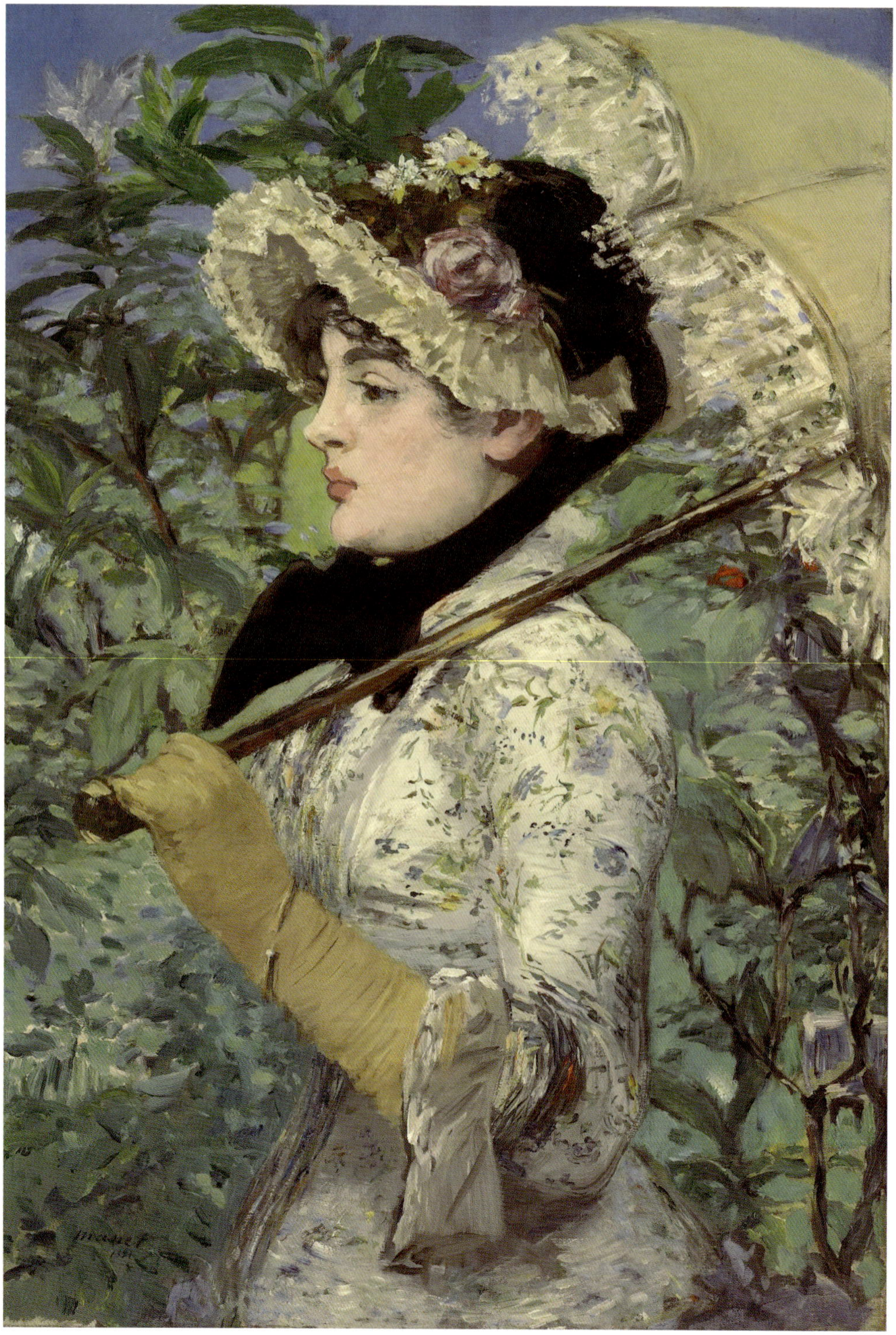

Jeanne (Spring), *1882. Critics praised this work, originally conceived as part of a decorative plan for the Hotel de Ville, Paris, which never materialized. The model, the young actress Jeanne de Marsy, is shown in fashionable bright attire against a backdrop of rhododendrons.*

Autumn (Méry Laurent), *1882. During the latter part of 1879, Manet worked on plans for a decorative scheme for the Hotel de Ville in Paris, showing allegories of the Four Seasons. Mery Laurent sat for him for the role of Autumn and, in contrast to* Jeanne (Spring), *she wears a black cloak and deep brown fur, while sitting against a decorative blue backdrop of aesthetic flowers.*

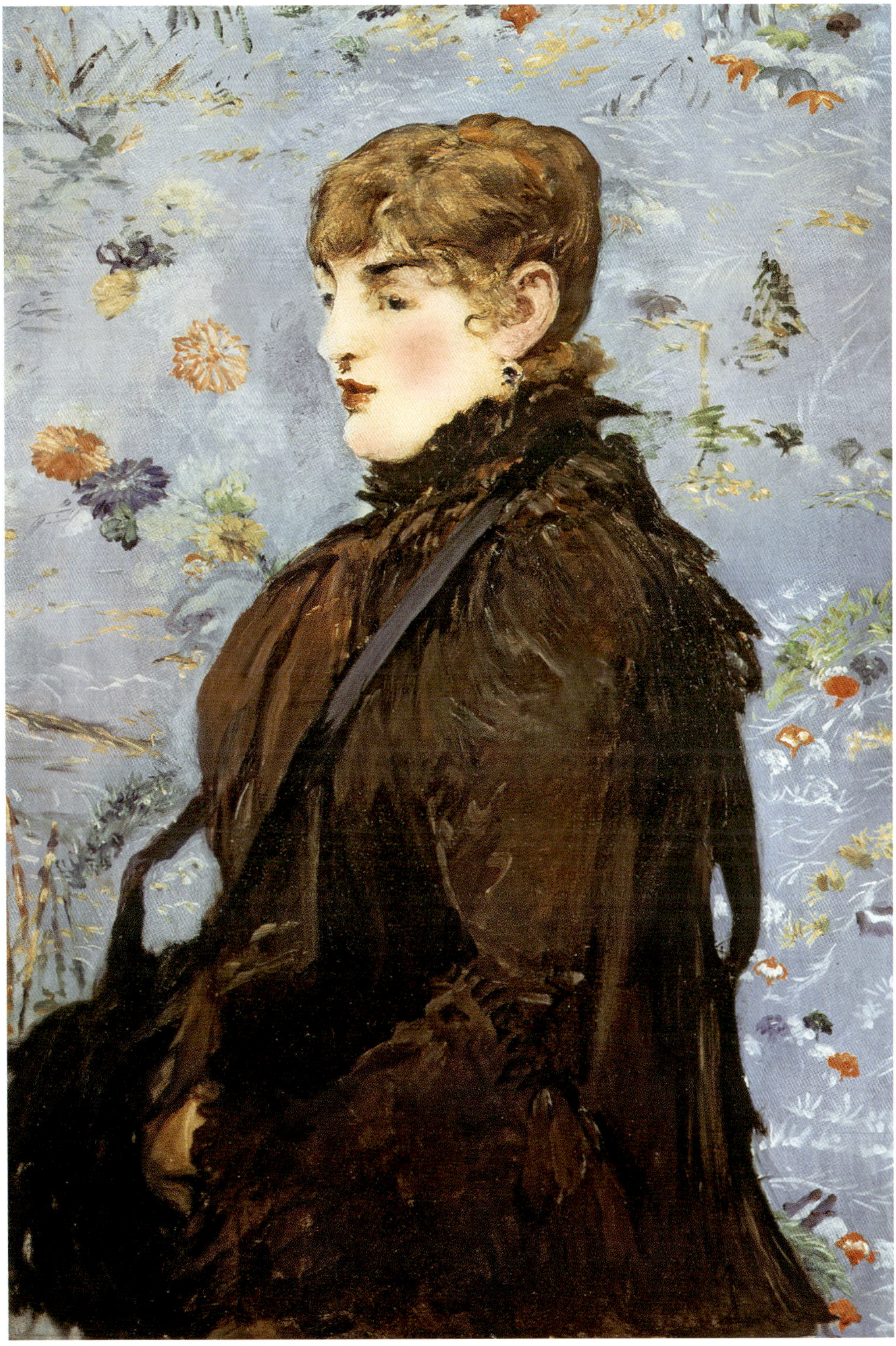

at the Folies-Bergère. All his faults. *Jeanne*. All his qualities… most legitimate success.'

Though much less known to us today, *Jeanne* (the title of *Spring* came a little later) was much admired at the time as a great triumph for Manet. For decades Manet's paintings had been either rejected by the Salon or met with controversy. But this work was the highlight of his Salon career, and it came not a moment too late – by the following spring he would be dead. The painting depicts a fashionable young woman in a day dress created from material with a design of delicate spring-like flowers, wearing a bonnet and carrying a parasol in a gloved hand. She is shown half-length in profile, looking ahead and set against a background of rich green foliage. He had personally scoured dressmakers' and milliners' shops to ensure her costume was exactly as he wanted; nothing with Manet was left to chance. He seems to have enjoyed painting the work, which demonstrates his extraordinary range of brushwork, especially in the thin touches on the dress to create the flower patterns which contrast with the smooth handling of Jeanne's face, and then the much broader strokes employed for the green foliage beyond. The sitter was the up-and-coming actress Jeanne de Marsy, who is shown as the embodiment of *Spring* – a title it was given at the memorial exhibition following Manet's death. His biographer Bazire confirmed in 1884 that 'Spring is indeed the name that Manet intended to give the portrait' and explained that it was the first of a planned series of the four seasons. However, only one other painting in the series was executed: *Autumn (Méry Laurent),* a beautiful painting which remained unfinished at his death. The seasonal series may have been undertaken at the suggestion of Manet's friend Antonin Proust, who purchased *Spring*, probably in 1882. That summer, Manet and Suzanne retreated from Paris so that he could rest, staying at Rueil. just west of Paris. There he occupied himself painting still lifes and occasionally the young Julie Manet, the daughter of his brother Eugène and Berthe Morisot, who were staying nearby at Bougival.

Manet had wanted to build on his critical success and was planning to enter pieces for the 1883 Salon. Before his summer break, he began work on but did not finish two paintings: *The Bugler*, and *Horsewoman, Full-face (L'Amazone)*. Both works are clearly unfinished, but the face and hat of the horsewoman are more complete in the latter painting, and the exact identification of the model

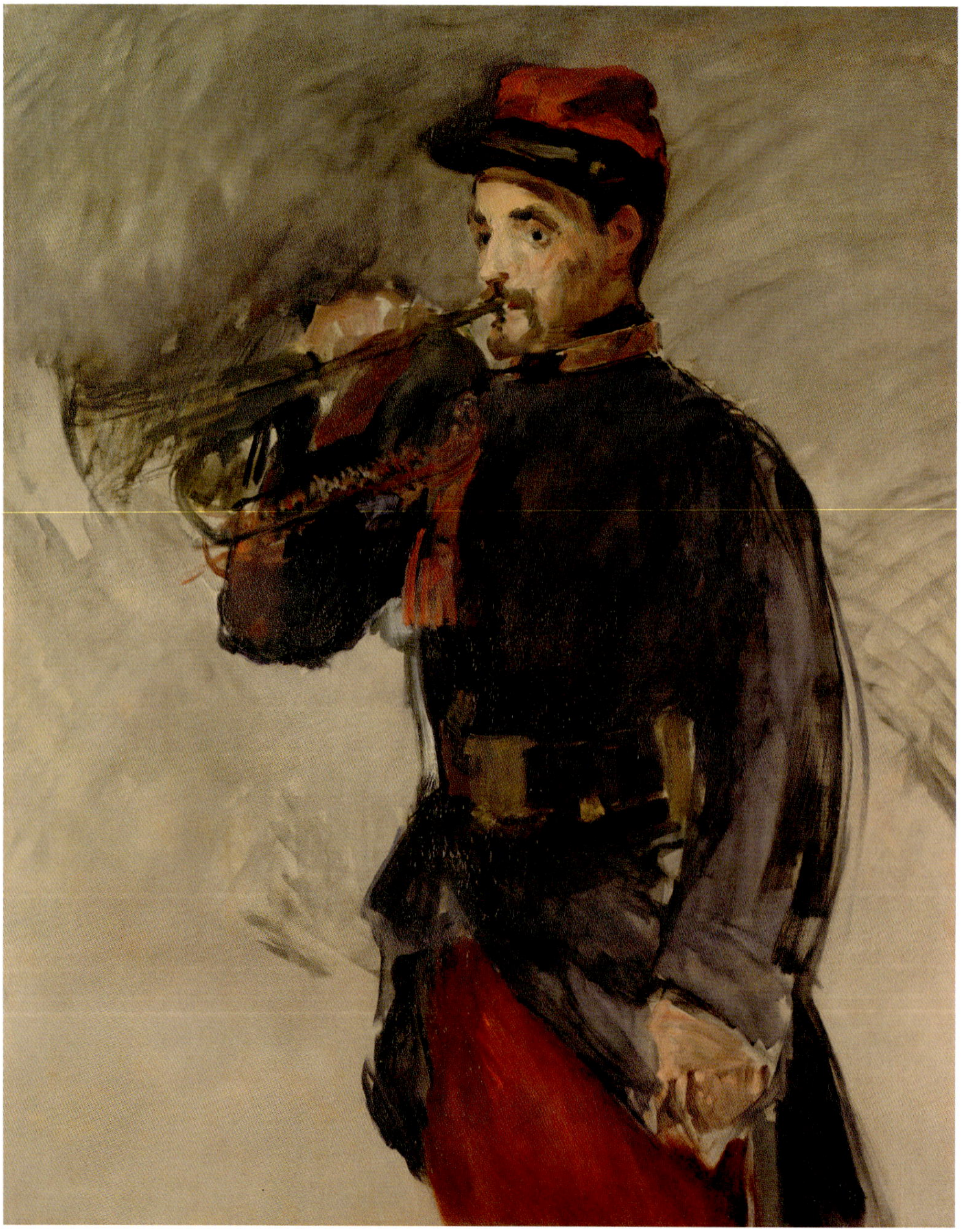

The Bugler, *1882. Painted in the last months of his life, Manet struggled to complete the work in his final year as his health deteriorated.*

remains uncertain. The work is the same size as *Jeanne (Spring)* and *Autumn (Méry Laurent)*, which has led some scholars to conclude that this was to have been part of the series, although Bazire stated that only two paintings in the series, *Spring* and *Autumn*, were attempted.

By September 1882, Manet knew he was dying and wrote his will, naming his wife Suzanne as his heir and Léon Koëlla as residuary legatee, and Duret as executor with responsibility for the sale of his work. He was clear that when Suzanne died, she would make Léon her only heir. In France this was significant because the law dictated that the estate passes unquestionably to children, legitimate or illegitimate. He added: 'I believe that my brothers will find these arrangements perfectly natural.' In other words, Manet was acknowledging Léon as his child. He returned to Paris in October still eager to return to the works he wanted to display in the Salon in 1883. He insisted on going to his studio each day, but once there was mostly confined to his couch and struggled to stand at his easel to paint. As Manet's health deteriorated further, it became clear that these works could not be completed and he devoted himself to smaller paintings. By early 1883, many of his friends and admirers were sending him flowers to cheer him. It was obvious he was dying of complications from syphilis, and he was in agonizing pain in his leg, but he wanted to paint the exquisite flowers

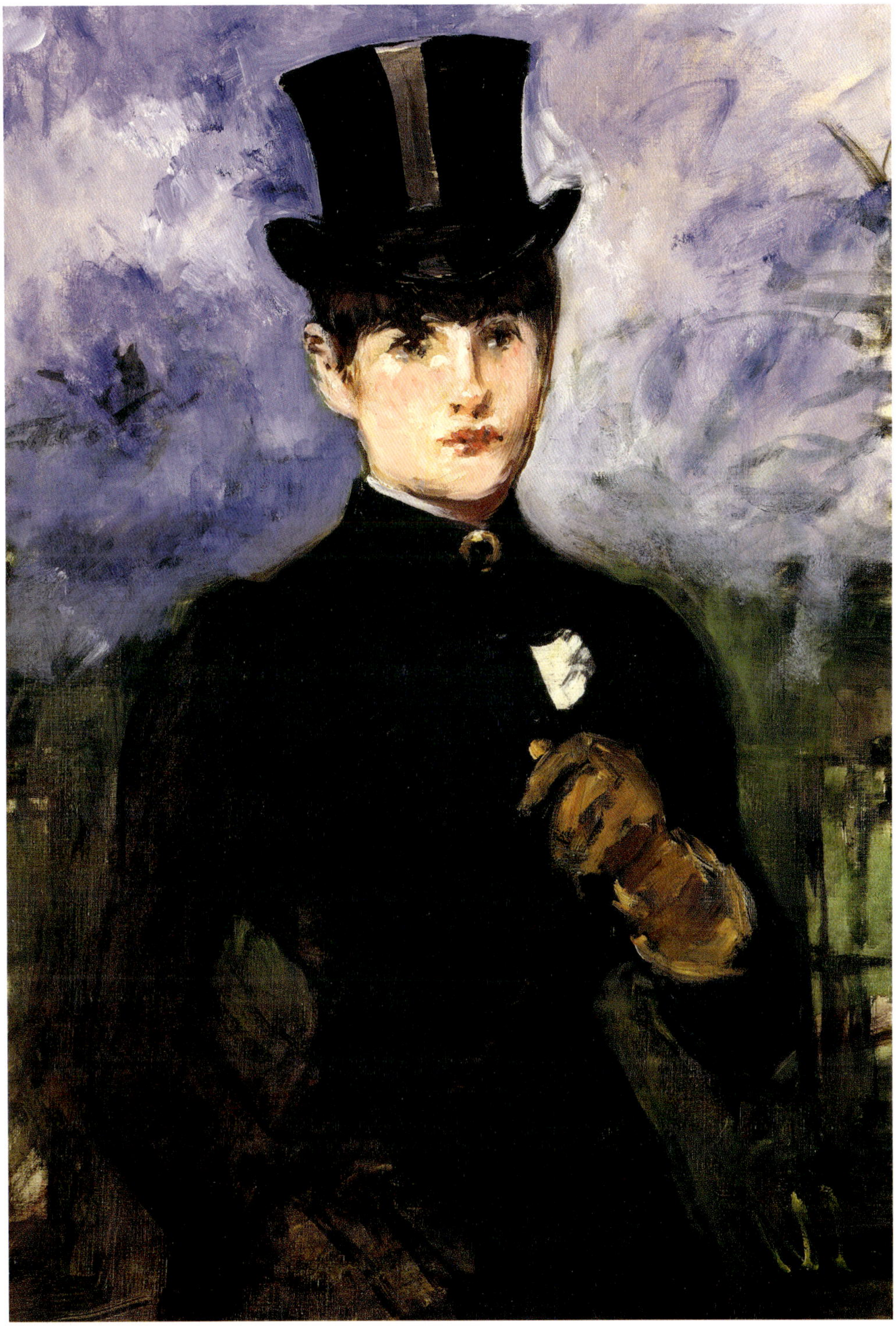

Horsewoman, Full-face (L'Amazone), c. *1882. This work is the same size as* Jeanne (Spring) *and* Autumn (Méry Laurent), *which may indicate that this was to have been part of the series, representing summer. The sitter was a less known model, the daughter of Madame Saguez, a bookseller in the rue de Moscou.*

surrounding him. Small intimate canvases were more suitable for his circumstances, such as *Vase of White Lilacs and Roses*, his second to last work, completed two months before his death. Studies of spring lilacs and roses appear in other paintings, as does also the same tall and narrow crystal vase. Such studies reflect nothing of his pain or suffering and sparkle instead with vibrant colour and vivid brushstrokes.

By March, Manet's health was of serious concern to his family and large circle of

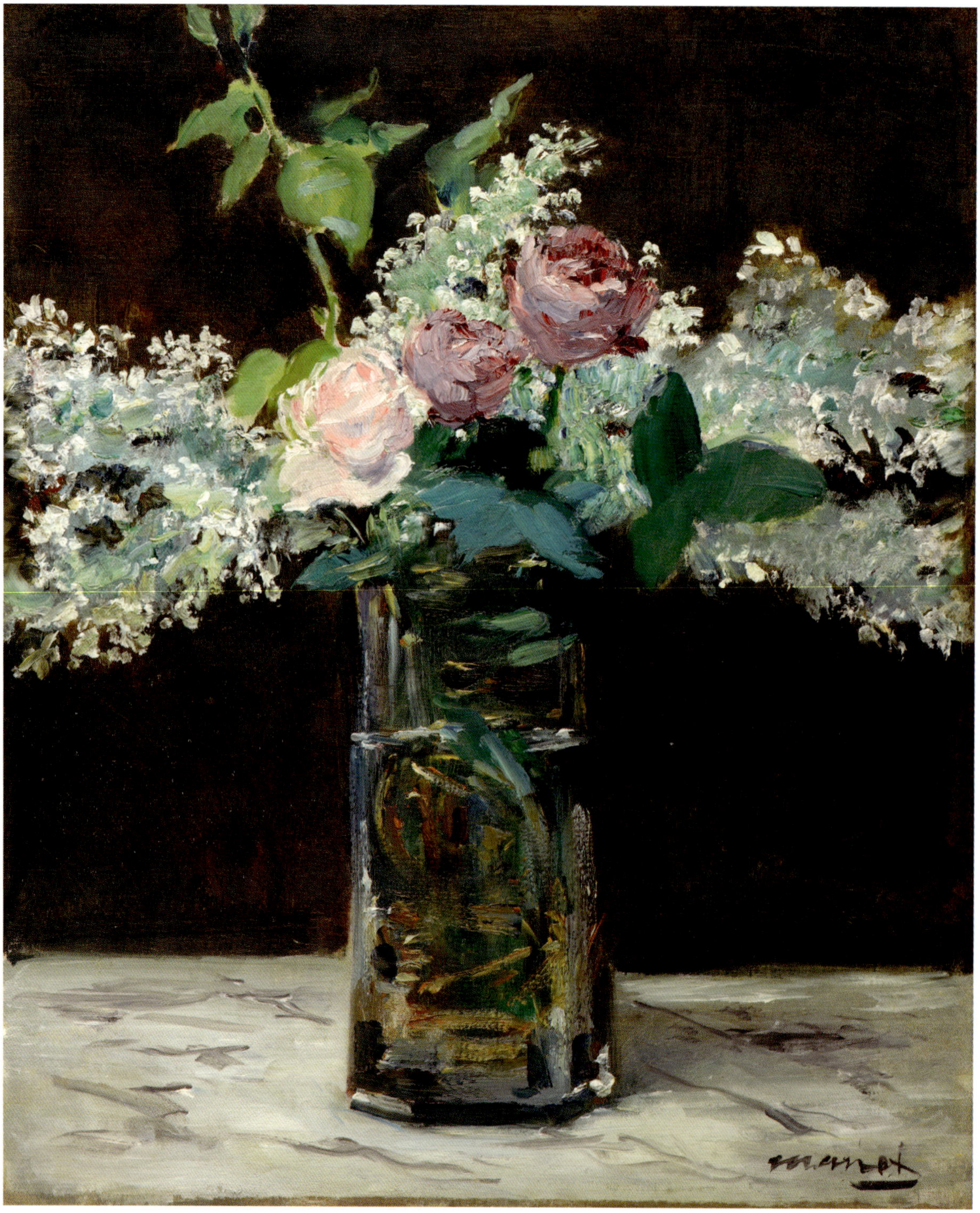

Vase of White Lilacs and Roses, 1883. *In his final months, Manet amused himself painting still lifes of the many flowers which his friends and admirers brought to his studio to cheer him up. This was his second to last painting before he died on 30 April 1883. Instead of his beloved peonies, he shows sparkling, vibrant springtime lilacs and roses, displayed in a cut-glass crystal vase.*

friends; gangrene had set into his leg. Pissarro wrote to his son Lucien, 'poor Manet is desperately ill. We are losing a great painter and a man of great charm.' On 19 April, after a visit from his great friend Antonin Proust, during which the artist enquired about the Salon that was about to open, his doctors amputated his leg below the knee. On the 20 April *Le Figaro* reported: 'Manet did not suffer. The day has been as good as one could hope and yesterday evening, when we asked for some news, his condition did not predict any severe complication.' However, this bulletin proved optimistic and Manet developed a fever. Suzanne, Léon, his brothers and Berthe remained at his bedside as Manet became weaker and delirium set in. He was in agony – and his death on 30 April 1883 was a release from his suffering. Berthe wrote to her sister, 'His agony was horrible, death in one of its most appalling forms.'

On that same evening the Salon preview opened and news reached the packed Palais de l'Industrie that Manet had lost his battle for life. A silence fell on the crowd of Parisians and men doffed their hats in respect. His presence was much missed and the Salon itself was diminished without him. Indeed, its own relevance was soon in question: it began to decline and its days were numbered. At his funeral on 3 May in the Batignolles, the pall-bearers for his coffin included his close circle of friends Antonin Proust, Claude Monet, Alfred Stevens, Fantin-Latour, Théodore Duret, Philippe Burty and Émile Zola. The chief mourners included his brothers and sister-in-law Berthe, and among those following the coffin were also Degas, Renoir, Pissarro and Puvis de Chavannes. Manet had been much loved, inspiring many fellow artists.

In the months and years following his death, Suzanne and Léon and his numerous artistic friends worked tirelessly to ensure his legacy was recognized and secured, through exhibitions, sales of his paintings, acquisitions by the French government for museums, and by the swift publishing of informed biographies. In January 1884, a posthumous exhibition of 179 of his paintings, pastels, drawings and prints was organized at the École des Beaux-Arts, and was a success. It was organized by a committee that included his brother Eugène and his wife Berthe, Antonin Proust (by then a former Minister of Arts), Alfred Stevens, the dealers Durand-Ruel and Georges Petit, and Zola, who wrote the introduction to the catalogue. At least one critic commented on the irony of the location for an artist whose works had been ridiculed and refused by so many Salon juries. The exhibition confirmed Manet as a great original artist, whose novel style and vision were finally being appreciated by the public and critics alike. On 4–5 February, a studio sale was held at the Hotel Drouot Paris, organized by Duret.

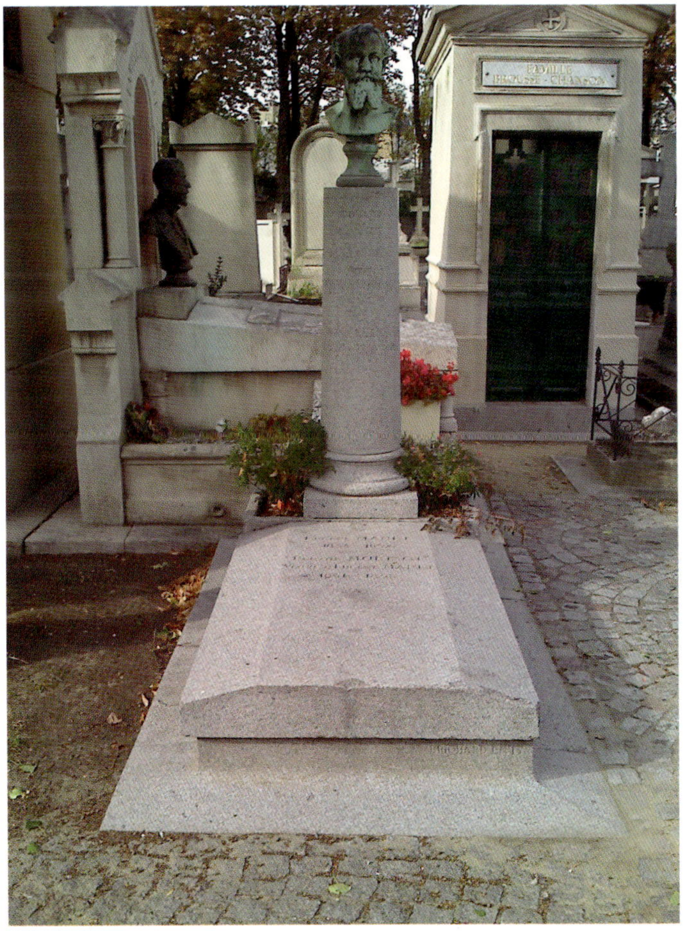

Manet's grave can be found at the Cimetière de Passy, near the Palais de Chaillot. The cemetery opened in 1820 in the expensive residential and commercial districts of the Right Bank near the Champs-Élysées and, by 1874, it had become the aristocratic necropolis of Paris. The tomb includes a column with a bust of the artist. Even in death it seems Manet was a stylish Parisian.

MANET'S LEGACY AND INFLUENCE

Despite a relatively short career, his works are now recognized as pivotal in the history of western art and held in most major international museums and galleries. He is considered by many art historians to be the father of modern art, and his influence on modernism is impossible to measure. Controversial paintings such as *Le Déjeuner sur l'herbe* and *Olympia* inspired the young Impressionist painters and are seen as watershed paintings that mark the start of modern art. American collectors appreciated Manet's art from the 1880s onwards, but in Britain only a few important collectors, such as Samuel Courtauld and the Davies sisters in Wales, did so. Dubbed 'the father of Impressionism', and the subject of blockbuster exhibitions, Manet remains intriguing, partly because he is not easy to pin down. His art is at once seductive and destructive. *Olympia* inverts the values embedded in the age-long pursuit of female beauty: neither passive nor idealized, nor the mere object of the male gaze, his nude sits up, flaunts on one raised foot a fashionable mule and coolly returns our stare. Some artists acknowledged their debt to him, such as William Orpen's *Homage to Manet* of 1909.

Homage to Manet, *William Orpen, 1909. Orpen depicts a room in the collector Sir Hugh Lane's home with one of Manet's most famous paintings hanging on the wall –* Portrait of Eva Gonzalès. *The Irish writer and art critic George Moore (*see *page 78) sits at one side of a breakfast table. He reads aloud from the newspaper to a gathering of forward-thinking art-grandees (*see *main text, left). Philip Wilson Steer and Walter Sickert, standing off to the right, had both travelled to France in the 1880s and encountered Manet's art and Impressionism, which influenced their work.*

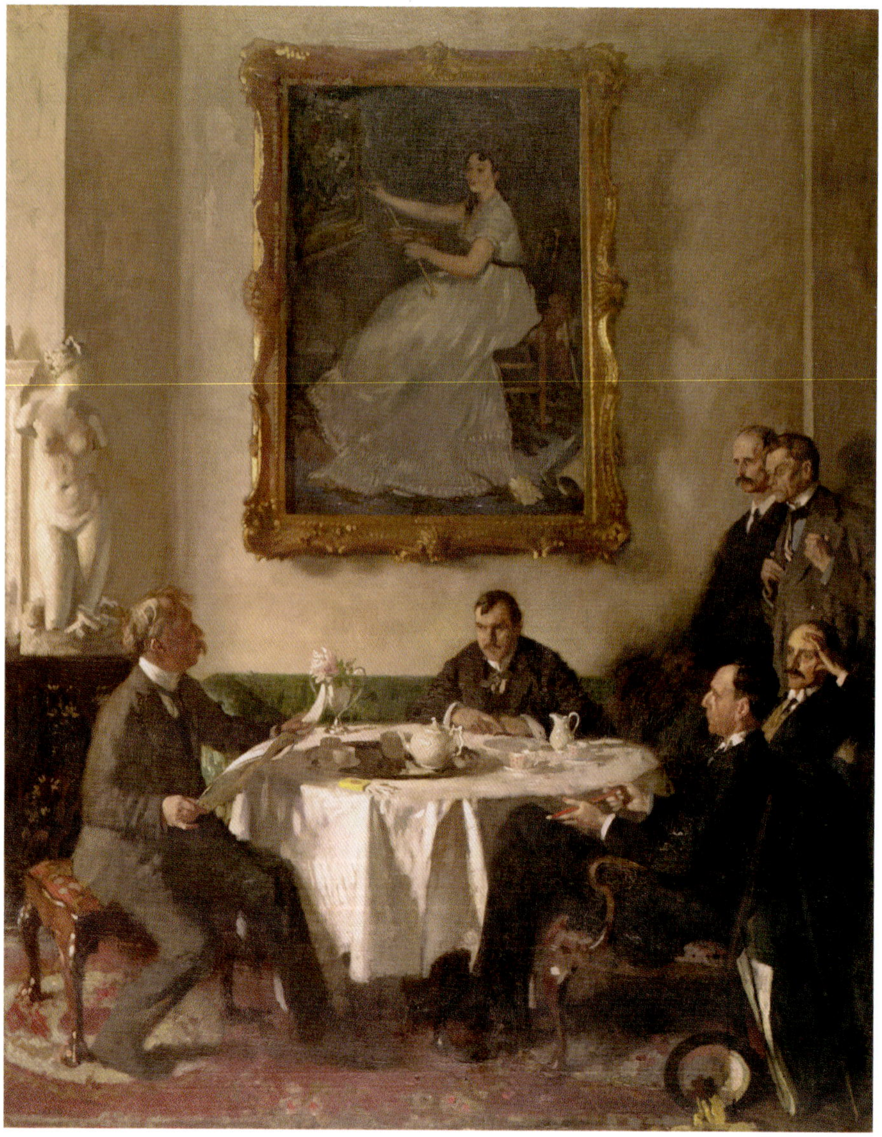

The Manchester painting depicts a group of formally dressed men sitting around a table, above which hangs his portrait of his pupil Eva Gonzalès. The room depicted is in Sir Hugh Lane's house in South Bolton Gardens, where the painting hung (and which was later acquired by Orpen and used as a studio). The fascination is the identity of these rather boring-looking men. The Irish writer George Moore, who had known the artist in Paris and sat for Manet in 1879 as a young man, reads aloud to the group from the newspaper in front of a model of a Greek statue. Listening to him across the table are the artists Wilson Steer, D. S. MacColl, W. R. Sickert, and Henry Tonks (left to right) and the collector Sir Hugh Lane himself, who did so much to popularize Impressionism in Britain. Since Lane's death in 1917, the painting has been shared between the Hugh Lane Gallery in Dublin and London's National Gallery.

Walter Sickert never actually met Manet, but as a young artist he tried to do so, calling at his home shortly before his death, when he heard his voice although was refused entrance to meet him. But Sickert was familiar with Manet's art and relayed his enthusiasm back in London to his friends Philip Wilson Steer and Henry Tonks at the recently formed New English Art Club. Indeed, photographs of Manet's work were shown at the club's early exhibitions. Sickert is thought to have been influenced by Manet's *Olympia* in his approach to nudes, especially those of prostitutes such as *La Hollandaise* (*c.* 1906) and the *Camden Town Murder* paintings (1908–9). These pictures, which referred to the recent local murder of a prostitute, caused a sensation when exhibited at the first Camden Town Group exhibition in June 1911. Philip Wilson Steer had also been greatly influenced by seeing works by Manet when he visited Paris. The influence is clear in *Two Girls Resting on the Grass* with its loose brushstrokes (*c.* 1900).

Only the year after Orpen executed his painting paying formal homage to Manet, the critic Roger Fry mounted his ground-breaking exhibition at the Grafton Galleries in London. 'Manet and the Post-Impressionists' created a sensation in London and saw Manet's art, including his great *Bar at the Folies-Bergère*, exhibited along with works by Seurat, Van Gogh, Gauguin, Cézanne, Matisse, Picasso and Vlaminck, already suggesting the breadth of the impact of Manet's influence. Many were outraged by what they saw and felt challenged by these artists who appeared to place form over content in their brightly coloured works. The British art-loving public and collectors were still relatively unaware of Manet even in 1910, except perhaps those few enthusiastic artists depicted by Orpen, which would explain why for many years Orpen's work was simply known as *A Portrait Group* and the significance of his original intention was lost.

Manet's *Olympia* has proved an enduring inspiration for his followers. Cézanne's *A Modern Olympia*, 1873–4, was shown at the First Impressionist Exhibition of 1874 and

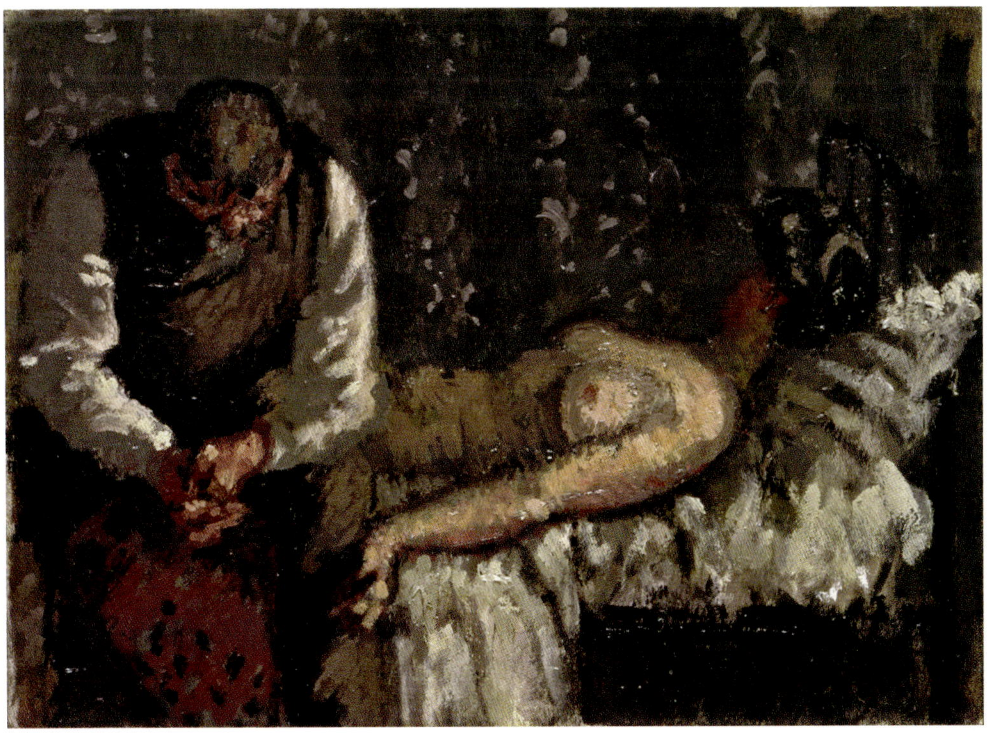

The Camden Town Murder (What shall we do about the Rent?), *Walter Sickert, c. 1908. Manet's portrayal of a fictitious prostitute in his* Olympia *transformed the way artists approached such subject matter. Manet undoubtedly influenced Sickert, who painted a series of nudes between 1905 and 1913, all posed on iron bedsteads which challenged artistic conventions, just as Manet had done in 1864. Four of these nudes are the provocative* Camden Town Murder *paintings. Here, Sickert has removed the direct gaze of the model, so we cannot view the details of her face, which is turned away.*

is a clear and daring reworking: a woman is uncovered by her black servant as a man in black (possibly Cézanne himself) looks on, thus creating a more erotic and theatrical scene. This extraordinary work was scorned by both public and critics in 1874. The Swiss painter Felix Vallotton created a much more direct tribute to Manet in 1913. In *The White and the Black* his debt to Manet is clear, although he significantly shifts the dynamic of the composition. A white model with flushed cheeks lies on a bed, without a velvet choker or high-heeled slippers, while a black woman is placed in the foreground, sitting on the bed. She appears relaxed, confident and smokes a cigarette, observing her dozing companion. The relationship between the two women is much more ambiguous. The blocks of pure colour in the green of the wall and dominant white of the bed sheet as well as the blue dress are all also reminiscent of Manet.

Perhaps not surprisingly, Manet's *Olympia* has endured as an inspiration for artists, who have explored the post-colonial and feminist issues it raises – such as the depiction of the female nude, prostitution and the male gaze. The American photographer Victor

The White and the Black, *Félix Vallotton, 1913. This homage to Manet's* Olympia *creates a relationship between the two women which is more ambiguous. The black servant at the back of Manet's work, offering the white flowers is now brought to the foreground, positioned much more prominently towards the right of the canvas, sitting on the same bed gazing at the reclining white female nude. This black woman wears a blue tunic dress and is shown smoking a cigarette. The blocks of pure colour, including the turquise green of the wall and dominant white of the bed sheet, are all a tribute to Manet, as much as the figurative composition.*

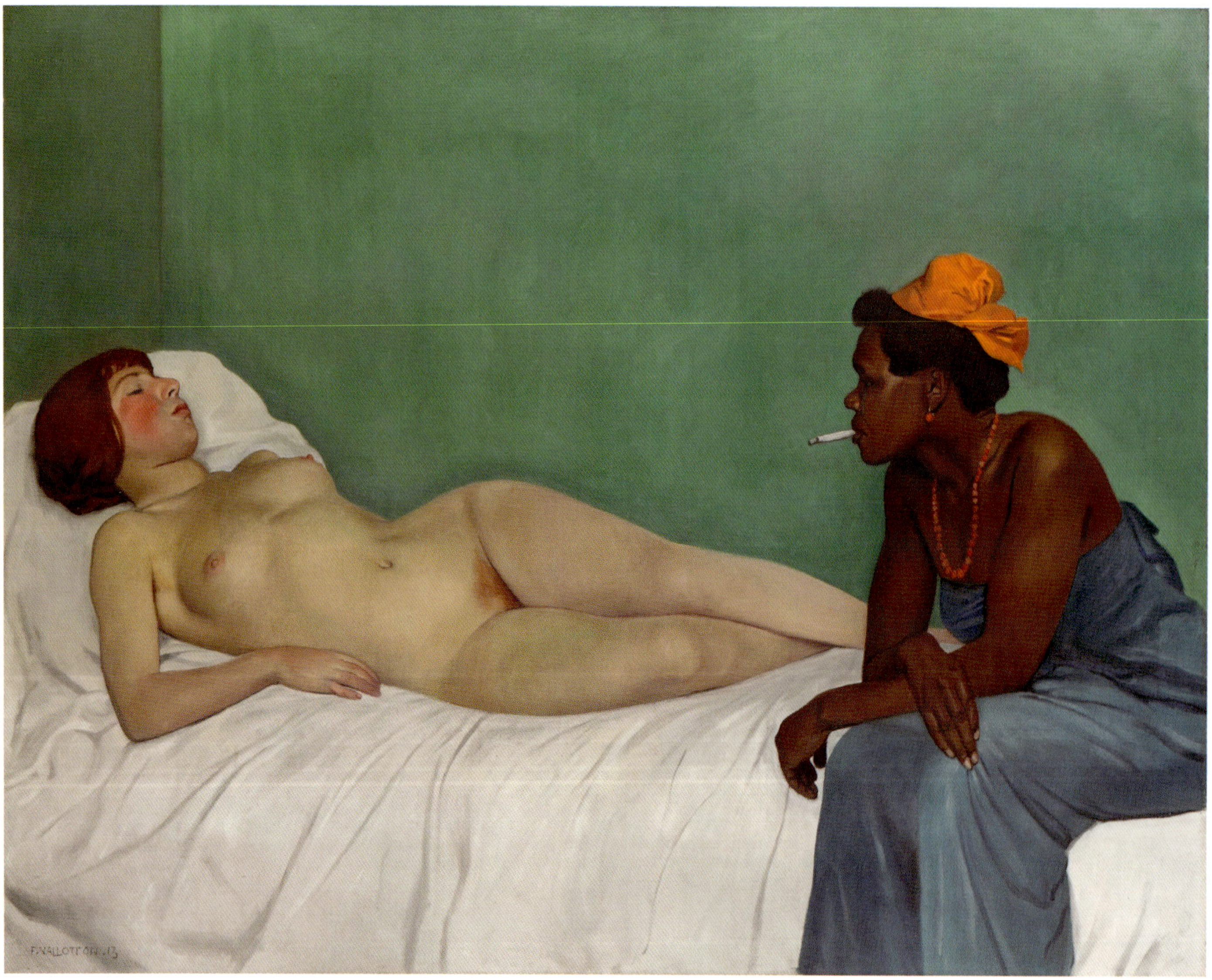

Burgin's tribute to Olympia clearly references Manet but also also makes reference to Alfred Hitchcock's film *Rear Window* and to E. T. A. Hoffman's story 'The Sand-Man'. The Japanese artist Yasumasa Morimura's unsettling photographic response, *Portrait (Futago)* (1988), further explores the female identity, playing with the gender of the nude figure. Morimura creates a new image with his body, wearing a wig and imitating a female gender role as a symbol of male sexual desire. The artist returned to the subject again in 2018, creating a chromogenic print entitled *Une Moderne Olympia*. Contemporary responses include the Luxembourg performance artist Deborah De Robertis who, in January 2017, laid naked in front of the painting at the Musée d'Orsay until she was arrested. There, in 2019, during the exhibition 'Black Models: From Géricault to Matisse', which focused on modern art's oft-unheralded black models, Manet's *Olympia* was retitled *Laure* for the duration of the exhibition, to acknowledge the black model.

Portrait (Futago), *Yasumasa Morimura, 1988. The Japanese photographer further explores the female identity, playing with the gender of the nude figure. Morimura creates a self-portrait with his own body, but wears a wig and dainty slippers, imitating a female, Westernized gender role as a symbol of male sexual desire, questioning as well the male gaze in Western art history. Manet's black cat is transformed into a popular Japanese waving or beckoning cat figurine, which in Japanese culture is believed to bring good luck to the owner. Yet the black woman remains in the background in her role as a servant offering flowers to the white, reclining woman figure.*

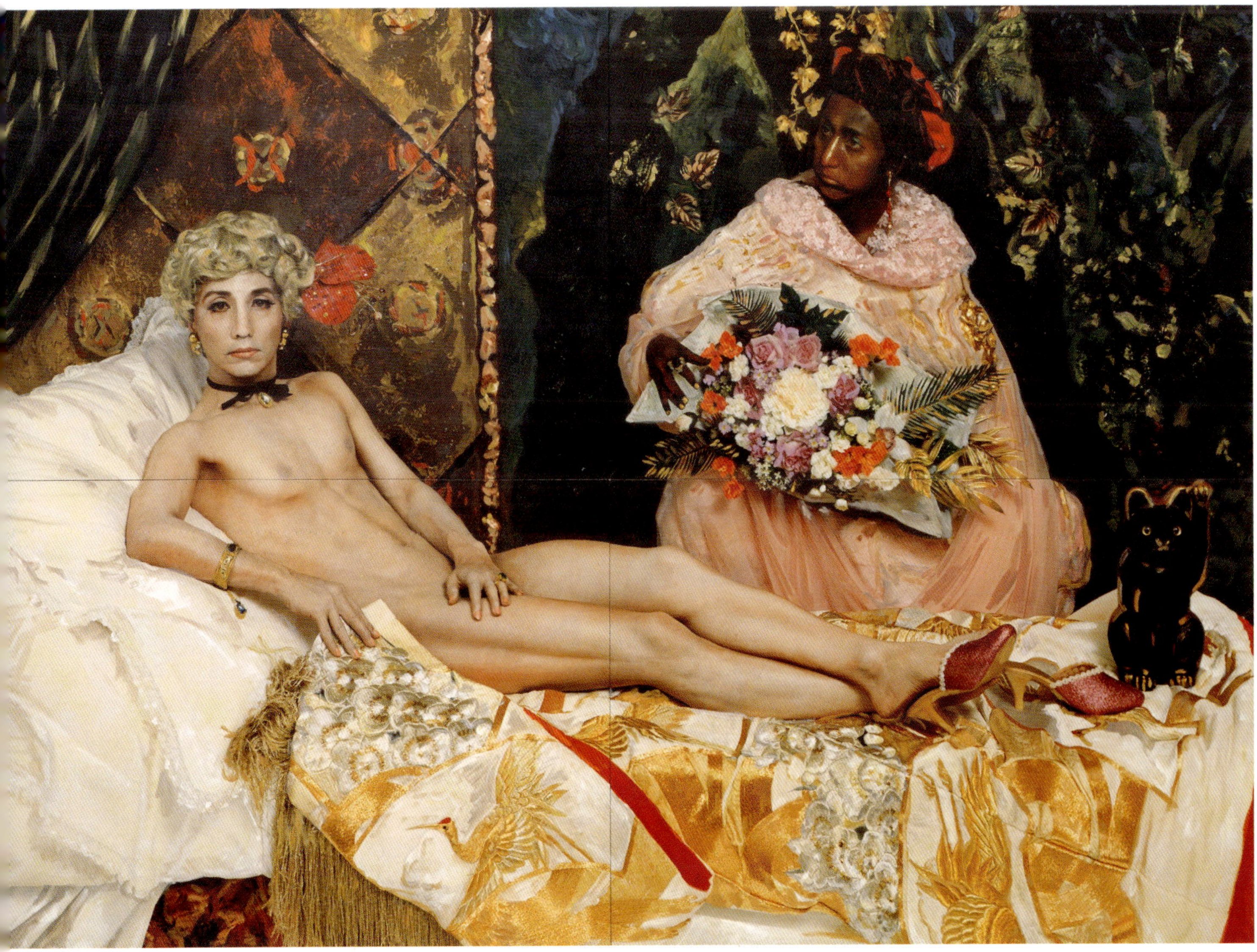

TIMELINE

1830s

'32 Édouard Manet is born in Paris.

'39 Attends the school of Canon Poiloup.

1840s

'44 Begins studying at Collège Rollin.

'48 Completes his studies and attempts to join the Navy.

February Revolution in France.

Creation of the French Second Republic.

'49 Manet decides to train as an artist after failing his naval examinations.

1850s

'50 Begins his training with Thomas Couture.

'51 Louis-Napoleon Bonaparte stages a self-coup.

Suzanne Leenhoff, a piano teacher and Édouard's future wife, is employed by the Manet family.

'52 Suzanne Leenhoff's son, Léon-Edouard Koëlla, is born.

Bonaparte becomes Emperor of the French, taking the regnal name Napoleon III.

Founding of the Second French Empire.

'55 Meets artist Eugène Delacroix, who will go on to support his work.

'56 Finishes training with Couture and sets up a studio with Albert de Balleroy.

'59 *The Absinthe Drinker* is rejected by the Salon.

1860s

'60 Paints *Portrait of Monsieur and Madame Manet* and *The Spanish Singer*.

'61 The Salon shows the two paintings; the latter wins an honourable mention.

'62 Death of Manet's father.

Paints *Music in the Tuileries Gardens*.

Meets the model Victorine Meurent.

'63 Manet's first solo exhibition in Paris at the Galerie Martinet.

The Salon des Refusés is held at the Palais de l'Industrie. Manet's painting, *Dejeuner sur l'herbe*, shocks both critics and the public.

Death of Eugène Delacroix.

Paints *Olympia*.

Marries Suzanne Leenhoff.

'65 *Olympia* is exhibited at the Salon.

Travels to Spain, where he meets Théodore Duret.

1860s continued

'67 *The Fifer* and *The Tragic Actor* are rejected by the Salon.

Excluded from the Exposition Universelle, Manet stages his own exhibition at great personal expense.

Maximilian I is executed by firing squad in Mexico. The event is depicted by Manet in four paintings and one lithograph.

1870s

'70 France declares war on Prussia. Manet remains in Paris during the Prussian siege and joins the National Guard.

Fall of Napoleon III marks the end of the Second French Empire.

Beginning of French Third Republic.

'71 France surrenders to Prussia, ending the Franco-Prussian war.

'73 Manet paints *The Railway*.

'74 First Impressionist Exhibition. Degas, Monet, Renoir and Morisot all participate, but Manet refuses to join them.

1880s

'80 First exhibition dedicated to Manet's work since 1867.

'81 *Portrait of Henri Rochefort* is awarded a second-class medal at the Salon.

'82 Paints his final masterpiece, *A Bar at the Foiles-Bergere*.

Manet's deteriorating health worsens and causes concern.

'83 Manet dies.

'84 A posthumous exhibition of Manet's works at the École des Beaux-Arts is a great success.

SELECTED READING LIST

Adler, Kathleen, *Manet*, Phaidon Press Ltd, London, 1986

Allan, Scott, Beeny, Emily A, Groom, Gloria, *Manet and Modern Beauty: The Artist's Last Years*, Yale University Press, New Haven and London, 2019

Armstrong, Carol , Bailey, Colin B, *Manet: Portraying Life*, Royal Academy of Arts, London. 2013

Brettel, Richard R, *Impressionion: Painting Quickly in France 1860–1890*, Sterling and Francine Clark Art Institute, Williamstown, 2000

Leribault, Christophe, *Fantin-Latour, Manet, Baudelaire: L'Homage à Delacroix*, Musée Delacroix, Paris, 2012 (French edition)

Locke, Nancy, *Manet and the Family Romance*, Princeton University Press, Princeton, 2001

Mauner, George, *Manet: The Still Life Paintings*, Harry N. Abrams, Inc., New York, 2001

Murrell, Denise, *Posing Modernity: The Black Model from Géricault to Matisse*, Yale University Press, New Haven and London, 2018 (exhibition catalogue)

Néret, Gilles, *Manet*, Taschen, Cologne, 2016

Orienti, Sandra and Pool, Phoebe (introduction), *The Complete Paintings of Manet*, Harry N. Abrams, Inc., New York, 1967

Patry, Sylvie (Ed.), *Inventing Impressionism: Paul Durand-Ruel and the Modern Art Market*, National Gallery, London, 2015

Richardson, John, *Manet*, Phaidon Press Ltd, London, 2015 (reprinted)

Roe, Sue, *The Private Lives of the Impressionists*, Vintage, London, 2007 (new edition)

Tucker, Paul Hayes, *The Impressionists at Argenteuil*, Yale University Press, London, 2000

FURTHER INFORMATION

Art institute, Chicago – artic.edu

The Clark (The Sterling and Francine Clark Art Institute) – clarkart.edu

Courtauld Gallery, London – courtauld.ac.uk

Metropolitan Museum of Art, new York – metmuseum.org

Musée d'Orsay – muse-orsay.fr

Museum of Fine Arts, Boston, Massachusetts, USA – mfa.org

National Gallery, London – nationalgallery.org.uk

Philadelphia Museum of Art – philamuseum.org

LIST OF ILLUSTRATIONS

Pages 6–7
A Bar at the Folies-Bergere, 1881–2, oil on canvas, 96 × 130 cm (37¾ × 51¼ in), The Courtauld Institute Galleries, London, United Kingdom. Public domain.

Page 8
Self-Portrait with a Palette, 1878–9, oil on canvas, 83 × 67 cm (32½ × 26½ in), Stephen A. Cohen Collection, Greenwich, Connecticut, USA. Public domain.

Pages 9
The Cats' Rendezvous, 1854, lithograph in black on ivory wove paper, 43.9 × 33.4 cm (17¼ × 13¼ in), John H. Wrenn Fund, Art Institute of Chicago. Public domain.

Page 10
Madame Manet at the Piano, 1867, oil on canvas, 38 × 46.5 cm (15 × 18¼ in), Musée d'Orsay, Paris, France. Public domain.

ages 11
Berthe Morisot with a Bunch of Violets, 1872, oil on canvas, 55 × 38 cm (21¾ × 15 in), Musée d'Orsay, Paris, France. Bridgeman Images.

Page 12
Portrait of Monsieur and Madame Auguste Manet, 1860, oil on canvas, 100 × 90 cm (39½ × 35½in), Musée d'Orsay, Paris, France. Bridgeman Images.

Page 14–15
The Romans During the Decadence, Thomas Couture, 1847, oil on canvas, 472 × 772 cm (186 × 304 in), Musée d'Orsay, Paris, France. Public domain.

Pages 15 (above)
Portrait of Antoine Étex, Thomas Couture, 1845–55, oil on canvas, 117.2 × 85.4 cm (46¼ × 33½ in), Birmingham Museums. Photo by Birmingham Museums Trust, licensed under CC0.

Page 15 (below)
Photograph of Thomas Couture, Étienne Carjat, *c.* 1860, Bibliothèque nationale de France. Public domain.

Page 16 (above)
The Barque of Dante, *c.* 1859, oil on canvas, 33 × 41 cm (13 × 16¼ in), Metropolitan Museum of Art, New York, USA. H. O. Havemeyer Collection, Bequest of Mrs H. O. Havemeyer. Public domain.

Page 16 (below)
The Barque of Dante, Eugène Delacroix, 1822, oil on canvas, 189 × 241 cm (74½ × 95 in), Musée du Louvre, Paris, France. Public domain.

Page 17
Boy with Cherries, *c.* 1858, oil on canvas, 65.5 × 54.5 cm (25¾ × 21½ in), Museo Calouste Gulbenkian, Lisbon, Portugal. Bridgeman Images.

Page 18
Woman with a Jug (Suzanne Leenhoff), 1858–60, oil on canvas, 61 × 54.5 cm (24 × 21½ in), Ordrupgaard, Charlotenlund, Denmark. Art Heritage/Alamy Stock Photo.

Page 19
The Absinthe Drinker, 1859, oil on canvas, 180.5 × 105.6 cm (71 × 41½ in), Ny Carlsberg Glyptotek, Copenhagen, Denmark. Public domain.

Page 20–1
The Old Musician, 1862, oil on canvas, 187.4 × 248.2 cm (73¾ × 97¾ in), Chester Dale Collection, National Gallery of Art, Washington DC, USA. Public domain.

Pages 23
The Spanish Singer, 1860, oil on canvas, 147.3 × 114.3 cm (58 × 45 in), Metropolitan Museum of Art, New York, USA. Gift of William Church Osborn, 1949. Public domain.

Page 24–5
Music in the Tuileries Gardens, 1862, oil on canvas, 76 × 118 cm (30 × 46½ in), The Hugh Lane Gallery, Dublin, Republic of Ireland. Public domain.

Pages 25, 26 and 27 (above)
Sections of *Music in the Tuileries Gardens*, 1862, oil on canvas, 76 × 118 cm (30 × 46½ in), The Hugh Lane Gallery, Dublin, Republic of Ireland. Public domain.

Page 27 (below)
The Little Cavaliers (after Velázquez), 1861–2, etching, first state, hand-coloured with watercolour, 24.5 x 38.7 cm (9½ x 15¼ in), Museum of Fine Arts, Boston, USA. Public domain.

Pages 28 (bove)
Young Woman Reclining in a Spanish Costume, 1862, black chalk, graphite, pen, brush and ink, heightened with white on laid paper, 29.6 × 58.5 cm (11⅝ × 23 in), Yale University Art Gallery, New Haven, Connecticut, USA. Pulic domain.

Page 28 (below)
Spanish Ballet, 1862, oil on canvas, 61 × 91 cm (24 × 35¾ in), The Phillips Collection, Washington DC, USA. Public domain.

Page 30
Lola de Valence, 1862, oil on canvas, 123 × 92 cm (35½ × 10⅔ in), Musée d'Orsay, Paris, France. Bridgeman Images.

Page 30–1
Le Déjeuner sur l'herbe, 1862–3, oil on canvas, 2.08 × 2.64 m (82 × 104 in), Musée d'Orsay, Paris, France. Public domain.

Pages 32 (above)
Le Concert champêtre, Titian (originally attributed to Giorgione), *c.* 1509, oil on canvas, 105 × 137 cm (41¼ × 54 in), Musée du Louvre, Paris, France. Public domain.

Page 32 (below)
The Judgement of Paris, Marcantonio Raimondi (after Raphael), *c.* 1510–20, pen and brown ink, white heightening on paper, 29.1 × 43.7 cm (11½ × 17¼ in), Metropolitan Museum of Art, New York, USA. Rogers Fund, 1919. Public domain.

Page 33
Homage to Delacroix, Henri Fantin-Latour, 1864, oil on canvas, 160 × 250 cm (63 × 98½ in),

Musée d'Orsay, Paris, France. Public domain.

Pages 34–5
Olympia, 1863, oil on canvas, 130.5 × 190 cm (51¼ × 74¾ in), Musée d'Orsay, Paris, France. Public domain.

Pages 36
Venus of Urbino, Titian, 1534, oil on canvas, 119 × 165 cm (43 × 65 in), Uffizi Gallery, Florence, Italy. Public domain.

Page 37
The Birth of Venus, Alexandre Cabanel, 1863, oil on canvas, 130 × 225 cm (51 × 88½ in), Musée d'Orsay, Paris, France. Public domain.

Page 38 (left)
Peonies, 1864–5, oil on canvas, 59.4 × 35.2 cm (23½ × 13¾ in), Metropolitan Museum of Art, New York, USA. Bequest of Joan Whitney Payson. Public domain.

Page 38 (right)
Vase of Peonies, 1864, oil on canvas, 93 × 70 cm (36½ × 27½ in), Musée d'Orsay, Paris, France. Bridgeman Images.

Pages 39
Guitar and Hat, 1862, oil on canvas, 77 × 121 cm (30¼ × 47¾ in), Musée Calvet, Avignon, France. Bridgeman Images.

Page 40 (above)
Still Life with Melon and Peaches, *c.* 1866, oil on canvas, 68.3 × 91 cm (27 × 36 in), National Gallery of Art, Washington DC, USA. Public domain.

Page 40 (below)
Still Life with a Salmon, *c.* 1868, oil on canvas, 72 × 92 cm (23¼ × 36¼ in), Shelburne Museum, Shelburne, Vermont, USA. Public domain.

Page 41
Portrait of Théodore Duret, 1886, oil on canvas, 60.1 × 45.6 cm (23⅔ × 18 in), Musée de la Ville de Paris, Musée du Petit-Palais, Paris, France. Bridgeman Images.

Page 42
The Dead Christ with Angels, 1864, oil on canvas, 179.4 × 149.9 cm (70½ × 59 in), Metropolitan Museum of Art, New York, USA. H. O. Havemeyer Collection, Bequest of Mrs H. O. Havemeyer. Public domain.

Page 43
Jesus Mocked by the Soldiers, 1865, oil on canvas, 190.8 × 148.3 cm (75¼ × 58½ in), Art Institute of Chicago, Chicago, Illinois, USA. Public domain.

Page 44
The Fifer, 1866, oil on canvas, 161 × 97 cm (63¼ × 38¼ in), Musée d'Orsay, Paris, France. Bridgeman Images.

Page 45
Portrait of Pablo de Valladolid, Diego Velázquez, *c.* 1635, oil on canvas, 209 × 123 cm (82¼ × 48½ in), Museo del Prado, Madrid, Spain. Public domain.

Page 46
The Tragic Actor (Rouvière as Hamlet), 1865–6, oil on canvas, 187.2 × 108.1 cm (73¾ × 42½ in), National Gallery of Art, Washington DC, USA. Public domain.

Page 47
Portrait of Édouard Manet, Henri Fantin-Latour, 1867, oil on canvas, 117.5 × 90 cm (46¼ × 35½ in), Art Institute of Chicago, Chicago, Illinois, USA. Public domain.

Page 48
Execution of the Emperor Maximillian, 1867, oil on canvas, 195.9 × 259.7 cm (77 × 102¼ in), Museum of Fine Arts, Boston, Massachusetts, USA. Public domain.

Page 49
Execution of the Emperor Maximillian, 1868, oil on canvas, 252 × 305 cm (99¼ × 120 in), Kunsthalle, Mannheim, Mannheim, Germany. Public domain.

Pages 50
Luncheon in the Studio, 1868, oil on canvas, 118 × 153.9 cm (46½ × 60½ in), Neue Pinakothek, Munich, Germany. Bridgeman Images.

Page 51 (above)
Majas on a Balcony, Francisco Goya, between 1800 and 1812, oil on canvas, 162 × 107 cm (63¾ × 42 in), Private Collection. Public domain.

Page 51 (below)
The Balcony, 1868–9, oil on canvas, 170 × 124.5 cm (67 × 49 in), Musée d'Orsay, Paris, France. Public domain.

Page 53
Portrait of Émile Zola, 1868, oil on canvas, 146.5 × 114 cm (57¾ × 44¾ in), Musée d'Orsay, Paris, France. Public domain.

Page 54
The Music Lesson, *c.* 1868, oil on canvas, 141 × 173.1 cm (55½ × 68¼ in), Museum of Fine Arts, Boston, Massachusetts, USA. Anonymous Centennial gift in memory of Charles Deering/ Bridgeman Images.

Pages 55
Eva Gonzalès at the Easel, 1888, oil on canvas, 191 × 133.4 cm (75¼ × 52½ in), National Gallery, London, UK. Bridgeman Images

Page 56
In the Garden, 1870, oil on canvas, 44.5 × 54 cm (17½ × 21¼ in), Shelburne Museum, Shelburne, Vermont, USA. Bridgeman Images.

Pages 57
Effect of Snow at Petit-Montrouge, 1870, oil on canvas, 61.6 × 50.4 cm (24¼ × 19¾ in), National Museum Wales, Cardiff, Wales, UK. Bridgeman Images.

Page 58
La Gare du chemin de Fer de Sceaux, 1870, oil on canvas, 50 × 60.5 cm (19¾ × 23¾ in), Private Collection. Public domain.

Page 59 (above)
The Repose (Portrait of Berthe Morisot), 1870, oil on canvas, 148 × 111 cm (58¼ × 43¾ in), Museum of Art, Providence, Rhode Island, USA. Bridgeman Images.

Page 59 (below)
Le Bon Bock, 1873, oil on canvas, 94 × 83 cm (37 × 32¾ in), Museum of Art, Philadelphia, Pennsylvania, USA. Public domain.

Page 60 (above)
On the Beach, 1873, oil on canvas, 95.9 × 73 cm (37¾ × 28¾ in), Musée d'Orsay, Paris, France. Public domain.

Page 60 (below)
Swallows, 1873, oil on canvas, 65 × 81 cm (25½ × 31¾ in), Emil Bürhle Collection, Zurich, Switzerland. Public domain.

Page 61
The Railway, 1873, oil on canvas, 93.3 × 111.3 cm (36¾ × 44½ in), National Gallery of Art, Washington DC, USA. Gift of Horace Havemeyer in memory of his mother, Louisine W. Havemeyer, public domain.

Page 62
Masked Ball at the Opera, 1873, oil on canvas, 59.1 × 72.5 cm (23¼ × 28½ in), National Gallery of Art, Washington DC, USA. Gift of Mrs Horace Havemeyer in memory of her mother-in-law, Louisine W. Havemeyer, public domain.

Page 63
Midnight at the Port of Boulogne, 1868, oil on canvas, 82 × 101 cm (32¼ × 39¾ in), Musée d'Orsay, Paris, France. Bridgeman Images.

Page 64
Impression, Sunrise, Claude Monet, 1872, oil on canvas, 48 × 63 cm (18¾ × 24¾ in), Museé Marmottan Monet, Paris, France. Public domain.

Page 65 (above)
Argenteuil – Boats, 1874, oil on canvas, 59.4 × 81.3 cm (23¼ × 32 in), National Museum Wales, Cardiff, Wales, United Kingdom. Bridgeman Images.

Page 65 (below)
Banks of the Seine at Argenteuil, 1874, oil on canvas, 62.3 × 103 cm (24½ × 40½ in), The Courtauld Institute Galleries, London, United Kingdom. Public domain.

Page 66
Boating, 1874, oil on canvas, 97.2 × 130.2 cm (38¼ × 51¼ in), Metropolitan Museum of Art, New York, USA. H. O. Havemeyer Collection, Bequest of Mrs H. O. Havemeyer. Public domain.

Page 67
Argenteuil, 1874, oil on canvas, 149 × 115 cm (58¾ × 45¼ in), Musée des Beaux-Arts, Tournai, Belgium. Public domain.

Page 68
Claude and Camille Monet in his Studio Boat, 1874, oil on canvas, 106 × 134 cm (28⅞ × 36¾ in), Staatsgalerie, Stuttgart, Germany. Public domain.

Page 68–9
Claude Monet Painting in his Studio Boat, 1874, oil on canvas, 80 × 98 cm (31½ × 38½ in), Neue Pinakothek, Munich, Germany. Public domain.

Page 70 (above left)
The Monet Family in their Garden at Argenteuil, 1874, oil on canvas, 61 × 99.7 cm (24 × 39¼ in), Metropolitan Museum of Art, New York, USA. Bequest of Joan Whitney Payson, 1975, public domain.

Page 70 (above right)
Madame Monet and her Son, Pierre-Auguste Renoir, 1874, oil on canvas, 50.4 × 68 cm (19¾ × 26¾ in), National Gallery of Art, Washington DC, USA. Ailsa Mellon Bruce Collection, public domain.

Page 70 (below)
Berthe Morisot with a Fan, 1874, oil on canvas, 61 × 50.5 cm (24 × 19¾ in), Palais des Beaux-Arts de Lille, Lille, France. Public domain

Page 71
The Grand Canal of Venice (Blue Venice), 1875, oil on canvas, 58.7 × 71.4 cm (23 × 28 in), Shelburne Museum, Shelburne, Vermont, USA. Gift of the Electra Havemeyer Webb Fund, Inc./Bridgeman Images.

Page 72
Faure as Hamlet, 1877, oil on canvas, 193 × 131 cm (76 × 51½ in), Museum Folkgang, Essen, Germany. Bridgeman Images.

Page 73
Nana, 1877, oil on canvas, 154 × 115 cm (60½ × 45¼ in), Kunsthalle, Hamburg, Germany. Public domain.

Page 75
Corner of a Café-Concert, 1878–80, oil on canvas, 97.1 × 77.5 cm (38¼ × 30½ in), National Gallery, London, United Kingdom. Bridgeman Images.

Page 76
At the Père Lathuille Restaurant, 1879, oil on canvas, 92 × 112 cm (36¼ × 44 in), Musée des Beaux-Arts, Tournai, Belgium. Bridgeman Images.

Page 78
Portrait of George Moore, 1879, pastel on canvas, 55.2 × 35.2 cm (21¾ × 13¾ in), Metropolitan Museum of Art, New York, USA. H. O. Havemeyer Collection, Bequest of Mrs H. O. Havemeyer. Public domain.

Pages 79
Plum Brandy, 1877, oil on canvas, 73.6 × 50.2 cm (29 × 19¾ in), National Gallery of Art, Washington DC, USA. Collection of Mr and Mrs Paul Mellon. Public domain.

Pages 80 (above)
Madame Manet (Suzanne Leenhoff) at Bellevue, 1880, oil on canvas, 80.6 × 60.3 cm (31¾ × 23¾ in), Metropolitan Museum of Art, New York, USA. The Walter H. and Leonore Annenberg Collection. Gift of Walter H. and Leonore Annenberg, 1997. Bequest of Walter H. Annenberg, 2002. Public domain.

Pages 80 (below left)
Letter to Eugène Maus, decorated with two apples, 1880, watercolour, pen and ink on woven paper, 20.1 × 24.8 cm (8 × 9¾ in), Metropolitan Museum of Art, New York, USA. Purchase, Guy Wildenstein, 2003. Public domain.

Pages 80 (below right)
Letter possibly to Madame Jules Guillemet, decorated with a snail on a leaf, 1880, watercolour, pen and ink on woven paper, 15.8 × 11.7 cm (6¼ × 4½ in), The J. Paul Getty Museum, Los Angeles, USA. Public domain.

Pages 81
Portrait of Henri Rochefort, 1881, oil on canvas, 81.5 × 66.5 cm (31¾ × 26¼ in), Kunsthalle, Hamburg, Germany. Bridgeman Images.

Pages 82
Jeanne (Spring), 1881, oil on canvas, 74 × 51.5 cm (29¼ × 20¼ in), The J. Paul Getty Museum, Los Angeles, USA. Public domain.

Pages 83
Autumn (Méry Laurent), 1882, oil on canvas, 73 × 51 cm (28¾ × 20 in), Musée des Beaux-Arts, Nancy, France. Bridgeman Images.

Pages 84
The Bugler, 1882, oil on canvas, 99 × 80.3 cm (39 × 31½ in), The Pauline Allen Gill Foundation, Dallas, Texas, USA. Public domain.

Pages 85
Horsewoman, Full-face (L'Amazone), *c.* 1882, oil on canvas, 73 × 52 cm (28¾ × 20½ in), Museo Thyssen-Bornemisza, Madrid, Spain. Bridgeman Images.

Pages 86
Vase of White Lilacs and Roses, 1883, oil on canvas, 55.8 × 46 cm (22 × 18 in), Dallas Museum of Art, Dallas, Texas, USA. Public domain.

Pages 87
Photograph of Édouard Manet's grave, Cimetière de Passy, Paris, France. Public domain.

Pages 88
Homage to Manet, William Orpen, 1909, oil on canvas, 162.9 × 130 cm (64 × 51¼ in), Manchester Art Gallery, Manchester, United Kingdom. Bridgeman Images.

Pages 89
The Camden Town Murder, Walter Sickert, *c.* 1908, oil on canvas, 25.6 × 35.6 cm (10 × 14 in), Yale Center for British Art, new Haven, Connecticut, USA. Paul Mellon Fund. Public domain.

Pages 90
The White and the Black, Félix Vallotton, 1913, oil on canvas, 114 × 147 cm (45 × 58 in), on loan to the Kunstmuseum, Bern, Switzerland from Fondation Hahnloser/Jäggli, Villa Flora, Winterthur. Public domain.

Pages 91
Portrait (Futago), 1988, colour photograph, 209.6 × 299.7 cm (82½ × 118 in). © Yasumasa Morimura; Courtesy of the artist and Luhring Augustine, New York.

INDEX

Numbers in italics denote illustrations